THE EMIL AND KATHLEEN SICK

LECTURE-BOOK SERIES IN

WESTERN HISTORY AND BIOGRAPHY

THE EMIL AND KATHLEEN SICK

LECTURE-BOOK SERIES IN

WESTERN HISTORY AND BIOGRAPHY

Under the provisions of a Fund established
by the children of Mr. and Mrs. Emil Sick,
whose deep interest in the history and culture
of the American West was inspired by their own
experience in the region, distinguished scholars
are brought to the University of Washington
to deliver public lectures based on original research
in the fields of Western history and biography.
The terms of the gift also provide for the
publication by the University of Washington Press
of the books resulting from the research
upon which the lectures are based.
This book is the twelfth volume in the series.

The Great Columbia Plain:
A Historical Geography, 1805–1910
by Donald W. Meinig

Mills and Markets: A History of the
Pacific Coast Lumber Industry to 1900
by Thomas R. Cox

Radical Heritage:
Labor, Socialism, and Reform
in Washington and British Columbia, 1885–1917
by Carlos A. Schwantes

CENTER FOR THE STUDY
OF THE PACIFIC NORTHWEST

in association with

UNIVERSITY OF WASHINGTON PRESS
SEATTLE *&* LONDON

BRINGING
INDIANS
TO THE
BOOK

ALBERT
FURTWANGLER

This book is published by the Center for the Study of the Pacific Northwest,

P.O. Box 353587, Seattle, WA 98195, in association with the University of Washington Press,

P.O. Box 50096, Seattle, WA 98145.

LIBRARY OF CONGRESS CATALOGING-IN-PUBLICATION DATA

Furtwangler, Albert, 1942–

Bringing Indians to the book / Albert Furtwangler.

p.   cm.   —(The Emil and Kathleen Sick lecture-book series

in western history and biography ; 12)

Includes bibliographical references and index.

ISBN 0-295-98523-2 (pbk. : alk. paper)

1. Indians of North America—Missions—Northwest, Pacific.   2. Indians of North
America—Northwest, Pacific—Religion.   3. Indians of North America—Northwest,
Pacific—History.   4. Missionaries—Northwest, Pacific—History.   I. Title.

E78.N77F87   2005

266'.0089'970795—dc22   2005002225

CONTENTS

PREFACE

THIS BOOK HAS COME TOGETHER IN A SMALL, BOOK-lined room in Salem, in a central neighborhood that still bears many reminders of the early Methodist mission in Oregon. Most Mondays I go to civic meetings at Jason Lee Manor, a nearby retirement home named for one of the first missionaries to settle in the area. Other days, I poke around in the libraries of Willamette University and so pass buildings that bear the names of other missionaries who were among the school's founders. My route to campus passes through the grounds of the state capitol, where one statue commemorates Lewis and Clark on horseback and another honors early circuit riders. A steady walk in another direction takes me to a pioneer cemetery and the graves of Lee and many of his associates. Mill Creek runs through this neighborhood, past my house, and down to the Willamette River. Its waters begin as soft Oregon rain and eventually flow on into the Columbia River and the Pacific; long ago it provided drinking water and powered the mission mills.

I work at home at a desk surrounded by books from several stages of an academic career. One block of bookshelves holds novels, plays, and poetry from my years as a teacher of literature. Another holds volumes of history, especially Western Americana. In 1993 I published a book about Lewis and Clark. Soon after moving to Oregon, I completed another about a famous speech attributed to Chief Seattle. Earlier, I wrote books about the American founders, including George Washington, Thomas Jefferson, and James Madison. I have shelves of books from those projects, too, to support a continuing interest in the origins of American institutions and the beginnings of what we call the American West.

One day I sorted through a shelf of academic journals and so came upon a review of Robert Boyd's *People of The Dalles*, a very informative book about missions and Northwest Indians. A week later, I was reading Boyd's pages, following his citations, and making connections from one shelf to another around the room.

Boyd's sources included Lewis and Clark, early missions along the Columbia, and further books and articles that linked Jason Lee to William Clark, Methodists to Presbyterians and Catholics, and local Indian customs to practices and literatures elsewhere in the world. As I traced this little web of connections and asked new questions, I began to feel a certain uneasiness. I had learned enough from my past work to notice errors in some of these materials and missed opportunities in others, but I was also embarrassed at how ignorant I had been about the Northwest at the time of its first white settlements. I made brief notes for a couple of articles I might write to make amends, and put in some requests for interlibrary loans.

As time passed, my design became more complicated. I thought about tensions that any good English teacher must manage between different kinds of learning. On the one hand is the library, on the other the direct, felt experiences we all have, which often seem hard to put into words. The missionaries were evidently caught between these opposite poles. They came to teach the Bible and to convert people in oral societies, but found that the natives baffled them with their indifference. They came west as bookish people and failed largely because of their resulting ignorance. Despite their own strong religious feelings and immersion in the oral life of vigorous preaching and shared hymns, they remained stiffly literate in their expectations. This was a severe disadvantage when they approached nonliterate native societies. The mission experiences therefore stood out for me as good material for studying a deeper American problem: the extension of literate institutions to the varied peoples and cultures of this continent.

Perhaps some captious critic will remark that I have thus become stuck in the ruts of my own advanced literacy—as a professional academic bookworm writing yet another book about readers and writers. I can only reply that all of us are now stuck in the complex, literate world of the twenty-first century, and that interpreting oral histories and material artifacts requires expert training very different from mine. I also respect the claims of many Native Americans that no outsider can properly comprehend their understanding of their past. To repair my own ignorance I have made a new upheaval in my own library, traced some new connections among books in much greater libraries, and revisited many Northwest scenes with new questions. From the printed page it is still possible to recapture the thinking that led young American adventurers into this region and the changes of mind and heart they recorded here. This has been my limited but telling subject. I have tried to bring their words to life and so bring out the sharply different ways people from the eastern United States first understood and inhabited the Northwest.

I have many people to thank for help and support, beginning with colleagues at Willamette University. Members of the English department, the late dean Lawrence Cress, and president M. Lee Pelton arranged to give me an appointment as a Willamette Independent Scholar, with faculty status for using the library and occasional secretarial services. All the staff librarians at the Hatfield Library have been helpful; Bill Kelm deserves special notice for tracing many citations that baffled others. Mary Plank in Eaton Hall handled duplicating and other chores very efficiently. Charles Wallace and Philip Hanni pointed out useful resources off campus. Ludwig Fischer lent books and discussed his own work in literacy and linguistics.

At the Oregon-Idaho Conference Archives of the United Methodist Church in Salem, Don Knepp, Shirley Knepp, and Ina Simms have frequently offered encouragement and useful advice. Dale Patterson and Tracy Del Duca responded to my requests for items from the United Methodist Church General Commission on Archives and History; so did Stephen Yale, at the California-Nevada Conference Archives, and Nancy Newins, at Randolph-Macon College.

Liisa Penner at the Clatsop County Historical Society pointed out obscure but valuable articles about the Frost, Kone, and Smith families.

For materials I could not find or have sent to Salem, I have relied on trips to the University of Washington library and courteous assistance from its staff in many departments.

Robert Moore at the Jefferson Expansion National Memorial in St. Louis organized a conference in 2004 on legacies of the Lewis and Clark expedition, where I presented my work on Clark and got helpful advice from William Foley, Jerry Garrett, and Landon Jones.

Two long-time friends have read almost all my past writings and pressed me to do more. Sally Bryan, once my teacher of both history and literature, has remained a steady correspondent through many decades. Robert Hunt has written many articles on Lewis and Clark and related topics; for over ten years he has also sent me clippings, raised new questions, and met me in Seattle for long conversations on Northwest history.

Once again I have enjoyed a strong working relationship with University of Washington Press. The expert readers for the Press have urged important revisions, and I owe particular thanks to Julidta Tarver for sponsoring this project from an early stage, to Molly Wallace for catching errors and helping me reconsider and improve many passages, and to Mary Ribesky for guiding me through the later stages of production.

My wife brought us to Salem through her own appointment at Willamette. We refrain from asking about each other's writings until they are published, but she has raised many good questions about the scenes around us and listened patiently as I have tried to work out straight answers. Questions of religious vocation, sense of place, teaching, and literature are abiding themes in our lives and daily talk.

BRINGING INDIANS TO THE BOOK

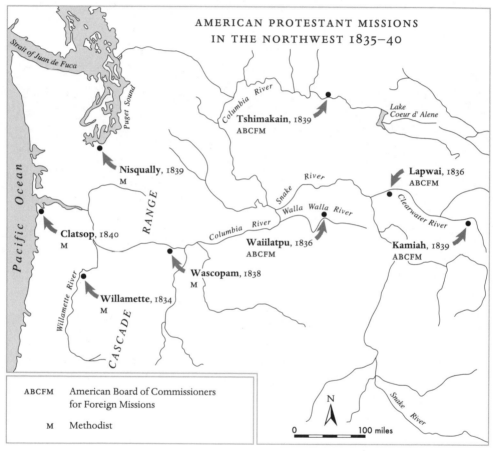

AMERICAN PROTESTANT MISSIONS
IN THE NORTHWEST 1835–40

Strait of Juan de Fuca

Puget Sound

Pacific Ocean

Columbia River

Tshimakain, 1839
ABCFM

Lake
Coeur d' Alene

Nisqually, 1839
M

Snake River

Lapwai, 1836
ABCFM

RANGE

Clearwater River

Walla Walla River

Columbia River

Clatsop, 1840
M

Kamiah, 1839
ABCFM

Waiilatpu, 1836
ABCFM

Wascopam, 1838
M

Willamette River

Willamette, 1834
M

CASCADE

ABCFM   American Board of Commissioners
         for Foreign Missions

M   Methodist

N

Snake River

0   100 miles

The Clatsop, Wascopam, Waiilatpu, Lapwai, and Kamiah missions were all
at sites along the Columbia River and its tributaries, where Lewis and Clark
had also had important encounters with Native American peoples.

INTRODUCTION

MERIWETHER LEWIS AND WILLIAM CLARK LED THEIR expedition west of the Rockies for just one winter, left very few marks on the trail, and then went home. Years passed before their discoveries were properly published—after many awkward delays and complications. Although the two young captains managed to stake some important political and intellectual claims, they hardly made a beginning at American domination of the West.

In 1805 Lewis and Clark had pushed beyond the limits of the Louisiana Purchase and reinforced Robert Gray's claims to the entire Columbia drainage area. Through close observation and careful record keeping, they also brought back a wealth of new information. They redrew the map of the continent, showed that there was no easy Northwest Passage, explained that the Rockies were a complex chain of high mountains, and supplied materials for the beginnings of far-Western botany, zoology, and ethnography. Yet more than twenty-five years passed before the first Americans crossed the continent to begin long-term agricultural settlements. When they arrived, they found that retired French-Canadian trappers had already built homes and plowed some choice acres along the Willamette River, and that the Hudson's Bay Company was very comfortably established at Fort Vancouver, had de facto authority over the entire region, and held monopoly advantages over goods they would need.

These first American settlers were Protestant missionaries, who struggled in their turn to make a significant mark in this region. Within a decade they had set up farms, mills, towns, and schools, and offered support to hundreds of new settlers who followed them over the Oregon Trail. They helped foster political arrangements so that Oregon soon emerged on American maps as first a coordinated settlement, then a territory, and finally (in 1859) a new state. An unbroken line runs from the arrivals of Jason Lee, Marcus and Narcissa Whitman, and Henry and Eliza Spalding to the spread of white American settlers across the Northwest.

In the end, all these first missionaries had to admit failure. Lee was dismissed from his post as ineffectual, and his successor dismantled his entire mission project. The Whitmans were killed by Indians who feared and hated them, and, in the resulting tensions between whites and Indians, the Spaldings were forced from their outpost. Many others abandoned mission work as hopeless, dispiriting, and exhausting.

Still, these mission efforts enlarged and implicitly challenged the work of Lewis and Clark. The explorers had come overland with the object of making exact observations, and they followed Thomas Jefferson's instructions to foster peaceful relations with native people, if only for the sake of their own survival and safe return. The next generation came west with much loftier aims. They wanted to save the world, beginning with the abject, disfigured savages they expected to meet here. The missionaries may have been ignorant, naive, and driven by a zeal that now looks very odd, but their explicit purpose gave them a completely different orientation to this landscape. They were not particularly mindful of plants, trees, minerals, animals, mountains, streams, or celestial observations for calculating latitude and longitude. They did not cock an eye (at least at first) at the potential for profit from salmon, beaver pelts, or trade routes. They came to live as model, civilized

Christians and to impart the highest wisdom they knew. These young men also brought young wives to the West and began to rear children here. They expected to transform raw wilderness into moderately comfortable spaces suitable for modern families. Even when wives, children, and close companions fell sick and died here, and when the Indians they met face-to-face proved indifferent, hostile, fickle, or exasperating, they persisted—believing that they were inspired and sustained by a special calling.

In short, Lewis and Clark came west under the authority of an intellectual American president, but the missionaries came, as they felt, by the will of God. The explorers came to survey the land and treat briefly with its people. The missionaries came specifically to engage with the people, and immediately found themselves entangled with the land—with hoes in their hands from the start.

The relations between the explorers and these early settlers are not just a matter of contrast, however. For these separate waves of early white invaders were both people of the book—readers, writers, and record keepers, with eyes trained to take in information that might well reach a wide public through print. Here in brief is the crux of the problems both addressed: they were to embrace the West for God and country, largely by writing about it and bringing past writings to bear on it. And in this effort they had to engage nonliterate people who had developed age-old ways of living here, ways unimaginable to the literate.

At this point we must frankly face our own prejudices as readers and writers, which is a root problem in dealing with this material as conscientious historians. In discussing the gap between white men's and Indians' minds in this period, even a very sharp critic can easily look past his or her own complicated involvement.

To cite a very influential example: Bernard DeVoto describes Jason Lee as an obtuse, well-meaning but inflictive intruder. Lee set out to save heathen souls, but he failed to understand that "heathen souls were inclosed in an envelope of personality, which in turn had been born of a savage culture." Such souls could not be converted except by what amounted to spiritual extermination. "You could not make Christians of Indians," DeVoto writes. "First you had to make white men of them."

Forty years of contact with traders, trappers, and explorers had already made Oregon Indians "into white men about as much as was possible, which is to say they were degenerate, debauched, diseased, despairing, and about to die." By coming to the Willamette Valley, Lee could

> set up his mission and serve God by making farmers, carpenters, herdsmen, users of soap, teetotalers, hymn-singers, monogamists, and newspaper readers of whatsoever Indians he might find there. This, he realized would be at best a small fraction of the universal hopes that had sent him West. But it would be a beginning and at least here was some hope, as assuredly there was no hope at all in the mountains, that it might succeed. That it could succeed only by means of the greatest cruelty men can inflict on other men, only by breaking down the culture that made them men—this mattered not at all, it was the end in view. (DeVoto 201–2)

This may seem an incisive judgment about a clash of cultures, but a careful reader must also frown over its evident display of writerly effects. This is a masterly page of DeVoto the rhetorician, building up an indictment with gifts of phrase learned through years of studying Mark Twain. In one line he rings out a chain of balanced alliterations about "degenerate, debauched, diseased, and despairing" Indians. In the next he creates a comic list of supposed traits of good American Methodist "farmers, carpenters, herdsmen, users of soap, teetotalers, hymn-singers, monogamists, and newspaper readers." The contrast is sharp and memorable. But we have to ask if it is not also inadequate and blind in its own way. Were all post-contact Indians debauched and doomed? Was there no hope for them or possibility of fruitful learning from the missionaries? Were the Methodists pious humbugs who believed merely in bubbles of soap and shrill little hymns?

DeVoto presses us to be more sophisticated—but to what end? He urges us to look back on the early missions with wry amusement or disgust, as superior onlookers observing a collision of the illiterate with the naive. But we should be aware that there are hazards in yielding to that pressure. If we agree that white teachers could introduce their kind of learning only by cruelty, and that their efforts were almost totally futile, then we face a daunting further problem: Even if the Bible could not be brought to the Indians, Indians would still be brought into white writer's books. They would be counted, described, quoted, represented, interpreted, and evaluated in the language of the literate. DeVoto himself is caught up in that process and so are we. At the time of white contact, were Indians noble or savage or debased or pitiable or simply inscrutable because they were beyond the knowing of the literate? No matter how we choose among these categories or try to shuffle and recombine them, we cannot help drawing on well-worn bookish formulas and literate patterns.

The circumstances that inspired the Oregon missions, however, point to possibilities beyond DeVoto's amusement or disgust. From the first, the missionaries were responding to a call from Indians who specifically sought literate teachers. Four Indians from beyond the Rocky Mountains had come to St. Louis in 1831 to plead for such help. Methodists and others not only publicized this striking appeal, they also worked to check its accuracy. Later, several missionaries in the field devoted years to projects of cultural translation, both to teach Indians and to learn from them. As a result we now have abundant materials for seeing into the thinking of these missionaries, and for sketching ethnohistories of many Northwest tribes. This evidence shows individual learners reaching from both sides of the literacy divide—Indians who claimed they gained something worthwhile from white men's books and missionaries who learned at least a little from Indians' ways.

The early missions to Oregon thus provide a particularly apt historical situation for looking into the values, costs, and distortions of literate learning—and so into problems that continue to trouble our thinking about clashes of cultures in America.

This study does not attempt to retell the story of the missionaries year by year, partly because good detailed narratives are already widely available. Many missionaries published their own histories of early Oregon and reprinted their own letters and sections of their diaries.

Clifford Drury has researched these materials to produce several volumes on missionaries of the Columbia Basin, and Cornelius Brosnan has written a good brief account of Jason Lee and his work. Alvin Josephy has woven all these materials as well as Indian oral histories into the very readable central chapters of *The Nez Perce Indians and the Opening of the Northwest*, which has recently been republished in paperback. Further caches of documents have come to light through the studies of Robert Loewenberg and Robert Boyd, based on missionary archives, and Theodore Stern, based on the records of the Hudson's Bay Company. The heroism or the shortcomings of the missionaries are not my focus here, either, nor is their role or motivation in developing an American stronghold in the West.

Instead of these long-argued concerns, this study looks hard at a preliminary point about all these records and studies—a point so obvious or transparent that it has easily been ignored. When the explorers and missionaries came west bearing books, they carried them not only in their baggage but in their most commonplace thoughts and habits. It had been through reading and writing in the first place that they set off on their dangerous trails. Written instructions and expectations continued to control their behavior. Particular methods of reading and writing shaped what they saw, recorded, and reported day by day. How they interpreted their books—military regulations, Bibles, law books, account books, scientific handbooks, committee minute books—determined how they organized their work, related to each other, and preserved their identities in new settings. Of course, it was with books in their hands and literate phrases on their tongues that they faced the Indians. They meant to impart written messages to them and to capture Indians' ways in books that they (and their sponsors) were creating. And in the long run it was through written documents that they held on to their Oregon experiences years later and thousands of miles away.

These literate conditions stand out sharply if we reread their writings in terms of four general themes. Two of these topics link the early missionaries directly to the explorations of Lewis and Clark. Two others link the missionaries to the concerns of modern readers and American citizens in the West.

The first is the remarkable incident that inspired the first Oregon mission. After the four Indians came to St. Louis in 1831, published reports stressed that they had made a long pilgrimage in quest of teachers of the white man's book. This was the specific point that the Methodists and others seized upon. At the heart of this incident, however, there sits an intriguing puzzle. Everything turns on the idea that they came into St. Louis and met directly with William Clark—and that he weighed and reported what the Indians wanted and needed. Yet Clark himself is absolutely unreachable on this subject. He left no written record of this meeting. The fact that it happened is confirmed by many contemporary documents, but all were written by others. As a result, we are left with a ring of interlocking documents, all claiming the authority of what William Clark said and meant about what the four Indians said and meant. Contemporary reports show that the learned and earnest men responsible for these documents sought solid information about the West, then elaborated what they had not quite heard or overheard or found in print. In the end they urged dozens of people to cross the continent with very illusory expectations.

The second is the odd geographical parallel between the explorer and missionary settlements. On the scene in Oregon, the missionaries developed several sites along the Columbia and its tributaries—very close to sites where Lewis and Clark had stopped and had significant encounters with Indians. So far as I can tell, no one has yet drawn the obvious lines of comparison between these parallel experiences. Both sets of records have been admired and quoted for their particular observations of native peoples' appearance and customs. But there is much more to be said about the ways each of these sojourns works as a critique of the other. It is easy to praise Lewis and Clark for their hardihood, shrewdness, and alertness about the Indians they met over the course of a few months. It is easy to fault the missions for all their lapses in dealing with the same groups years later. The records, however, tell a different story, or complex of stories. Both sets of observers were limited in what they could see by preconditions they had accepted before they set out. Both were hard-pressed and distracted by the struggle for survival in a new place. And the missions had a further burden of social organization, as they grew in size and their members kept writing about each other, and warily rewriting the terms of their commitment.

This writing and rewriting highlights my third theme, the missionaries' dilemmas as people of the printed word who were attempting to address the nonliterate. These Protestants took their religion from the book, and, no matter what their particular denomination, their habits were deeply bookish. They expected to live under fixed laws, to keep accurate records and accounts, and to stay in touch by means of far-flung correspondence. Above all, they regarded themselves as figures in history and geography—history on a scale of millennia, with a definite beginning, middle, and end; and geography that embraced all the continents on the globe. They came to impart salvation to the Indians, but salvation as they understood it included this literate worldview. How could they begin? The Indians beyond their doorways were transient hunters, fishers, and gatherers, evidently ill clad, often hungry and marked by disease. It was manifestly futile to offer dying adults the letters *A B C* on a slate. Many mission leaders simply lost heart. A few hit upon fortuitous convergences of Indian and Christian patterns. Some were ingenious. Some held fast through years of disillusionment. Some turned to the whip—or the whip writ large in bureaucratic form, the federal Indian agent's armed patrol.

My final theme is the distortion and even blindness of literate thinking. Two centuries after Lewis and Clark we still face problems they busily scratched at with their pens. The Indians they saw in Oregon looked deformed to them. At dramatic moments, the explorers felt their human sympathies drop and they closed their minds and fortress gates against them. The same must be said about the missionaries of the 1830s. They often saw Indians only as sick, indifferent, lawless people, who exasperated them and defeated the lofty convictions they thought they were bringing to the wilderness. What admonition should we take from their experience? What can we claim to know about peoples who know the world differently, evidently suffer from our infliction and invasion, and by turns appeal for our help and spurn it? To put it more forcefully: what can we learn from them, especially if we have the nerve to go on dwelling where our predecessors pushed them out of the way? The Oregon missions press these questions to an extreme. They began with a strange double prejudice: With their heads pressed flat in infancy, these natives seemed deformed in body and probably in brain; yet they were nonetheless God's children and capable of salvation. Jason Lee capitalized on this paradox—quite literally—by bringing flat-headed but articulate companions along on his fundraising appeals in the East. Other strange developments followed. If there were great seasons of achieved salvation, as the missionaries claimed, these were also times of shared holiness, which the whites felt among Indians. Through years of cramped subsistence living at the outposts, there were also long periods of shared grief, hardship, disease, and squalor. One or two missionaries saw the inadequacies of translating the Bible into local languages, and some admitted the vanity of preaching against local ways, however cruel and outrageous they might seem. A few were caught up in Indian rituals and mysteries. They resisted and rejected them, of course, but also took pains to write them down and thereby hold on to them. These few years forced a few young white idealists into intimacy with people they looked upon as wretched, and forced them to think again. They force us to think again, too, if we pay close attention to their records.

I

ON THE AUTHORITY
OF WILLIAM CLARK

WILLIAM CLARK NEVER WENT BACK UP THE MISSOURI River to the Rockies after his famous expedition with Meriwether Lewis. Soon after his return in 1806 he settled in St. Louis and began a long career there as a chief officer of the federal government. President Jefferson made him a militia general, he succeeded Lewis as the appointed governor of Missouri Territory, and after statehood in 1820 he continued for many years as superintendent of Indian affairs over a vast region. He was no longer William Clark, the younger brother and much junior officer to George Rogers Clark, the great hero of the Old Northwest. After the sobering death of Lewis in 1809, Clark also left behind the celebrity they had shared as young men. He married, fathered several children, and settled into years of official duty—surviving many presidential administrations as a leading public figure in middle America. He took part in dozens of controversies and developments: fur trading ventures, Indian disputes, preparations against British threats during the War of 1812, treaty councils, territorial politics, state elections, the Missouri Compromise, Indian removals to lands west of the Mississippi, and the framing of new federal laws. He thus became a conspicuous authority for easterners to consult about the West. At the same time, he remained the well-known, approachable agent to whom Indians could come in hopes of finding seasoned understanding.

In 1831, near the end of his career, Clark met with four Indians from beyond the Rocky Mountains, who may have come into St. Louis specifically to see him. A published report of this visit created a sensation many months later, for it stated that the Indians had come on a spiritual quest, to ask Clark about the truth of the white men's religion. This influential report also summarized Clark's reply—to the effect that there was indeed a book among white men that provided clear rules for conduct in this life as a means to a happy and eternal afterlife. Clark also imparted a brief historical outline to these visitors, from the fall of man to the advent of the savior, and he mentioned moral precepts that would serve to prepare them for the last judgment.

The report appeared on the front page of a widely circulated Christian weekly newspaper, and it immediately inspired a drive to send missionaries into the far West. Funds were subscribed, young men were recruited, and in 1834 Jason Lee and his adult nephew Daniel joined a fur trader's party and made their way across the Rockies, down the Columbia River, and into the Willamette Valley. Over the course of the next decade, the Lees and others set up several missions along the Columbia and its tributaries. Some came with young wives; some married young missionary women who came west months later. Soon there were several families with children, and the mission compounds included shops, farms, schools, and mills. These settlements marked the beginning of a permanent American presence in Oregon—the long-delayed sequel to Lewis and Clark's bold push to reach the Pacific and survive there in the winter of 1805–6.

The sensational report in the *Christian Advocate* may seem absurd on its face. Months and years later, there were doubters who found it hard it believe that four Indians crossed the plains just to ask Clark their famous questions, and that through an interpreter he replied with a full account of Christian theology. In fact, however, other witnesses confirmed many elements in this incident. Four Indians did come from the Rockies to St. Louis in 1831. They did express an interest in white men's religion, and they did meet with Clark. Other details also tally between independent reports and the *Christian Advocate* account. The crucial issue is what Clark and the Indians said to each other, and even on this point there is some indirect positive evidence. Missionaries heading west stopped in St. Louis and met with Clark; mission supporters also wrote to St. Louis to learn more about this story as it spread across the country. At no time did Clark deny what the most famous report had said. He rather confirmed it, according to several inquirers. It was because of his authority, and seemingly with his support, that the missionaries proceeded on up the Missouri as they did.

Of course, no one directly transcribed Clark's interview with his four visitors, and he himself left no written record of it. But the surviving records point to that meeting as a crucial moment for his mediation. To Indians who lived hundreds of miles away and had never seen him, Clark was still known: He had passed among their people, would listen and tell the truth. And to white readers hundreds of miles away in the other direction, Clark was the experienced sentinel: Who better could vouch for what conditions were really like beyond the horizon? Again and again writers referred to Clark as the central figure who had met these Indians and first ministered to them.

Did Clark then foster Christianity as well as American settlement beyond the Rockies? The records do not quite provide a straight answer. Instead they show people from both sides of the Mississippi reaching far in the hope that he would answer—and give an affirmative answer—to deep questions in their lives. This incident also shows how impossible it was for anyone at this time to embrace both East and West, literate and oral peoples, Christians and non-Christians, as Clark was supposed to have done. The missions set off with convictions based on complicated misinformation. The remaining certainty is that Clark was in the middle of it and much cited as its source.

Rumors, examples, and some direct teaching of Christianity had infiltrated the far West by the early decades of the nineteenth century. They came from many points of contact. Individual trappers and traders had carried Bibles in their packs and tried to impart the gospel message to native people from time to time. Wherever the Hudson's Bay Company established its posts it also instituted Sunday services as a matter of policy and required every man, woman, and child to attend, including any Indians "whom it may be proper to invite" (Vibert 108). Many men at these posts fathered children with Indian women and were expected to teach them in English and to develop their moral character. Hundreds of Indians from eastern Canada, many of whom were Christian converts, also moved west with the fur trade. In 1825 a few boys were selected from western tribes and sent to board at a school at the Red River trading post at Fort Garry, near modern Winnipeg. Two of these boys—renamed Spokane Garry and Kutenai Pelly, after Hudson's Bay Company officers—came from the Columbia Plateau region. When they returned in 1829, they carried Bibles and other religious books, and began to preach and demonstrate the power of white men's learning.

It is impossible to define exactly how these various influences reached the regions beyond the Rockies or what effects they had. Some modern researchers have claimed that there was already an indigenous, widespread religious system on the Columbia Plateau, which anticipated white attempts at domination and even foretold them. An often-quoted Spokane prophecy declared, "Soon there will come from the rising sun a different kind of man from any you have yet seen, who will bring with them a book and will teach you everything, and after that the world will fall to pieces" (Wilkes 4:449 quoted in Spier 58).[1] These words were first recorded in 1841, however, from an informant who said he had heard them proclaimed when he was a boy, about fifty years earlier (Appleman 115). Other prophecies and descriptions of precontact religious beliefs are also vulnerable to modern skepticism. We can now repeat and discuss them only because, at some point, they became written records—at some point, that is, after books and Christian teachings were known among Indians and were affecting the ways they reshaped their beliefs.

It could well be that, as early explorers claimed, Indians who met them regarded them as supernatural beings or messengers, in keeping with indigenous beliefs and prophecies. Certainly Christian teaching could be intelligible at first only in terms that matched and reinforced local ceremonies and practices. But how important could books or Bibles have seemed to any group of Indians before literate invaders began to appear? How could the idea of a book even be taken in or expressed among people who did not read or observe others reading?

As the first glimmers of Christian teaching reached this region, other forms of European power were also touching Indian life and effecting great changes. Contact with white explorers brought the spread of new and devastating diseases. Some time in the eighteenth century, herds of horses were traded to Indians of the Columbia Plateau, opening new possibilities of hunting, warfare, trade relations, and long-distance travel. Later, the fur trade introduced new trade goods, including cloth blankets, guns and ammunition, metal tools, alcohol, and refined tobacco. Fur company posts also demonstrated a different way of life, based on both local agriculture and the global exchange of luxury items. All these forces came into play before the direct teaching of Christianity and literacy, and they make it impossible to disentangle the power or appeal of white religion from other Euro-American cultural influences.

Acquiring power or material goods was commonly what mattered, on both sides, in early dealings between natives and whites. Some material goods were also spiritually significant, or were adapted for spiritual purposes. As early as 1827, for example, an Okanagan leader insisted very forcefully that tobacco was to his people what the Bible was to white people. A Hudson's Bay trader reported his argument and seemed to be both astonished and amused by it:

> [Nkwala] very ingeniously maintains that he and those of any good sense among them smoak Tobacco from a *much different* and better motive [than mere pleasure]—that which moves the white people to look in the Great Fathers Book: for the moment *he* takes his Pipe, he cannot help thinking of the Great Creation of the world and the number of good things done for their benefit

the Indians cannot understand. I never saw a Savage that seems more consumed in the power of a Supreme being. He is convinced the Indians bring much of their present misery upon themselves by a total neglect of the great good conferred upon them and especially in showing too much levity in the very act of smoaking! (Hudson's Bay Company Archives, quoted in Vibert 153)[2]

A modern reader is left to wonder whether Nkwala was slyly suggesting that the Bible was a form of white people's addiction.

Nevertheless, when Christianity was introduced—whether by traders, eastern Indians, or the students who returned from the Red River school—it surely troubled some Indian minds. And it was out of this tension that the four Nez Perces resolved to make their way to St. Louis. With the aid of Nez Perce informants and the scant records of contemporary fur traders and missionaries, Alvin Josephy has tried to piece together what can be known of these men. He stresses that their motives are now impossible to determine, but he points out that they all came from the upper reaches of the Clearwater River in present-day Idaho. Here "the people had been greatly influenced" by Spokane Garry's recent teaching, and many leaders still warmly remembered the long stay of Lewis and Clark in 1806 (Josephy 94, 96). According to one report, a party of twenty Flatheads and Nez Perces initially set out to head east with a group from the Rocky Mountain Fur Company headed by Lucien Fontenelle and Andrew Drips. In the end, just four of these men went with Fontenelle all the way to St. Louis. Josephy identifies them as follows:

> One of them was a Nez Perce warrior of about 44 years of age from the Kamiah Valley, who was known as both Tipyahlanah (Eagle) and Kipkip Pahlekin, a term whose meaning is not known today. He seems to have come from the village of the powerful Kamiah leader whom Lewis and Clark had met and called Tunnachemootoolt [the journals also refer to him as Broken Arm]. The others were two young Nez Perces, each about 20 years old, named Hi-yuts-to-henin (Rabbit Skin Leggings) and Tawis Geejumnin (No Horns on His Head, or Horns Worn Down Like

Those on an Old Buffalo); and a second older Indian named Ka-ou-pu (Man of the Morning, or of the Dawn Light), the son of a Nez Perce buffalo hunting leader from the Kooskia-Stites area of the upper Clearwater, and of a Flathead woman. Hi-yuts-to-henin was related to Tipyahlahnah, and it may have been that the entire mission was concocted and carried out in behalf of only a limited number of Nez Perces, possibly the leaders of the villages in the Kamiah-Kooskia-Stites region. (96)

In 2003, the Nez Perce people dedicated an eight-foot granite monument to these men at Calvary Cemetery in St. Louis, where two of them are now buried. This monument lists the names somewhat differently:

Black Eagle—Tipyeléhne Cimúuxcimux
Speaking Eagle—Tipyeléhne 'Iléesenin
(also called Man-of-the-Morning—Ka'áwpoo)
Rabbit-Skin-Leggings—Hey'úuxctohnin'
No-Horns-On-His-Head—Téewis Sisímnim'

The monument also carries a brief, carefully worded description of their aims: "Feeling pressure from an encroaching white presence in their homeland, these men sought information on the white man's culture and a greater understanding of the 'Book of Heaven.' Knowledge was power—power to assure their families thrived and that their way of life continued."

This, in brief, is the background information that can be found about the four Indians who met with Clark. It confirms that they set out with some kind of religious questioning, but also suggests that they represented a small number of Indians on the west side of the Rocky Mountains, not a deliberative council of people from across a great region. Their number included one member whose parent was a Flathead, but none of these four had a flattened head or came from the lower Columbia where infant head flattening was practiced.

When the Indians reached St. Louis they reportedly approached several leaders and tried to learn about Christianity. Though according to one later account they visited every church in the city, direct reports describe only their meeting with Catholic priests and with William Clark and his visitor William Walker. These accounts provide some intriguing details, and show that both Catholics and Protestants seized on this event and began to imagine a vast field opening for missions in the far West.

Rev. Joseph Rosati was the first bishop of the new diocese of St. Louis, and in 1831 he was busy there with many projects. At the end of the year he composed an annual report letter for the mission society in France, which would be published in *Annales de la Propagation de la Foi*. He noted that work was proceeding on a hospital, an orphanage, two colleges, and three large stone churches, including a proper cathedral near the waterfront. Like many a year-end report, Bishop Rosati's letter makes an appeal for more support. It ends by stating that the old church is too cold for winter services and the priests have barely managed to say Sunday Masses there for the past two months. Yet despite all this business and pleading, the report devotes about half its space to another matter—the arrival of the four Indians a few months earlier, and the wonderful opportunity they seemed to signal.

Bishop Rosati's report opens with a long, rambling, somewhat tangled sentence. I translate it here phrase by phrase, and retain the original punctuation:

> Some months ago, four Indians who live on the other side of the Rocky Mountains, near the Columbia River, arrived in St. Louis, after having visited General Clark, who in his famous expedition saw their people and was well treated by them; they came to see our church and seemed to be extremely pleased by it; unfortunately there was no one who understood their language. (Rosati 599)

L. B. Palladino has translated this passage by breaking it into three distinct sentences and adding an explanatory parenthesis—but with some revealing distortions as a result:

> Some three months ago four Indians who live across the Rocky Mountains near the Columbia River (Clark's Fork of the Columbia) arrived in St. Louis. After visiting General Clark who, in his celebrated travels, has visited their country and has been well

treated by them, they came to see our church and appeared to be exceedingly well pleased with it. Unfortunately, there was no one who understood their language. (Palladino 11)

Palladino is historically accurate here: the Indians came from an upper tributary of the Columbia, and they came to St. Louis, then to see Clark, and then to the church. But Rosati's original French does not quite put it that way; a French reader might easily suppose that the visitors came from somewhere along the Columbia near the Pacific coast and that seeing Clark was their first object, even before they came into St. Louis. In Rosati's long sentence, the Indians make a more sweeping movement. They come from the most remote part of the West to reach St. Louis and his church; they come by way of a visit with Clark; and they express pleasure at what they find, even though there is a language barrier. Writing to his French sponsors, Rosati could be implying that Clark helped direct the visitors toward what they were seeking. Rosati was, after all, reporting here to the Society for the Propagation of the Faith, an international mission society that had no Protestant equivalent in the West at this time.

Though the priests could not speak to these Indians directly, they kept up contact once they had met. Rosati continues his account:

Some time later, two of them fell dangerously ill. I was then absent from St. Louis. Two of our priests visited them, and these poor Indians seemed delighted by their visit. They made signs of the cross and other gestures which seemed to have some relation to baptism. This sacrament was administered to them; they showed their satisfaction at that. A little cross was presented to them, they seized it eagerly, kissed it often, and it could not be taken from their hands until after their death. It was very distressing to be unable to speak with them. Their bodies were carried to the church for burial which was done with all the Catholic ceremonies. The other two Indians attended with great simplicity. They have returned to their country. (Rosati 599, my translation)

Several points stand out here. One is that the priests kept up contact for weeks after the Indians' first visit, continuing to minister to them through illness and death. Parish burial records show that the two older men died in October and November, but not before both had received baptism and one had "l'estreme onction" (Palladino 10; Behrmann 28–29). Moreover, the Indians seemed to welcome this attention. Their signs and gestures imply that Christianity was not entirely strange to them: they had some preparation for Catholic sacraments, and they sought this form of service and were grateful to receive it. On the other hand, there is no mention whatever here of their asking for a white man's book or formal teaching.

> We later learned, from a Canadian who has gone through the country where they live, that they belong to the nation of the Flat-heads, which as well as another called the Black-feet, has received some ideas of the Catholic religion from two Indians who had been to Canada and told them in detail what they had seen there, making striking descriptions of the beautiful ceremonies of the Catholic worship, telling them that this was also the religion of the whites; they remembered as much as they could, they learned to make the sign of the cross and to pray. (Rosati 599–600)

These lines make it appear that the Indians came east seeking Catholic teaching or ministry. They also refer to these people as Flat-heads, though there is no mention of their having any flattened or disfigured features. The priests learned this name from some unnamed Canadian (i.e., *Canadien*, French-speaking fur trapper)—which could imply that they did *not* consult William Clark or learn much, if anything, directly from him. Very likely the term "Flatheads" (*Têtes-Plattes*) was mentioned to the priests by Fontenelle or one of his companions. Yet there are also other terms used in the burial records: "Nez Perce" and "Chopweck" (no doubt a garbled spelling of Chopaneche or Choppunish) are versions of the names first used by Lewis and Clark for the people they came to know well in the Rocky Mountains (see Moulton 5:224n17; Josephy 645–46).

The priests saw a wonderful opportunity in this incident—and again it is important to weigh Rosati's account line by line.

These nations have not yet been corrupted by commerce with others; they have gentle manners and are very numerous. We have conceived the most powerful desire not to let slip such a fine opportunity. [Father] Condamine has offered to go there next spring with one other. Meanwhile we are going to gather information about what we have been told and on the means of making the trip. It will be necessary to pass through the regions of several intensely fierce tribes, and we will do all in our power to go to their aid. (600, my translation)

"These nations have not yet been corrupted . . .; they have gentle manners." Here, they come seeking Christianity, "and they are numerous." The priests could hardly hesitate to leap at such an opportunity, for it touched a longing older than Columbus—to find an isolated enclave of numerous western souls, all yearning sweetly, appreciatively, and docilely for the gifts of baptism and Christian teaching, or who were already holy without knowing it. This idea has persisted into recent times in the myth of a Shangri-La, in popular accounts of Tibet and the Dalai Lama, and in reports of a gentle people in the remote Philippines who seemed to meet the outside world for the first time in the 1960s. But accounts of such pure, remote peoples can also be found in the fourteenth-century *Travels of Sir John Mandeville*, which stitched together dozens of ancient legends. In the far isle of Bragman or Brahmin, one passage reported, the people "even if they are not Christian nevertheless . . . live a commendable life, are folk of great virtue, flying away from all sins and vices and malice, and they keep the Ten Commandments well. . . . They do nothing to another man that they would not have done to themselves. . . . They believe in God who made all things, and worship Him with all their power" (Mandeville 178). In short, in far places were pure-living heathens just ripe for the final touch of salvation, the arrival of a kindly mission to reinforce all their natural goodness and unite them with the gospel.

But Bishop Rosati and his companions could not immediately act on this romantic possibility. Just as the Protestants would do a short time later, they waited to gather more information, especially about a barrier of hostility that might block their way. Besides, at this time Rosati led only a small band of mission priests at St. Louis; they were just raising the walls of their own much-needed churches. Catholic missionaries would not arrive at the Columbia until many years later; in a letter of 1839, Rosati would appeal to the Jesuit Order to send missionaries in order to answer the pleas of three successive Indian "deputations" that had come to St. Louis by then (reprinted in Blanchet, *Historical Sketches* 43–44).

Bishop Rosati's original report weaves together threads of wonder, puzzlement, hope, and yearning—all of which are echoed in the Protestant account that came out many months later, in 1833. That front page of the *Christian Advocate* is much more complicated, however. It does not have just one author, as the Rosati letter does, but consists of one letter enclosed in another, and both those letters refer to further background materials and play upon current issues in American Indian policies and Methodist missions. Both letters also refer directly and extensively to William Clark, presenting him in passages of twisted or unreliable information.

The two letters filled three front-page columns of the *Christian Advocate and Journal* of March 1, 1833; I have reprinted them in full from that source in the Appendix.[3] The covering letter was written by Gabriel P. Disosway of New York, a merchant who had financed the founding of the Methodist Missionary Society in 1819 and remained active on mission boards.[4] This letter introduces and then reinforces a letter written to Disosway by William Walker, an Indian agent in Ohio. Walker's letter develops what he calls an anecdote. Walker had gone to Missouri on official business to survey western lands for the Wyandots, and in St. Louis he had seen William Clark in the fall of 1831. During his visit, Walker writes, he saw "chiefs of the Flat-head nation" who were staying at Clark's house—and all of them indeed had flattened heads. They had come to St. Louis as a delegation to learn of white men's religion, and Walker learned from Clark that the latter had given them very positive instructions in Christian doctrines.

As these letters are arranged on the newspaper page, Walker's letter fills the middle of the three columns, and smack in the center of his column is a sketch diagram, in profile, of a flattened head, with dotted lines to show "the usual rotundity of a human head."

Certainly Walker did not see all that he claimed to see here. For reasons that will unfold in a moment, he may have been confused at the time by being suddenly exposed to a lot of new information, and he may have jumbled his recollections months later, as he wrote them out for Disosway. Nevertheless, his eye-witness account was combined on the printed page with the striking image of a flattened head and a couple of paragraphs explaining the flattening process "produced by a pressure upon the cranium in infancy." At the heart of his story was this sensational exotic touch.

Walker and Disosway both intended their letters to be published— and to stir up support for a new mission effort. Walker certainly knew that Disosway had the influence to reach a wide audience through his church. At the end, he apologizes for his hasty "rough and uncouth scroll" and concludes: "You are at liberty to make what use you please of it."

Disosway chose to make use of it in two distinct ways, and probably Walker had both of them in mind. They nicely balance each other on the page. Disosway wrote an introduction of six paragraphs, and then presented Walker's long letter in full; afterwards, he went on with another long column of information about the Flatheads and exhorted: "Let the Church awake from her slumbers and go forth" to save these people. The first parts of both his and Walker's letters are, however, not about Flatheads at all, but about the Wyandots of Ohio. About half of the whole article, then, is a report on the Wyandots, and half develops the anecdote of Walker's visit with Clark.

These halves are connected historically by the fact that Walker met with Clark regarding his surveying trip to the West as a Wyandot agent. But there is also a possible rhetorical connection, which would catch the interest of Methodist readers of the *Christian Advocate*. The Wyandot report is a success story about a recent Methodist mission in Ohio, and so it makes a fitting preface to the exhortation to go farther west and reach another promising Indian people. In his opening section, Disosway also points to failures in secular Indian policies, most notably the pressure to expel all the eastern tribes to lands west of the Mississippi.

Disosway refers to the removal policy in his first paragraph and immediately praises the Wyandots for holding out against it. "Among those who still remain are the Wyandots, a tribe long distinguished as standing at the head of the great Indian family." After sketching their early history, he repeats this point: "The Wyandots, amounting to five hundred, are the only Indians in Ohio who have determined to remain upon their lands." They have been offered western lands, he explains, but they "wisely resolved to send agents to explore the region offered them in exchange, before they made any decision." The exploration proved that the land was unsuitable, and so they rejected the offer.

Disosway then goes on to suggest that the Wyandots have become shrewd Americans largely as a result of recent missions among them.

> The wonderful effects of the Gospel among the Wyandots are well known. Providence has blessed in a most remarkable manner the labors of our missionaries for their conversion. Knowledge, civilization, and social comforts have followed the introduction of Christianity into their regions.

The Wyandots have thus become capable of dealing with even the most initially attractive but ultimately specious propositions.

> To all of the Indians residing within the jurisdiction of the states or territories the United States propose to purchase their present possessions and improvements, and in return to pay them acre for acre with lands west of the Mississippi river. Among the inducements to make this exchange are the following: perpetuity in their new abodes, as the faith of the government is pledged never to sanction another removal; the organization of a territorial government for their use like those in Florida, Arkansas, and Michigan, and the privilege to send delegates to congress, as is now enjoyed by the other territories. Could the remaining tribes of the original possessors of this country place implicit reliance upon these assurances and prospects, this scheme to meliorate

their condition, and to bring them within the pale of civilized life, might safely be pronounced great, humane, and rational.

But, Disosway continues, the Wyandots have been wise enough to look before they leapt—and they have refused the government offer.

Walker's letter then bolsters Disosway's by providing details about the rejected land. It had little timber and no soil suitable for long-term agriculture; even where there was timber, the land was rough and broken. Furthermore, the whole large area between western Missouri and the Rockies was already inhabited by "wild, fierce, and warlike people." Beyond that barrier, however, there might be a different prospect. "West of the mountains reside the Flat-Heads, and many other tribes, whose names I do not now recollect." This line brings Walker to a new topic, his anecdote about Flatheads and General Clark.

A modern reader needs some background information at this point about matters that many of Walker's readers would have recognized immediately. The mission to the Wyandots was in fact a very famous effort the Methodists had organized among American Indians. Both Disosway and Walker had been involved in it, and it sprang from another strange and improbable tale, the career of a powerful preacher named John Stewart.

Stewart was a freeborn mulatto from Virginia who experienced a sudden religious conversion near Marietta, Ohio, and soon afterwards heard a voice directing him to press on to the northwest. He made his way to Sandusky in 1817, right to the doorstep of William Walker, the Indian subagent of the time and the father of Disosway's correspondent. Walker helped him find an interpreter and begin meetings with the Wyandots. After several months of preaching, Stewart applied to become a properly licensed Methodist minister. His mission soon drew support from Ohio Methodists and stimulated the founding of the Methodist Missionary Society in 1819—with financial support from Disosway. Stewart died at age thirty-seven in 1823, but the Upper Sandusky mission continued to develop with a school, a church, a house for a resident missionary family, and productive farms. By the time of the removal pressures in Ohio, the Christian Wyandots included many well-educated and effective resisters. The younger William Walker compiled a little memoir of John Stewart in 1827, and his story was a well-known object lesson in how the most unlikely missionary could achieve wonders if he followed a true calling.[5]

Disosway drums on that same topic at the close of his article, but, in his second section, he also develops a theme we have already seen in Bishop Rosati's report: that the Flatheads are especially appealing because they are isolated, virtuous, and even holy people already. To make this point, Disosway calls upon expert witnesses. Unfortunately, he cites them in a brief footnote reference that has often been omitted in later reprintings of his letter, and he uses no quotation marks.[6] His authorities are Lewis and Clark and Ross Cox, a fur trader who had published a book about the Columbia region in 1830. Disosway copies passages from both sources and runs them together to create a simple but regrettable confusion. He quotes Lewis and Clark about flat-headed Indians of the lower Columbia, near the Pacific, and Cox about the Flat-head tribes of the western Rockies.

Disosway lifted the Lewis and Clark passage almost verbatim from the *History of the Expedition,* which was digested from the explorers' journals. The passage describes the process of infant head-flattening which was widely practiced by Chinooks, Clatsops, and others along the Columbia River from the Cascade Mountains to the Pacific coast. (See Coues 774–75; and compare Moulton 6:433.) The Cox passage praises the inland Flathead tribes for their striking virtues. Disosway joins these ideas by saying that the astonishing "deformity . . . of the Flat-Head Indians is redeemed by other numerous good qualities. Travellers relate that they have fewer vices than any of the tribes of those regions." Then he proceeds to summarize, paraphrase, and directly quote Cox (see Cox 219, 230–31):

> They are honest, brave, and peaceable. The women become exemplary wives and mothers, and a husband with an unfaithful companion is a circumstance almost unknown among them. They believe in the existence of a good and evil Spirit, with rewards and punishments of a future state. Their religion promises to the

virtuous after death a climate where perpetual summer will shine over plains filled with their much loved buffalo, and upon streams abounding with the most delicious fish. Here they will spend their time in hunting and fishing, happy and undisturbed from every enemy; while the bad Indian will be consigned to a place of eternal snows, with fires in his sight that he cannot enjoy, and buffalo and deer that cannot be caught to satisfy his hunger.

A curious tradition prevails among them concerning beavers. These animals, so celebrated for their sagacity, they believe are a fallen race of Indians, who have been condemned on account of their wickedness, by the great Spirit, to their present form of the brute creation. At some future period they also declare that these fallen creatures will be restored to their former state.

Disosway no doubt added these passages as a supplement to Walker's account, simply to explain head-flattening and supply the most recent information about the people who practiced it. But by running Lewis and Clark together with Cox he created a people who never existed, a people both glamorous and grotesque in his view:

They are not ignorant of the immortality of their souls, and speak of some future delicious island or country where departed spirits rest. May we not indulge the hope that the day is not far distant when the missionaries will penetrate into these wilds where the Sabbath bell has never yet tolled since the world began? There is not, perhaps, west of the Rocky mountains, any portion of the Indians that presents at this moment a spectacle so full in interest to the contemplative mind as the Flat-Head tribe. Not a thought of converting or civilizing them ever enters the mind of the sordid, demoralized hunters and fur trader[s]. Those simple children of nature even shrink from the loose morality and inhumanities often introduced among them by the white man. Let the Church awake from her slumbers, and go forth in her strength to the salvation of these wandering sons of our native forests.

Walker's long letter in the *Christian Advocate* thus appears encircled, as it were, by this halo of Disosway's letter.

Like Disosway's letter, Walker's contains glaring mistakes; yet Walker also includes so many accurate details that one must wonder how, exactly, he came to write such distortions. In the first place, he sensibly explains that he carried an official introduction to Clark and got further letters from him to Indian agents in the west. But then he goes on to describe seeing the "flat-headed" Indians at Clark's house:

> While in his office and transacting business with him, he informed me that three chiefs from the Flat-Head nation were in his house, and were quite sick, and that one (the fourth) had died a few days ago. They were from west of the Rocky Mountains. Curiosity prompted me to step into the adjoining room to see them, having never seen any, but often heard of them. I was struck by their appearance. They differ in appearance from any tribe of Indians I have ever seen: small in size, delicately formed, small limbs, and the most exact symmetry throughout, except the head.

Other evidence contradicts this passage. As we have seen, Bishop Rosati makes no mention of odd head shapes. The painter George Catlin later met and painted the two surviving visitors, and recorded no irregular head shape. Evidence collected much later in the west enabled Josephy and others to identify all four visitors as Nez Perce, with possibly some connections to the nearby Flathead people of the Rockies. Yet Walker states that he saw these men himself, and he accurately notes that they had been sick and one had died.

Walker confuses fact and fiction again when he presents the reason for their visit.

> The distance they had travelled on foot was nearly three thousand miles to see Gen. Clarke, their great father, as they called him, he being the first American officer they ever became acquainted with, and having much confidence in him, they had come to consult him as they said, upon very important matters. Gen. C. related to me the object of their mission, and, my dear friend, it is impossible for me to describe to you my feelings while listening to his narrative. I will here relate it as briefly as I well

can. It appeared that some white man had penetrated into their country, and happened to be a spectator at one of their religious ceremonies, which they scrupulously perform at stated periods. He informed them that their mode of worshipping the supreme Being was radically wrong, and instead of being acceptable and pleasing, it was displeasing to him; he also informed them that the white people *away* toward the rising of the sun had been put in possession of the true mode of worshipping the great Spirit. They had a book containing directions how to conduct themselves in order to enjoy his favor and hold converse with him; and with this guide, no one need go astray, but every one that would follow the directions laid down there, could enjoy, in this life, his favor, and after death would be received into the country where the great Spirit resides, and live for ever with him.

Upon receiving this information, they called a national council to take this subject into consideration. Some said, if this be true, it is certainly high time we were put in possession of this mode, and if *our* mode of worshipping be wrong and displeasing to the great Spirit, it is time we had laid it aside, we must know something more about this, it is a matter that cannot be put off, the sooner we know it the better. They accordingly deputed four of their chiefs to proceed to St. Louis to see their great father, Gen. Clarke, to inquire of him, having no doubt but he would tell them the whole truth about it.

Here Walker seems to be summarizing what Clark told him, including misinformation that originated elsewhere. It could have come from faulty interpreters or from members of the fur trading party that had brought the Indians to St. Louis. The Catholic priests heard a different account, confirmed by other sources—that the challenge arose from boys who had gone to the Red River school, not from a white spectator at Indian ceremonies. The priests also said nothing about a white men's book. The sentence about the four Indians being "deputed" by a "national council" is also very misleading. Josephy and others have reasoned that the four Indians represented just a small group of villages

(Josephy 96). In fact, the "national council" arrangement rather mirrors Walker's own situation as part of a deputation from a council of the Wyandots. The Wyandots also had held full meetings in earlier years to debate the merits of white men's religion of the book. Such meetings are fully described in Walker's memoir of Stewart.

Still, Walker could be right in saying that the four came on purpose to see Clark, for Clark was indeed known and warmly remembered decades after his expedition. And both this account and Rosati's agree that the Indians came hundreds of miles, from the other side of the Rockies, on some kind of quest for religious teaching.

Walker's understanding of what he observed in this moment could have been distorted for many reasons. He was startled by what he saw and heard. "I was struck by their appearance," he says of the visitors. "They differ from any tribe of Indians I have ever seen." This is a weighty sentence from someone who had lived among Indians all his life. Later he adds, "It is impossible to describe to you my feelings while listening to his narrative." What he heard was filtered through Clark, a legendary figure himself, and through accounts Clark must have heard from others. Finally, Walker met Clark in Clark's office, which was in his house, with the Indians in an adjoining room, lying ill. These points taken together give an impression, which Walker may have felt, that Clark was acting personally as well as officially in caring for these men— going far beyond his duty in giving them shelter and support.

For all these reasons, Walker could have seen, heard, and felt more than he could hold in a coherent memory. As beginning psychology and law students often learn from dramatic experiences in class, eye-witness accounts vary greatly. They can be conditioned by suggestions from figures of authority. They can also become bizarre when they describe startling, baffling, novel incidents. If Clark said to Walker that there were "Flathead" Indians in the next room, and "quite sick," perhaps Walker looked in very briefly and cautiously, expected see flat-headed Indians, and so saw shapes that he later recalled as flat-headed and emaciated.

By describing people "small in size, delicately formed, small limbs, and the most exact symmetry throughout, except the head," Walker seems to imply that he looked very closely, in fact took time to walk around standing figures. But these lines could mean only that he relied on Clark's word for what they looked like—and remembered some of Clark's printed words, too. In the *History* of the expedition, the main published record of Lewis and Clark in this period, the Indians of the Pacific coast are sometimes described as diminutive, though not at all delicate or symmetrical (Coues 2:755, 773).

To complicate matters, there is Walker's accurate description of Clark's house, including the office and an adjoining room. Clark also maintained an elaborate museum there, a well-known repository of Indian artifacts, often visited by curious travelers. According to a survey of the available records about the museum, it "occupied a brick structure about 100 feet long and 30 feet wide, attached to the south end of his residence on the southeast corner of Vine and Main Streets. The building also served as a council chamber where Clark met members of the many Indian delegations who came to St. Louis to confer with him" (McDermott 370; Ewers, "William Clark's Indian Museum"). Travelers recorded seeing hundreds of items there, including mounted animal specimens, minerals, and Indian artifacts, especially a great variety of native costumes. In 1833 Prince Maximilian of Wied noted "portraits of the most distinguished Indian chiefs of different nations" in the council room (McDermott 372). Perhaps Clark was deliberately creating a western version of Charles Willson Peale's famous museum in Philadelphia, where the main hall displayed portraits of the greatest Americans along with cabinets of American birds, animals, and other objects of natural history—including many items Peale had received from Lewis and Clark.

Another visitor noted a particular curio at Clark's museum at about this time. He dined with Clark in 1834 and then went into the council chamber, where the walls "were completely coated with Indian arms and dresses, and the mantelpiece loaded with various objects of curiosity connected with the aborigines. Among the latter was that celebrated piece of pottery that has caused so much idle speculation among the curious—a small vase formed by three perfect heads blended in one, the features being marked, and wholly dissimilar from those of any existing race of Indians" (McDermott 372).

Walker was thus surrounded by images of Indian features, especially heads of various shapes and histories, when he met with Clark and heard the strange story of his visitors. Little wonder if an hour later, let alone a full year later, his memory was too crowded to be accurate.

Now to Walker's account of the crucial interview containing Clark's replies to the seekers:

> They arrived at St. Louis, and presented themselves to Gen. C. The latter was somewhat puzzled being sensible of the responsibility that rested on him; he however proceeded by informing them that what they had been told by the white man in their own country, was true. Then went into a succinct history of man, from his creation down to the advent of the Saviour; explained to them all the moral precepts contained in the Bible, expounded to them the decalogue. Informed them of the advent of the Saviour, his life, precepts, his death, resurrection, ascension, and the relation he now stands to man as a mediator—that he will judge the world, &c.

This account of Clark's message looks absurd after a moment's reflection. He was not a minister; he did not know the Indians' language; and these ideas of salvation history are much too complicated to explain briefly, through an interpreter. These and other objections come to mind almost immediately. Here, it seems, Walker has to be embellishing his report.

On the other hand, Clark must have said *something* to the visitors, and it is very doubtful that he would have *denied* the truth of the Christian message. Clark was at least a nominal Christian, "one of the organizers of and a pew holder in Christ Church," the Episcopal congregation in St. Louis, as well as a charter member of a Masonic lodge there (Johnson 196). We should bear in mind that St. Louis was founded by French Catholics, and for a long period the Catholic church was the sole agent of Christian teaching there, though in the early years even Catholic services were sporadic. Clark and his wife thus seized the occasion—and wrote their conspicuous signatures in the parish records—to have their three children baptized at the Catholic church during the visit of a bishop in 1814 (Behrmann 18). Moreover, Clark was an important public official and a business partner and ally with many well-known Catholic citizens. He had ample reason to keep on good terms with Catholics and with all other denominations that came into St. Louis as American Protestants moved west (Foley 201, 256).

As Walker presents the situation, the Indian visitors let Clark know that they already had some ideas of Christianity. Bishop Rosati's account confirms that they arrived with some understanding of the cross and baptism. What, then, would Clark have said in reply to their questions? If he affirmed that "what they had been told in their own country was true," he would have had to go on to make some further explanation of the Christian message. Walker's description of his answer is therefore not entirely fanciful. In any case, there is no knowing what the Indians heard or understood through translation.

The *Christian Advocate* article added many new touches to the story of Clark and the four Indians. It presented Walker's first-hand experience of seeing three of them, and it related this incident to the famous and providential mission of John Stewart to the Wyandots. Disosway reiterated the importance of mission work in preparing Indians to gain political and economic independence, especially in the face of current pressures to drive them off their lands. He also raised the idea that a peaceful, holy people was awaiting the Gospel in the far West. In the middle of these writings was the sensational image of a flattened head, with accompanying detailed descriptions and the news that a delegation of flat-headed Indians had come from the other side of the Rockies and received assurances from William Clark about the truths of Christianity. Of all these new touches, which was the most distorted or misleading? It is hard to choose.[7]

These touches also kindled new flames of imagination. The *Christian Advocate and Journal*, as its title implies, was a religious paper, published in New York and circulated across the United States for the Methodist Episcopal Church. At this time, it had the largest circulation of any periodical in the world, but its chief readership was Methodist. For present purposes the core of Methodist beliefs can be reduced to three main points: (1) all people are capable of salvation; (2) God works directly in the world, to touch individual souls and achieve astonishing reformations; (3) evangelism can be effected through ministers who are not highly educated or specially trained but who impart the power of their own personal transcendent experience. Readers with these beliefs could take in the Walker and Disosway letters not as mere reports, but as glimmers of a present-day miracle or revelation. To some, it seemed that God's will was working through the Indians from out of the West, and through Clark's response to them.

Among Methodists this incident soon became known as the "Macedonian call" or the "Macedonian cry." In Acts 16 the apostle Paul tries to preach to and convert gentiles, people of a radically different faith, but an unseen power stops him and redirects his route until he receives a vision that leads him into Greece:

> And they went through the region of Phyrgia and Galatia, having been forbidden by the Holy Spirit to speak the word in Asia. And when they had come opposite Mysia, they attempted to go into Bithynia, but the Spirit of Jesus did not allow them; so, passing by Mysia, they went down to Troas. And a vision appeared to Paul in the night: a man of Macedonia was standing beseeching him and saying, "Come over into Macedonia and help us." And when he had seen the vision, immediately we sought to go on into Macedonia, concluding that God had called us to preach the gospel to them. (Acts 16:6–10, Revised Standard Version)

To many in 1833 it seemed that this same call was renewed. Just as Paul's steps into Macedonia had started the spread of Christianity across the Roman Empire and into Europe, so this call could begin the spread of the gospel across America to the Pacific.

Like Paul, later missionaries were driven by Jesus' command at the end of the gospels: "Go therefore and make disciples, baptizing them in the name of the Father and of the Son and of the Holy Spirit, teaching them to observe all that I have commanded you" (Matthew 28:19–20, RSV). Within weeks of the Walker letter, moneys were being collected and candidates sought for a mission to the Flatheads. On March 22, another letter appeared in the *Christian Advocate* to second

Disosway's ringing appeal. Wilbur Fisk, the new president of Wesleyan University, wrote that he had already proposed the idea to his former student, Jason Lee:

> Let two suitable men, unencumbered with families, and possessing the spirit of martyrs, throw themselves into the nation. Live with them—learn their language—preach Christ to them—and, as the way opens, introduce schools, agriculture, and the arts of civilized life. The means for these improvements can be introduced through the fur traders, and by the reinforcements with which from time to time we can strengthen the mission. Money shall be forth coming. I will be bondsman for the Church. All we want is the men. Who will go? Who? I know of one young man who I think will go; and of whom I can say, I know of none like him for the enterprise. If he will go, (and we have written to him on the subject), we only want another, and the mission will be commenced the coming season. . . . Bright will be his crown, glorious his reward.

Some readers, however, questioned Fisk's plan, beginning with the Mission Board of the Methodist Church. Its minutes of March 20, 1833, recorded a resolution that the corresponding secretary should "open a correspondence with General Clark, the Indian Agent, and with any other person he may judge expedient" in relation to the mission Fisk had proposed (Minutes of the Board of Managers 174). No documents from such a correspondence can be found, but in May the *Christian Advocate* printed three letters with further information about Indians and the hardships of living in the West. Another such article has been traced to a newspaper in Illinois, near St. Louis. Later publications questioned whether the "delegation" to Clark was a myth. Writer after writer, however, turned to William Clark for first-hand confirmation of the Indians' visit and what it meant. According to these published reports, Clark changed a few details in the Walker account, but on the whole he affirmed that the story of the four Indians was true. On the strength of these repeated assurances, Jason Lee passed through St. Louis on his way to cross the Rockies.[8]

Three interrelated letters appeared in the *Christian Advocate* of May 10, 1833 The first, from E. W. Sehon in St. Louis, reported a meeting with Clark, who had already received numerous inquiries:

Dear Brethren:—The communication respecting the Flat Head Indians which appeared a few weeks since in your paper and the call of Dr. Fisk, have excited considerable attention. I have just received a letter from Brother Brunson, propounding several questions, which he wished me to have answered here, so that the desired information might be rendered available to the Christian public. I called immediately upon Gen. Clark, who received me kindly. He informed me he was just answering, or has just answered some communications on the subject. I was struck with the propriety of an immediate communication from this place; I therefore send you his, sincerely wishing it may be useful.

Gen. Clark informed me that the publication which had appeared in the Advocate was correct. Of the return of the two Indians nothing is known. He informed me the cause of their visit was the following: Two of their number had received an education at some Jesuitical school in Montreal, Canada, had returned to the tribe, and endeavored as far as possible to instruct their brethren how the whites approached the Great Spirit. The consequence was, a spirit of inquiry was aroused, a deputation appointed and a tedious journey of three thousand miles performed, to learn for themselves of Jesus and him crucified.

This much is directly to the point and straightforward. It sounds stilted to say of the Indians that "a spirit of inquiry was aroused, a deputation appointed and a tedious journey . . . performed," but Clark's reply is otherwise plain—and noteworthy for two reasons. First, it fits with Bishop Rosati's account about Indians educated in Canada (at Red River rather than Montreal). Second, the fact that Clark makes this correction seems to imply that he endorses the rest of Walker's letter; he states that the article as a whole "was correct" and that the aim of the Indians was to learn about Christianity. Moreover, Sehon found Clark friendly and freshly prepared to answer just these questions. (If Clark wrote out answers to any inquiries they have never been found, though his papers have been thoroughly searched for any scrap about this incident. See Josephy 102n36.)

Sehon concludes by introducing another source of information about the West, a letter answering his (or perhaps "Brother Brunson's") particular questions. The author is Robert Campbell. Sehon calls him an intelligent, gentlemanly, reliable man and "one of the first traders among those Indians."

Dear Sir:—In compliance with your request I shall give you a very few brief answers to the questions you have put respecting the Flat Head Indians.

1. Prospects of a mission? I cannot pretend to say what prospects there would be in a religious point of view. The Flat Head Indians are proverbial for their mild disposition and friendship to the whites, and I have little hesitation in saying a missionary would be treated by them with kindness.

2. Distance from St. Louis to Council Bluffs? The distance is about five hundred miles.

3. Whether suitable interpreters can be obtained for the Flat Head Indians? There would be some difficulty to have religious matters explained, because the best interpreters are half-Indians, that you could not explain to their minds the matter you would require to have told to the Indians.

4. The number of the Indians? There are about forty lodges of these Indians, averaging, say seven Indians to a lodge.

5. Do steamers go as far as the Council Bluffs? With the exception of the American Fur Company's steamboats, which ascend as high as the Yellowstone, none go as far as the Bluffs.

6. Do fur traders go to the Flat Head country, and at what season of the year, and will they allow the missionaries to go in their company? There is every season one or more companies leaving St. Louis in the month of March and I doubt not but they would willingly allow a missionary to accompany them, but the privations that a gentleman of that profession would have to

encounter would be very great, as the shortest route that he would have by land would be not less than one thousand miles, and when he reached his destination he would have to travel with the Indians, as they have no permanent villages, nor have the traders any houses, but like the Indian, move in their leather lodges from place to place throughout the season.

Looked at dispassionately, these questions seem random and naive; these answers, polite but terse. Altogether Campbell offers a fair warning: You will have to travel far—then keep traveling and live a comfortless existence—just to reach a few dozen Indians and struggle to make yourself understood.

The eager desire of many Methodists, however, can be gauged from a further letter in the *Advocate*, printed right after Campbell's and vigorously denying his cautions. The writer, one A. M'Allister, has been reading his Lewis and Clark, and he finds thousands of souls out west ripe for the evangelist. "The Cho-pun-nish or Pierced Nose Indians, are about seven thousand in number according to Gen. Clark's account." Moreover, "The Indians residing on the tide water of the Orregon [i.e., the Columbia] and below the great falls are about eight thousand in number. Those residing on the north west of the Oregon, on the coast of the Pacific number about six thousand. Those on the south-south west on the same coast number about ten thousand two hundred. . . . Gen. Clark discovered on the waters of the Origon and coast of the Pacific more than sixty tribes of Indians, numbering about eighty thousand souls."

It does not occur to M'Allister that eighty thousand souls might resist or overwhelm a handful of missionaries, that Lewis and Clark's numbers might be decades out of date, and that the explorers themselves had a miserable, cold, wet, hungry winter at the mouth of the Columbia. He presses on with "highly probable" numbers and denies any hint that missions might fail. To M'Allister's reading, recent events spell out a sign from God:

How ominous [i.e., providential] this visit of the Cho-pin-nish and Flat Head Indians! How loud the call to the missionary spirit of the age! It calls to my mind a declaration made by Bishop Soule when preaching at a camp in this country. Speaking of the missionary zeal of the Methodist preachers, of their extended field of labor, their untiring perseverance to compass the earth and spread Scriptural holiness through all the world, "We will not cease," said he, "until we shall have planted the standard of Christianity high on the summit of the Stony Mountains."

Already it would seem that a door is open, and the Indian[s] from the lofty summit of the Rocky Mountains, look far east with burning desire to behold the coming of the messenger of God.[9]

These three letters thus pass from Sehon's sensible questions, through Campbell's laconic cautions, to M'Allister's lines of sheer rhapsody. The *Christian Advocate* editors evidently stressed M'Allister's point of view, for they shortened other pieces to make space for these letters. They again printed the sketch of the flattened head, and beneath it they introduced these columns as follows: "The following correspondence and communication will be read with great interest. Is it not the voice of Heaven to us? The field opens gloriously. Read Mr. M'Allister's letter below. The men are ready: let the Missionary Society have the means. Let the whole Church become a missionary band."

Such were the exaggerations that attached themselves to the story of Clark and the Indians, even through efforts to qualify and question Walker's report. This credulity might seem touching or amusing, but it soon carried dozens of young men and women into months of hardship, sickness, and frustration, and led many of them and their children to early graves.

Combined with this missionary passion was a complex impulse of expansionist patriotism. Even if missionaries did not save souls, they might teach and subdue some fierce Indians and so save white settlers from bloodshed. This is the main thrust of a further attempt to get at the truth of Walker's article, a committee report of October 1833 published in the Jacksonville *Illinois Patriot*.

A meeting was held in this place a few weeks since, by some gentlemen who felt anxious to bear their part in Christianizing and civilizing the Indians of this country, and particularly those who have expressed a desire to become acquainted with our religious institutions. A committee was appointed by the meeting to make the necessary investigations. This committee, consisting of the Rev. Lucian Farnam and Mr. Julius Reed, visited St. Louis, and there made such inquiries of individuals who had become personally acquainted with the character and locality of the tribes in the vicinity of the Rocky Mountains, and consulted such authorities as the object of their investigations seemed to demand. . . .

This committee made a report, an extract from which will be found below. We publish this extract because it contains much interesting and authentic information in regard to a portion of our country which is, at no distant day, to be occupied by citizens from all parts of the United States. If any benevolent individuals are disposed to go out as pioneers among the tribes who inhabit these regions, and shall become instrumental in so subduing their natural ferocity as to induce them to "beat their swords into ploughshares and their spears into pruning hooks," they should be looked upon as contributors to the happiness and prosperity of the nation at large. In so doing, they will save the lives and property of many who would otherwise fall a prey to savage barbarity in its natural state. (Reprinted in Mowry 37–39)

The committee report itself opens by dwelling on a single point: the committee did its best but could not find out every detail or reach every source. "The facts which we procured, were drawn from several sources, and those among the best that are to be found. And the inquiries of the committee were as extensive and minute as their time and the nature of the case would permit."

This could mean that the committee saw Clark but not Bishop Rosati, or it could mean that it neither met with Clark nor with other witnesses. The report mentions Clark but with a maddening vagueness:

It is a fact that in the autumn of 1831, four Indians from beyond the Rocky Mountains came to General Clark, in St. Louis, for no other ostensible purpose than to make inquiries concerning our religion. The circumstances which led to this visit are already before the public. Three of these Indians were from what is called the Flathead tribe, and one of them from another tribe, which I do not recollect that General Clark mentioned—probably, however, from the adjoining tribe, called Pierced-Nose Indians. They remained several months with General Clark, and attended all the places of worship in the city. During their stay two of them died; in the spring the others returned to their countrymen, very favorably impressed, and highly gratified with the kind treatment they had received. The ideas they obtained on the subject of their embassy must have been very limited and indistinct, from the difficulty both of understanding the particular points of their inquiries, and of communicating to them the answers in such terms as they could comprehend. And even had they been adept in our language, and had they possessed every facility for instruc-tion, the time was so short, that they could have carried back to their nation but a very imperfect sketch of the Christian religion. From anything that could be learned on the subject, it does not appear whether these Indians were a delegation from their tribe, or whether, being of a more inquisitive turn of mind than their brethren, and having their curiosity excited by the white man's story, they came as mere adventurers to gratify their curiosity. Nor does it appear whether those who returned, received such an impression in regard to the Christian religion as that they would prefer it to their own superstitious rites. (Quoted in Mowry 39)

The sober, cautious questioning here is evidently meant to tone down the reports "already before the public" from the pens of Walker and Disosway. The idea of a "delegation"—of the Indians' having come on a definite religious quest rather than out of general curiosity—and the notion of their receiving clear religious teaching are questioned.[10] Did Clark speak to these issues directly; are his words somehow behind this report? His openness to other inquirers makes it likely that the committee saw him, and the report's one clause written in the first person—"I do not recall that General Clark mentioned"—could be a telling slip in this otherwise guarded paragraph. In any case, two new details emerge here: the Indian visitors "remained several months with General Clark, and attended all the places of worship in the city." These points evidently support Walker's claims that he saw them in Clark's house and that they came with a deep religious interest.

These are the documents that appeared and either confirmed or qualified the Clark-Walker-Disosway story during the time that the Methodist plans for a mission were taking shape. But the church and its leaders were also alert to what they took as another divine intervention.

In 1832, Nathaniel J. Wyeth had managed to lead a small band of adventurers across the Rockies to the Columbia, and when he returned to Boston, late in 1833, he brought along two Indian visitors—"a halfblood Flathead boy named Baptiste, the son of a Hudson's Bay Company employee, François Payette, and a twenty-year-old Nez Perce youth" (Josephy 106). Wyeth was planning to return to the Oregon country to set up a trading company, which would be supported by an annual ship from Boston to the Columbia River. This was urgent news for the Methodists. Jason Lee was about to go to St. Louis in November to gather information and make proper plans for his mission, but the mission board directed him to go to Boston to meet with Wyeth instead. Thus Lee spent hours learning about first-hand and recent experiences in the far West, and the two men worked out plans for crossing the continent together the following spring and for sending out a supply ship to meet them on the lower Columbia. Lee also wrote a full letter for the *Christian Advocate* (February 21, 1834) describing the animated spirit of the younger Indian boy—"Me want to learn to drive, me want to learn to read, me want to learn *every* thing"—and the more "stoical" but still impressionable manner of the older youth, who had a head "literally flattened by compressure." Out of his experiences in Boston, Lee assured his readers yet again that "the providence of God has been strongly marked in the developement of this enterprise from its commencement."

Years later, Lee's nephew, Daniel Lee, looked back on this period very differently. In 1844 Jason Lee was dead, the Methodist missions in Oregon had collapsed, and Daniel Lee had survived his own frustrations.

He had good reasons for writing that the original Walker-Disosway letters amounted to a "high-wrought account" and not a "divine mandate," after all. Yet despite his obvious bias his version of what Clark knew and said in 1831 has its own revealing touches, if it is read in full.

An event took place in the year 1832 which directed the attention of the American churches to Oregon, as a vast field of benevolent enterprise, ripe for the introduction of the Gospel among its benighted inhabitants. Four Indians, from beyond the Rocky Mountains, belonging to one of the tribes (for there are several) who flatten their heads, probably the "Nez percé" tribe, accompanied some of the white trappers from the buffalo country down to the city of St. Louis. The resident United States' Indian agent, General Clark, was known to them as the first great chief of the white men who visited their nation. He had been seen by their fathers, who had often told them of his greatness, and it was natural they should desire to see him. They also expected to return to their own land, and make known their interview, as among the most interesting occurrences of their toilsome journey. Having great confidence in him, they made inquiries about the book of which they had been informed by the hunters, which the Great Spirit had given to the white men to teach them his will. The answers they received were in accordance with what had been told them. The writer saw General Clark in 1834, two years after their visit, and learned from him these particulars in relation to it. Two of them became sick, and died in St. Louis, and the other two started to return to their own land. It has been reported that one of them died on the way, and the other reached his tribe. As to the truth of this report, some have doubts. That both perished in the wilderness, the victims of sickness, famine, or war, appears more probable. A high-wrought account of the visit of these Indians to St. Louis, by some writer in the vicinity, was published in the Christian Advocate and Journal, New-York city, in March, 1833.

This is the most important periodical in the Methodist Episcopal Church. The sum was this: that these "red men" were from the Flat-head tribe, in the interior of Oregon, beyond the Rocky Mountains, from whom they had been sent by a council of their chiefs, as delegates to St. Louis, to inquire concerning the Word of the Great Spirit; that in prosecution of their great object they had travelled two thousand miles, through rugged mountains and barren plains and dangerous enemies, enduring cold and heat, thirst and hunger, and many hardships, and reached their destination in safety; and that having made known the object of their visit to General Clark, and gained the information they sought, two of them were snatched away by death, not being permitted to carry back the "glad tidings" to their anxious countrymen. These incorrect statements receiving the fullest confidence, many believed that the day had come, and that the call was imperative, to send the gospel to Oregon. First among these was that excellent man of God, Wilbur Fisk, D. D., at that time president of the Wesleyan University, Conn. Alive to everything favourable to the advancement of the kingdom of Christ, and seeing before the church "an open door" to the "red man" of the "far west," the "fields there white to harvest," he could not be silent. The Macedonian cry, as it seemed, reached him as a divine mandate. Immediately his voice was heard rousing the churches; especially did he urge on the Methodist Episcopal Church an immediate response. His appeal was heard: and the Missionary Society of the Methodist Episcopal Church determined to attempt the establishment of a mission among the Flat-head tribe of Indians, in Oregon; that tribe, for reasons before stated, appearing to demand their first missionary efforts in the country. (Lee and Frost 109–11)

It is hard to catch Lee's tone here. Some stilted phrases and brief quotations may make him sound caustic. Perhaps he was simply weary and disillusioned as a missionary. This passage also falls into two parts, with different tones, divided by the sentence naming Clark as the source of Lee's true particulars. It is the second, very critical part that has often been quoted, but Lee does not attack Clark even here; he rather laments the excesses in the *Christian Advocate* and the mistaken enthusiasm that ensued—the fact that incorrect statements inspired overconfident responses from Fisk and the Mission Society.

In the first part of this passage, Lee evidently means to set out the true information, with Clark as his direct authority. What does he affirm? At the very least, Lee states that the Indians came by choice to see Clark, they asked about religion and mentioned the white men's holy book, and "the answers they received were in accordance with what had been told them" by other informants. In short, Lee confirms the gist of Walker's letter. The new possibility he introduces is that the Indians might have traveled east just to visit Clark out of a natural desire to see a man who remained famous among their people, and that the religious questions emerged in the course of a more secular meeting.

But was religion merely an incidental matter in this famous incident of 1831, something of an afterthought? That hardly seems possible given the many other questionings and documents we have examined. Bishop Rosati's letter, E. W. Sehon's letter, and the committee report in the *Illinois Patriot* all reinforce Walker's report that the Indians traveled far with the specific aim of finding out about Christianity. The afterthought theory does not even fit well with the fact that Daniel Lee met with Clark in 1834. At that time, the Lees were about to embark from St. Louis—after making famous and elaborate arrangements— and their whole purpose was to answer what they and their sponsors took as a specific and deliberate Indian appeal. Clark must have known this: the plans of the Methodists were widely published, and when the Lees passed through St. Louis there was a large send-off meeting at the Methodist church. Daniel Lee spoke at that meeting, offering to visit the spot where the Indians were buried and "on his knees beg the God of missions to aid in the mighty undertaking which lay before them." After he spoke, the local Presbyterian minister encouraged the mission effort and recalled the Indians' visit "of which fact General Clark had assured him." (Reported in a letter from E. W. Sehon to *Zion's Herald*, reprinted in Hulbert and Hulbert 5:126–30)

One other point worth stressing is that it was William Clark's duty to know the missionaries' purposes before approving their traveling up the Missouri into Indian country (Jackson, *Voyages* 29–30). Yet he apparently made no attempt to dissuade the missionaries or dampen their spirits. Lee mentions nothing of the sort, though the long passage in his memoir is precisely the spot for him to do that.[11]

A definite religious quest by the Indians also appears in another crucial document—a version of the story printed years later by the artist George Catlin. He had met the two Indians who survived the winter in St. Louis, for he "travelled two thousand miles, companion with these young fellows, towards their own county, and became much pleased with their manners and conversation." Catlin documented their three months together aboard the American Fur Company steamboat *Yellow Stone*; he published portraits of both men, which show that neither of them had a flattened head. He also supplied their names—as "Hee-oh'ks-te-kin (the rabbit skin leggings) and H'co-a-h'co-ah'cotes-min (no horns on his head)"—identified them as Nez Perces, and reported that one of them died on this voyage, near the mouth of the Yellowstone River (Catlin 2:108–9).

According to Catlin, "These two men were part of a delegation that came across the Rocky Mountains to St. Louis, a few years since, to enquire for the truth of a representation which they said some white man had made amongst them, 'that our religion was better than theirs, and that all would be lost if they did not embrace it.'" A paragraph later he adds this crucial line: "When I first heard the report of the object of this extraordinary mission across the mountains, I could scarcely believe it; but in conversing with General Clark on a later occasion, I was fully convinced of the fact" (2:109).

Catlin's sentence seems very positive, but it, too, raises some questions. No one has ever doubted that he met the two Indians, learned a version of their names, painted their portraits, and rightly reported the death of one of them. But he writes of the other: "I have since learned [that he] arrived safely among his friends, conveying to them the melancholy intelligence of the deaths of all the rest of his party; but assurances at the same time from General Clark and many Reverend gentlemen, that the report which they had heard was well founded; and that missionaries, good and religious men, would soon come amongst them to teach this religion, so that they could all understand and have the benefits of it" (2:109). Here Catlin is spreading hearsay at best. It is also certain that he knew William Clark and could easily have asked for confirmation of the religious quest story. He had come to St. Louis in 1830 seeking Clark's support for his project of setting up as an artist of western Indians. He secured Clark's very friendly aid, traveled with him to treaty councils, painted Indians who posed for him in Clark's St. Louis chambers, and completed a portrait of Clark himself. He boarded the *Yellow Stone* as a guest of the American Fur Company, thanks no doubt to Clark's connections and good words on his behalf. But why then did Catlin first learn of this fascinating Indian visit—a ripe subject for his particular interests—only on board the steamboat, and from Clark many months later? The answer may be that the Indian visit was one of dozens of pressing matters on Clark's schedule in 1831, and became a famous incident only through Walker's letter in the *Christian Advocate*— a full year after the *Yellow Stone* left St. Louis with Catlin aboard.

One further item also points to Clark as the authority who confirmed the *Christian Advocate* account. In 1838 Jason Lee came east to meet with his mission board and conduct a fund-raising tour. Soon after he reached St. Louis, he addressed a large audience in the main church of Peoria, Illinois, and a local newspaper printed a detailed report of what he said. This report begins with the story of the Indians coming to meet with Clark, but contains an obvious error: it states that six Indians came east, three died in St. Louis, and one made it home safely. The Indians are correctly identified, however, as "of the Flat Head and Nez Perce tribes," and what follows this first paragraph seems more reliable. Here the report turns on what Lee recalled of his own experience as a beginning missionary: how exciting Walker's report was, how it was doubted at the time, and how Clark's reassurances tipped the balance:

This event created quite a sensation in the Christian community throughout the U.S.A. It was considered so remarkable that doubts were expressed by some whether the design of the Indians was really what it professed to be; and this skeptical feeling increasing, an inquiry was set on foot which resulted in the perfect establishment of the fact. In this inquiry the friends of Christianity were greatly aided by Gen. Clark. . . . He was acquainted, from personal experience, with the tribes spoken of, and became satisfied of the sincerity of the deputation shortly after their arrival at St. Louis. The event, therefore, was regarded as an intimation that Providence was opening the way for a mission to the tribes of Indians more immediately referred to, and to the tribes generally of that region—an intimation which Christians did not fail to obey with all reasonable expedition. (*Peoria (Illinois) Register and Northwestern Gazetteer*, October 6, 1838, quoted in Mockford 22)

In Lee's mind at least, Clark had confirmed Walker's story. Moreover, Lee and his nephew Daniel Lee began to read what little they could find about the West, and again turned to Clark. "The two ministers left New England with no other knowledge of the country than what they had gathered from Lewis and Clark's Travels, and one or two other works." They could find no better information in New York, or anywhere, until Providence stepped in once more and led them to Nathaniel Wyeth, freshly returned to Boston from beyond the Rockies (*Peoria Register*, quoted in Mockford 22–23).

Taken one by one the various records of the incident remain puzzling. They do not yield a consistent and satisfying account, even when read line by line, sifted together, and scrutinized for consistencies and telltale hints. Each of them is either sketchy, sensational, or colored by eager ideas for a mission or a western settlement. And every one strikes at least one note that does not ring true.

Perhaps the best way through this problem is to make a shift of focus. It is impossible to know exactly what the Indians asked Clark and what he replied, and why. But it is quite evident that they came to Clark with some kind of seeking, and white men later came to him with another. Both quests were rooted in troubled ignorance, and Clark was trusted to have the means to a good answer. The incident thus serves as a telling anecdote of a different kind. It shows how little could be known about the extremes of east and west in America in the early 1830s, despite conspicuous efforts to get at the truth.

In the West, Indians were troubled by the puzzle of white men's literacy. As nonliterate people, they must have been awkwardly challenged, and not just by students from Red River or literate traders they occasionally met. They were outside the world of books and there was no direct or easy way to get in. They were even at a loss in knowing how to ask the right questions. Decades of white invasion had brought other novel challenges and means to power: horses, firearms, metal goods, cloth blankets, alcohol, devastating illnesses. Many of these could be absorbed or withstood. Literacy, however, was impossible to master, though it must have seemed an important clue to white power, a key skill that related readers to the most powerful gods. Many Indians must have wondered about the mystery of marks on paper. But where could they turn for answers? Most white men they met were traders who came west to press their own advantage. The British and the Americans displayed rough and confusing animosities toward one another. Even the young men returning from school at Red River might be unwitting dupes of white indoctrination. Yet several lines of thought could well have led inquiring spirits to look toward St. Louis and William Clark.

First and foremost, Clark had been known across the West for generations, since the time of his expedition with Lewis. Some elders had met him when they made their first contact with whites. On many famous occasions he had practiced arts of healing, shared in the hunt, and listened attentively to learn local ways and put them into practice. His frank generosity had not entirely faded from living memories.

Years later he was still dealing with Indians month after month in St. Louis. It had long been a government practice to bring Indian groups to the eastern states. Clark helped provide interpreters and other support. He had been an intermediary who ensured their safe travel and sometimes made special exertions for their safe return. Indeed there were four such Indian visitors aboard the *Yellow Stone* along with Catlin and the two Nez Perce men in 1832; they were being escorted back from a visit to official Washington.[12]

Clark had also made personal gestures to particular Indians. Most notably, he had persuaded Sacagawea and Toussaint Charbonneau to bring their infant son to him, soon after the end of the expedition in 1806. Young Charbonneau grew up in St. Louis and received an education there at Clark's expense. By 1832 Charbonneau had returned to the West after years in Europe, in the household of a German duke who met him during an excursion up the Missouri.

One after another, these lines of connection kept Clark's fame alive among Indians and gave his authority a turn of personal warmth. He was a long-tested white man, a courageous young explorer who had become a respected elder; he had often worked to understand Indians and personally liked many of them. He might well have seemed a reliable source for a straight answer to a hard question.

Meanwhile, in the East the American reading public also needed a figure with authority. Twenty-five years after the Lewis and Clark expedition, few people knew much about lands west of St. Louis. The explorers' records had been published, but in a much-edited, much-delayed, and incomplete form in 1814—in a press run of only a few hundred copies. By the time those volumes appeared, the War of 1812 had wiped out the American fur trade outpost on the lower Columbia. The treaty of 1818 provided for "joint occupancy" of the Pacific coast region, but in fact it would remain under the control of the Hudson's Bay Company for over twenty years. At this time, travel and communication were slow and chancy even within the settled states east of the Mississippi; to go further west required the daring and skills of a fur trapping party or other experienced adventurers. We have seen that the *Yellow Stone* carried an artist or two up the Missouri in 1832 (John James Audubon was another passenger, along with Catlin), but that was the first long ascent of that little steamboat and it took three months just to reach the mouth of the Yellowstone River. When Catlin took out his brushes along the route, he felt he was the first to paint terra incognita. Karl Bodmer went up the Missouri on the *Yellow Stone* a year later, and his paintings too would long serve as essential early records of this region and its people. When Jason and Daniel Lee headed west with the Wyeth party, they were also joined by John Kirk Townsend and Thomas Nuttall, two naturalists who would follow Lewis and Clark's lead in describing birds and plants in the Oregon country.

The missionary beginnings reflect an almost hopeless ignorance— and credulity—about the West. Not one loud voice rose to challenge the dubious notion that four Indians represented thousands yearning for Christian conversion. No one caught the confusion between Flat-head Indians of the Rockies and flat-headed Indians of the Pacific coast. No one picked up Robert Campbell's brief hints or pushed hard on Nathaniel Wyeth's recent experiences, to argue that western trails were hardly the place for a tenderfoot armed with a Bible and the good wishes of a mission board in New York. Along the eastern seaboard, decision makers could consult only a very few writings about the West, and those few were likely misquoted, truncated, or confused.

Often the best that writers and planners could do was to invoke the name of William Clark. We have found these references scattered through various documents, but when brought together they add up to a strong chorus. "The four Indians," wrote Bishop Rosati, "visited General Clark, who in his famous expedition saw their people." "Gen. C. related to me the object of their mission," wrote William Walker. Gabriel Disosway described the practice of head-flattening and cited his source: "Vide Lewis and Clarke's Travels." The Methodist mission board directed their secretary to correspond with Clark and other experts he might name. E. W. Sehon reported further information: "I called immediately upon Gen. Clark, who received me kindly . . . [and] informed me that the publication which had appeared in the Advocate was correct." A. M'Allister criticized Campbell's information by using numbers "according to Clark's account." A circumspect committee intimated in the *Illinois Patriot* that they had consulted Clark during the "intensive and minute" researches they made in St. Louis. Jason and Daniel Lee "saw General Clark in 1834 . . . and learned from him these particulars." George Catlin could scarcely believe the delegation story "but in conversing with General Clark . . . was fully convinced." Along with these testimonies, there was the evidence of his meaningful silence. Nowhere did he protest against the famous Walker letter or take any step to dampen the missionary flames that it kindled. Indeed, in Jason Lee's recollections, Clark definitely confirmed what Walker wrote.

Where would this story have gone, we must wonder, without Clark at its center? The course it eventually took reechoed his fame and authority years after his death. At Jefferson's command, Clark and Lewis had descended the Columbia and reached the Pacific—and so made a bold move for American empire. By encouraging the Protestant missions, Clark fostered a further bold step, which was followed by another and another: American missions, American settlements, American migration, and eventually full American possession of the area that is now Washington, Oregon, and Idaho.

And another dramatic moment was to occur there, when the first official Indian agent arrived in Nez Perce country. This was Elijah White, a physician from New York state who had already served for a time as the doctor in Jason Lee's mission at the Willamette. In 1842 he responded to attacks against two inland missions by coming up the Columbia and the Clearwater to their support. What he found there, at the mission compound of Henry Spalding, very much surprised him. Young Nez Perce students appeared much advanced in their schoolwork, and there was one Indian on hand—"a sensible man of thirty-two, reading, speaking, and writing the English language tolerably well" (Allen 182, 186–87). This man had been renamed Ellis or Ellice in 1830 when he was sent off by the Hudson's Bay Company to the Red River school. He soon became White's trusted interpreter, and so led an uneasy life as an intermediary between white men's laws and his own people's ways.

But the most astonishing surprise took place in a formal council, when Ellis's grandfather rose to speak. Hohots-Ilppilp had known Lewis and Clark, and in White's arrival he saw history coming full circle.

His name meant red or bleeding grizzly bear; among whites he was called The Bloody Chief. He was a famous warrior. When Lewis and Clark met him in 1806 they took note of his regalia: "I observed a tippit woarn by Hohastillpip, which was formed of human scalps and ornamented with the thumbs and fingers of several men which he had slain in battle" (Moulton 7:253–54). The explorers spent over three weeks camped near his village on the return trip, because they could not proceed through the snow-packed Bitterroot Mountains. During this time Clark gave medical treatments to many of the local people, managed to help a long-paralyzed chief who was carried into their camp, and so developed an exalted reputation as a healer. According to claims made much later, Clark also fathered a child at this time in a liaison with Hohots-Ilppilp's sister (7:241n5). The Nez Perce had welcomed the party very generously, even though they arrived hungry with little to trade. They heard the white men's plea for fresh meat and immediately brought them "two fat young horses" as a gift. "This is a much greater act of hospitality than we have witnessed from any nation or tribe since we have passed the Rocky Mountains," Lewis wrote; "in short be it spoken to their immortal honor it is the only act which deserves the appellation of hospitallity which we have witnessed in this quarter" (7:238). A few days later Hohots-Ilppilp gave more; he "told us that most of the horses we saw runing at large in this neighborhood belonged to himself and his people, and whenever we were in want of meat he requested that we would kill any of them we wished; this is a peice of liberallity which would do honor to such as bost of civilization" (7:290). This chief received a peace medal from the captains and sat in council with them when they laid out a map of the West and promised that goods would soon flow into the region through trading posts on the upper Missouri. In one council, his old father spoke for the nation and pledged "their warmest attachment" and "every assistance in their power" (7:238, 242–43, 247–48).

It was from this background that Hohots-Ilppilp rose to speak to Elijah White — or to let history speak through him (and an interpreter) in 1842. White recorded his full speech as follows:

> Soon the Bloody Chief arose—not less than ninety years old—and said: I speak to-day, perhaps to-morrow I die. I am the oldest chief of the tribe; was the high chief when your great brothers, Lewis and Clarke, visited this country; they visited me, and honored me with their friendship and counsel. I showed them my

numerous wounds received in bloody battle with the Snakes; they told me it was not good, it was better to be at peace; gave me a flag of truce; I held it up high; we met and talked, but never fought again. Clarke pointed to this day, to you, and this occasion; we have long waited in expectation; sent three of our sons to Red river school to prepare for it; two of them sleep with their fathers; the other is here, and can be ears, mouth, and pen for us. I can say no more; I am quickly tired; my voice and limbs tremble. I am glad I live to see you and this day, but I shall soon be still and quiet in death. (Allen 185)

2

COLUMBIA REDIVIVA

AMERICAN CLAIMS TO THE PRESENT PACIFIC NORTHWEST
began with Captain Robert Gray of Boston, who named the
Columbia River soon after piloting his ship across its bar in
1792. Many other explorers had searched the north Pacific shoreline
for a Northwest Passage, but Gray found what others had missed. He
trusted his instincts, made a closer approach, and found both the large
bay that is still named Gray's Harbor and a broad river estuary farther
south, where he remained for several days. To name a landmark was
to claim it, as Gray knew. He also knew that British and Spanish rivals
were nearby, charting and claiming other channels and harbors for their
empires. Even more was at stake in finding this great river of the West,
for to claim it could be to assert a claim as well to all the lands it drained.
There was also the lingering chance that somewhere deep inland the
Columbia might reach an easy point of connection to tributaries of the
Mississippi or St. Lawrence river systems.

The surviving logbook entries are so brief that it is impossible to
know how deeply Gray pondered the name he assigned. The most

explicit record states only this: "Captain Gray gave this river the name of *Columbia's River*, and the north side of the entrance *Cape Hancock*, the south, *Adams's Point*" (Howay 438). It seems obvious that he named the river for his ship, the *Columbia*, but could he have held other thoughts in the moment? "Columbia" is a poetic term for America and an echo of a name for the whole New World that had been claimed by Christopher Columbus. Did Gray have America and Columbus in mind? The simultaneous naming of the entrance capes for John Hancock and John Adams bespeaks a flash of patriotism. The *Columbia* was also a celebrated ship already, and an American symbol. On his first voyage in 1787–90, Gray had taken furs from the Northwest coast to China and traded them at a profit before returning to Boston—making the *Columbia* the first United States ship to sail round the globe.

From Columbus the explorer to "Columbia" as a continent to *Columbia* as a ship and an American symbol—the name had layers of history and significance. And there was more. In its log and other official papers the ship was simply the *Columbia*, but technically it was named *Columbia Rediviva*. That was the full name painted or gilded across its transom: Columbia renewed or reborn. To some, this name has suggested that the ship was an older vessel, rebuilt for Gray's backers (Scofield 43; Howay vi). When the ship was outfitted in 1787, the name might just as well have referred to America reborn—that is, to the newly established United States, in that year of the Constitutional Convention. With Gray's discovery of the great western river, at any rate, Columbia was reborn across the continent, as a new region for American development.

The idea of Columbia reborn would unfold again and again in the early nineteenth century as successive groups traveled to and staked claims in the area. In 1805 Lewis and Clark came down the western slopes of the Rockies, made canoes for descending the Columbia River, and wintered near its mouth, flying a fifteen-star American flag over Fort Clatsop. In 1811 John Jacob Astor's agents established Fort Astoria at a site nearby and tried to develop an American trading operation. It foundered in 1813 when no supply ships came and the British North West Company made an offer the surviving agents could not refuse.

The War of 1812 was settled by the Treaty of Ghent, which permitted both British and American settlements, but for decades the Hudson's Bay Company dominated the Columbia from a comfortable base or factory at Fort Vancouver. Then came the Methodist missionaries— Jason and Daniel Lee and two companions—in 1834.

Dr. John McLoughlin, the chief factor at Fort Vancouver, welcomed the missionaries generously. They could hardly have seemed a threat to his operations. He even directed them to a likely site, some miles up the Willamette River, where a few French Canadians had settled with their Indian wives after leaving the company. Perhaps McLoughlin shrewdly directed the Lees up the Willamette in order to keep intrusive Americans out of the richer fur country in the Columbia Plateau; perhaps Lee settled there out of the practical need to be at hand when Wyeth's supply ship arrived. There were also advantages to the site he chose. Flat-headed Indians could be found nearby as well as along the Columbia, and this location would not be as isolated and dangerous as an outpost farther inland. The missionaries could easily meet annual supply ships, and of course they could also buy supplies directly from Fort Vancouver, using drafts on their mission board.

From this tiny beginning, Lee managed to develop an expanding American presence. He soon called for reinforcements, which included a novel means for upsetting the balance of power. After months at sea, two ships arrived in 1837, bearing new ministers, a doctor, a blacksmith, a carpenter—and several women and children. More mission families arrived in the Great Reinforcement of 1840, which also brought more single women to join the single men available at the new settlements. With growing families to consider, the missions took on a new aspect, including immediate needs for creature comforts and long range hopes for land titles and other protections under American law.

Meanwhile the American Board of Commissioners for Foreign Missions had sponsored Presbyterian and Congregational mission couples, who came overland to sites east of the Cascade Mountains. The result was that by 1840 a chain of mission compounds stretched along the route Lewis and Clark had traced three decades earlier, a small but significant rival to the chain of Hudson's Bay Company posts and operations. On the Columbia proper, the Methodists had one mission near the old site of Fort Clatsop and another at The Dalles. Marcus and Narcissa Whitman were established at Waiilatpu on the Walla Walla River. Henry and Eliza Spalding were in Nez Perce country a few miles upstream from the mouth of the Clearwater; and for a time Asa and Sarah Smith were farther inland, at Kamiah. All these groups were in touch with each other and with the principal Methodist station on the Willamette at present-day Salem, Oregon.

This little network of missions gave a new turn to "Columbia Rediviva." Where Lewis and Clark had passed a few hours or months at most, the families planned to stay for years. Their experiences were also different in kind from those of military explorers. Both the explorers and the mission parties consisted of bright young Americans, purposeful, resolute, and resourceful. In different ways, both parties came to claim the Columbia region. Both came with pen and ink, prepared to keep observing, recording, and reporting—and so to take in the land and its inhabitants, just as Captain Gray had done by describing the river in his log book. But the missionaries did that work in a much more complex way. On the expedition only the captains and a handful of enlisted men kept journals. Among the missionaries, there was constant flow of ink as ministers, laborers, wives, teachers, and children wrote out records, diaries, letters, and reports.

These two American parties differed along very evident lines of purpose, organization, discipline, engagement with Indian people, and capacity to survive. Their separate experiences therefore illuminate each other by providing a balance or contrast that brings out their different strengths and shortcomings. In surprising ways, their experiences also converged at particular geographical spots along the route up the Columbia to the Rockies. Standing in the same places, looking out at the same settings, they often seized similar means for getting through a day or the next stages of a task, yet they adapted their advantages to attain very different results.

Perhaps the best way to bring out the leading differences is to begin with a contrast in organization. Lewis and Clark led a select military expedition to the Pacific, with all the advantages that implies. Their instructions came directly from President Jefferson, whom Lewis had recently served as private secretary. Clark had been Lewis's friend and fellow officer. Their soldiers were recruited by both captains and disciplined for their task through a long trial period. After a winter encampment in Illinois across from the mouth of the Missouri, the men who could not measure up were left behind. On the first leg of the journey, to reach the next winter camp on the upper Missouri, rules were enforced through courts-martial and corporal punishments, and a final band of adventurers was selected for the trek to the West. The others were sent back down the river in the spring of 1805. At that point Lewis could write in his journal: "The party are in excellent health and sperits, zealously attatched to the enterprise, and anxious to proceed; not a whisper or murmur of discontent to be heard among them, but all act in unison, and with the most perfect harmony" (Moulton 4:10). Lewis noted this esprit de corps again and again through many hardships in the months that followed.

Jason Lee had no such authority and no such morale. Once he was established in Oregon, his followers came to him in irregular groups and were often chosen by a mission board that ignored his stipulations. Robert Loewenberg has shown in detail how unfitted many of them were for mission work. Many applicants were erratic, chronically ill, notorious for their debts, or otherwise intractable (Loewenberg, *Equality* 125–27). Many arrived complaining about disputes that had broken out aboard the ships on the long journey round Cape Horn. Lee could not settle these quarrels, and in other ways he lacked a firm hand. He could make assignments and spell out large plans, but he had strong-willed fellow ministers, heads of families, and rivals as his outspoken critics. Twice he left Oregon to raise funds and face his board in the East, leaving others in charge during his long absence. And he expected his several mission stations to operate without close supervision. Finally, many of the women who went west did so halfheartedly, soon regretted it, pined for home, and pled with their husbands to abandon their commitment. Lee stressed these lines of weakness in his final statement to the Methodist mission board.

If my associates had stood firm to their post, and persevered willingly in the work consigned them, I have not a doubt but far more favorable accounts would have reached you from that distant country. The plans, I assert [were] well formed and had I been sustained the object would have been accomplished. A great mistake was made in selecting some of those who were sent out. I allude not to the number but the qualifications of certain individuals. I forewarned the Oregon Committee that if the persons who applied for situations were not examined by a proper committee the plan would fail. Such proved to be the case. As proof I aver that we had not reached our first stopping place in South America, before some desired to return to the United States, and even after touching at the S[andwich] Islands before we had reached Oregon one wanted to return and secure the Chaplancy at the Islands. I have had much to contend with and I regret that men of more steadfast minds had not been chosen. Such persons do more injury to a distant Mission than they do good, and no one knows the difficulties I have had to pass through.

. . .The Oregon Committee must remember that I told them that the first question to be asked the applicant should be, "Does your wife want to go?" and a negative answer should satisfy the Committee that such a person ought not to be sent. What was the fact in the case, why a number of females were unwillingly dragged thousands of miles from home into a strange and savage country—and some of them, I know, would gladly have returned in the very steamer that took us to the Ship. It is a hard lot to go so far from home free from care and anxiety, but to endure such a voyage, with a companion all the time looking back to home, and reproaching one for having drawn her from that home, is more than almost any one can endure. (Lee's address to the mission board, July 1, 1844, in Brosnan 248–49)

There were similar woes and tensions in the American Board missions of the Whitmans and the Spaldings. The two couples traveled overland together in 1836, even though they knew that Henry Spalding had once proposed to Narcissa Whitman and been rejected. Spalding was a short-tempered man by nature and the others were all strong willed. The two couples chafed as they crossed the country; they agreed they could not share a common mission, and so set up sites a good distance apart. The fifth member of their party, William H. Gray, also needed his separate space. And so it went. When new members came west they set up further isolated missions, and all watched each other and reported sharp criticisms back to the board.

Lewis and Clark had very clear and full instructions, in which Jefferson stressed three general aims. The captains were to trace the Missouri River to its source and reach the Pacific coast if possible; they were to develop friendly relations with the Indians they met; and they were to record close observations of almost everything in sight: geographical features; minerals; vegetation; animals; climate; and native peoples, including their appearance, numbers, language, beliefs, customs, and diseases. Given these definite tasks, the explorers achieved definite results, and more. They brought back records, maps, and specimens that have long served—and often delighted—later geographers, scientists, and ethnographers.

The missionaries lacked such clear directions. Their general aims were to go west, minister to Indians, and lead them to salvation, but they frankly stated that they put faith in God to guide them in this work. Many believed that God directed all their important steps. Jason Lee, for example, told his mission board that he had never sought to lead or become a mission superintendent. "They had made him a superintendent without his solicitation and knowledge. Since his conversion he had never taken one step towards an appointment. He went nowhere, except God first opened the door. In this case God opened the door and the church pushed him in" (Brosnan 266). Similar expressions can be found on dozens of pages from the missionaries. Their impulse to go west stemmed from the astonishing call of the Indians who had come to St. Louis, and they answered it without pausing to spell out what definite results should ensue. As years passed, mission boards began to expect some tangible results for their investments. Lee notoriously failed to provide any. But how could he? Could he or any other mission leader report the numbers of the definitely saved, or measure their spiritual progress?

As soon as they arrived, the Methodists saw that no vigorous, earnest, flat-headed Indians were expecting them. The Indians of the Willamette Valley were indifferent to them, or came to their camps weak with hunger or disease. Just as immediately, the Lees saw that they would have to postpone their lofty aims in order to meet pressing needs of their own. They cut down nearby trees, started work on a mission house, and began to till the ground.

The following winter, Jason Lee wrote to Wilbur Fisk seeking support for aims very different from Fisk's original idea. Fisk had recruited Lee in 1833 while rousing the church with his plan: "Let two suitable men, unencumbered with families, and possessing the spirit of martyrs, throw themselves into the nation. Live with them—learn their language—preach Christ to them and, as the way opens, introduce schools, agriculture, and the arts of civilized life" (*Christian Advocate*, April 22, 1833). Now Lee proposed to invert this arrangement, and begin with agriculture—and model families—and then mission work. "We have been labouring hard to build a house, and prepare ground for a crop," he wrote. "We shall probably cultivate 20 acres this season. I have requested the Board to send a man with a family to take charge of the farm, and by the time one can arrive we shall have it so arranged that it will not be so difficult as it now is. Though we think this establishment essentially necessary to the successful prosecution of our object, yet we still have our eyes on other places where the Indians are more numerous and enterprising than they are here" (Lee to Fisk, February 6, 1835, in Brosnan 73).

Lee was hatching the idea of a long-term settlement that would eventually support traveling ministers or satellite missions. In his request for "a man with a family," he also opened a more radical proposition— to bring white women to the West to set an example of civilized marriage and child rearing. "I have requested the Board not to send any more *single* men," he went on, "but to send men with *families*."

I have also advised that Daniel's *chosen* be sent as soon as possible. A greater favour could not be bestowed upon this country, than to send it pious, industrious, inteligent females.

I am not singular in this. The Gov. and other Gentlemen of the H. B. Co. (though they have native wives) say that white females would be of the greatest importance to the mission, and would have far more influence among Indians than males.

If your opinion accords with ours I beg you to use your influence with the Board to cause them to send out some as soon as possible. (Brosnan 73)[1]

With this change of plans, the Methodists committed themselves to a very long undertaking. The call for auxiliaries—and the arrival of mission couples farther inland—resulted in abiding complications. The mission settlements became ends in themselves, and the ministers' energies went into housing, feeding, nurturing, and administering their own little communities. Many complained of lacking the time to reach many Indians directly.

In addition to differences in aims and organization, there were also sharp differences in observation and interpretation between the explorers and the missionaries. Meriwether Lewis often looked out at the world with a naturalist's eye; he was eager to spot and record all kinds of new phenomena. The missionaries had no such drive; their deepest concerns were otherworldly. They could fill reams of paper with notes about particular characters and their collisions, yet scarcely notice if a rare bird flew into view. On the other hand, the explorers leave a reader wondering about the day-to-day human dynamics in their camps. Such matters seldom touched the work of exploration enough to get a mention in the journals. Finally, Lewis and Clark were firm skeptics about the mysteries that faced them. When they were told of spirit mountains or heard strange rumblings in the distance, their first impulse was to seek out a rational cause or explanation. For the missionaries, the extraordinary was likely to be an intimation of the divine. They too were skeptical about Indian myths and mysteries, yet they watched and sometimes leapt at coincidences that might indicate God's will.

As a result, the two groups engaged very differently with Indians. Lewis and Clark were eminently practical and matter-of-fact. They took in details of Indian life in much the same way they noticed details in nature. They studied the ways of bands and villages, and later compiled long inventories and descriptions of regions and their inhabitants. When the captains met with particular tribes, they acted as official representatives of President Jefferson. They quickly pressed to meet with headmen, and if good will developed into personal friendship, so much the better for supporting the explorers' long-range purposes. They had proclamations to make, or they needed information, shelter, horses, canoes, or foodstuffs. Always they were passing through, hurriedly taking in what they could, knowing that they would come this way but once or twice. Some of the men had sexual relations with Indian women; the captains record treating them for venereal diseases. But there could be no enduring ties. The party would have to move on down the trail—just as the Indians would move on in their seasonal cycles—and they would part, probably forever.

The missionaries, on the other hand, came specifically to live among Indians, know them individually, and remain among them for years. When missionaries set up schools and began their own families, they committed themselves to long seasons with Indians as close neighbors. Some ministers applied themselves to learn the local languages— which Lewis and Clark never managed to do. A few paid close attention to local customs and beliefs, and then had to cope with some resulting shocks. Many hardened in their attitudes and abandoned mission work, or escaped either to another part of the world or into a safe, secluded corner for reading and writing. These responses will be discussed more fully in later chapters. For now we should notice that instead of meeting headmen in council, the missionaries typically met weaker, more vulnerable, and hence more approachable Indians: the sick, the young, the outcast, the dying. They understood their duty to be to address Indians' needs and meet them soul to soul.

One way or another, the first missions along the Lewis and Clark route all knew grief. The explorers were a different story. They brought their party over the mountains and down the Columbia; suffered through a cold, wet, hungry winter; then returned. Some became ill, some were injured, but no one died. Back beyond the Mississippi they met a heroes' welcome and were soon compensated by a special act of Congress. The missionaries spent years in Oregon and faced terrible losses. Jason Lee outlived two wives and a child but died of tuberculo sis at the age of forty-one. Daniel Lee left Oregon pleading his wife's broken health and his own. Their first associate, Cyrus Shepard, died after an amputation. Other missionaries lost wives and children to disease and accidents, and suffered chronic ailments. One committed suicide. Several people drowned.

For the survivors there were further wrenches. The Methodist missions were curtailed in 1843. The Whitmans were killed by Cayuse Indians four years later, and the Spaldings were forced out of Idaho as a result. By that time Catholic priests had set up rival missions across the Northwest, the American boundary had been drawn at the forty-ninth parallel, and hundreds of families had come over the Oregon Trail. The idea of isolated Indian missions was soon swept away by robust new settlements, political arrangements, and secular aspirations.

The early Protestant missions thus flourished for just a few years. Their results were hard to measure, their costs high. Still, those results deserve a close review, for these settlers came west as idealists, hoping to embrace both a new region and its people. They saw this world as explorers had not and could not have seen it. Here and there they fitted their steps into the same contours of the land, but with a difference. They taught lessons, instituted policies, built lasting structures, and touched lives—with the result that their presence was still palpable long after the traces of the explorers had vanished. Even their failures can be telling. Their accidents, quarrels, illnesses, and blunders point up the narrow edge of good fortune by which other adventurers escaped disaster.

In 1803 Jefferson asked Congress for a special appropriation to support the new project to be led by Captain Lewis. His message also discussed general policies towards Indians. Jefferson urged the development of trading posts, which would induce them to leave off hunting, take up farming, and learn to trade for manufactured goods. "In leading them thus to agriculture, to manufactures & civilization, in bringing together their & our settlements, & in preparing them ultimately to participate in the benefits of our government, I trust and believe we are acting for their greatest possible good" (Jefferson to Congress, 18 January 1803, in Jackson, *Letters* 1:11). In effect, the Oregon missions put Jefferson's plans to a severe and surprising test, for his words frame the hard question that arose when missionaries followed Lewis's path to the west: How well could educated, white Americans take up farming, trade for necessities, and maintain the comforts of civilization? Thousands of miles across the continent, the missions faced bitter struggles over just these tasks.

We can trace these struggles in detail at four crucial sites along the Columbia and its tributaries, places where Lewis and Clark had important and varied experiences with native peoples. Years later, the missionaries came to these same settings and faced some of the same challenges, but with very different preparation and results.

At the Pacific: Gloom and Revulsion

November rain and cold had set in when Lewis and Clark reached the mouth of the Columbia in 1805, so they quickly scouted sites for a winter camp. They chose a spot on a small river east of Point Adams where they expected to hunt enough elk to offset a diet of fish, roots, and dogs. Here they could also keep watch in case a trading ship crossed the bar and brought goods they could trade on their way back. (Jefferson had provided letters of credit for just this purpose.) They built Fort Clatsop, a small rectangular compound of huts, and settled in until March.

The journals record a miserable winter. Rain fell almost every day. Leather goods rotted and fell apart. The hunters brought in little meat, and it spoiled quickly. The nearby Indians were used to dealing with white men on fur-trading ships; they demanded high prices just when the captains' stores of trade goods had run low. The last drops of whiskey had been drunk months before. By Christmas the huts had been roofed but there was little cheer within them. "We would have spent this day the nativity of Christ in feasting," Clark wrote, "had we any thing either to raise our Sperits or even gratify our appetites, our Diner concisted of pore Elk, so much Spoiled that we eate it thro' mear necessity, Some Spoiled pounded fish and a fiew roots" (Moulton 6:138). During the weeks that followed, men fell ill and took a long time to recover. Wet winds swept over the fort day after dismal day.

The captains used this time to consolidate their records, but a new tone poisoned their pages—frequent notes of ill temper towards Indians. They admired many things about Indians of the lower Columbia: their beautiful, seaworthy canoes and the expert ways they handled them; the tightly woven hats and garments that kept them dry; the even balance of tasks between men and women. The journals noted these positive features and others. But now for the first time the party was camped for a long period among people to whom they could hardly speak, for lack of translators. Trade was sharp and unfriendly, and there was petty pilfering, as there had been on the route down the river. With prices high and trade goods exhausted, every lost item counted.

On January 1, an order was given to keep Indians out of the fort, except by special permission. On February 20, Lewis wrote out a long journal entry stating his deep distrust of the local people. After a visit from an apparently friendly party, the sun went down and, Lewis recalled,

we desired them to depart as is our custom and closed our gates. we never suffer parties of such number to remain within the fort all night; for notwithstanding their apparent friendly disposition, their great averice and hope of plunder might induce them to be treacherous. at all events we determined allways to be on our guard as much as the nature of our situation will permit us, and never place our selves at the mercy of any savages. we well know, that the treachery of the aborigenes of America and the too great confidence of our countrymen in their sincerity and friendship, has caused the distruction of many hundreds of us. so long have our men been accustomed to a friendly intercourse with the natives, that we find it difficult to impress on their minds the necessity of always being on their guard with rispect to them. this confidence on our part, we know to be the effect of a series of uninterupted friendly intercouse, but the well known treachery of the natives by no means entitle them to such confidence, and we must check it's growth in our own minds, as well as those of our men, by recollecting ourselves, and repeating to our men, that our preservation depends on never loosing sight of this trait in their character, and being always prepared to meet it in whatever shape it may present itself. (Moulton 6:330–31)

"Well known treachery" as a "trait of character" had not been mentioned this way among Indians of the Plains and Rocky Mountains. But here Lewis sat at his desk after weeks of cold, wet, gray weather, suspended between arduous travels west and east, and surrounded by people who spoke a strange language, looked different from other Indians, and kept up confusing maneuvers of theft, trade, and gift giving. His mind closed down against them.

He saw them as ugly. Just a few days before the party departed in March, Lewis wrote out a long description of the local people. This essay seems to be a set piece that he had prepared over time and now copied out in final form, because Clark copied it on two separate dates and with some intriguing variations.[2] In any case, this long entry is Lewis's attempt at a balanced assessment. He makes several thoughtful remarks about why people dress and behave as they do, including an account of the head-flattening process and very detailed descriptions of clothing, tattooing, and body piercing with dentalium shells. Nonetheless, he says that to his eye they are "illy shapen" people at best:

> The Killamucks, Clatsops, Chinnooks, Cathlahmahs, and Wâc'-ki-a-cums resemble each other as well in their persons and dress as in their habits and manners.—their complexion is not remarkable, being the usual copper brown of most of the tribes of North America. they are low in statue reather diminutive, and illy shapen; possessing thick broad flat feet, thick ankles, crooked legs wide mouths thick lips, nose moderately large, fleshey, wide at the extremity with large nostrils, black eyes and black coarse hair. (Moulton 6:432–33)

Lewis goes on to describe the process of head flattening, then takes special note of the women. They have swollen, "deformed" ankles by choice, he notes, because they tie a cord tight there; also, "their method of squating or resting themselves on their hams which they seem from habit to prefer to siting, no doubt contributes much to this deformity of the legs by preventing free circulation of the blood" (6:433–34). They wear scanty clothing. Their breasts are exposed "and from the habit of remaining loose and unsuspended grow to great length particularly in aged women in many of whom I have seen the bubby reach as low as the waist" (6:435). Also, their cedar bark skirts hide little from view from the waist down: "the whole thing being of sufficient thickness when the female stands erect to conceal those parts usually covered from formiliar view, but when she stoops or places herself in many other attitudes, this battery of Venus is not altogether impervious to the inquisitive and penetrating eye of the amorite." Lewis later added a final personal judgment, which appears in full only in Clark's copy: "The women Sometimes wash their faces & hands but Seldom. I think the most disgusting Sight I have ever beheld is those dirty naked wenches" (6:440).

Lewis here seems confused in his impulses. At one and the same time he works both to dress and to undress these figures, both to expose them and to cover them up, both to confess a prurient attraction and to wince at the sight of filth. Lewis could hardly be called squeamish—certainly not at this point. He had spent months on the trail butchering and eating whatever came to hand, sharing close quarters with naked Indians, and treating them and his men for putrid, smelly diseases. In this entry he does not flinch at seeing a "bubby reach as low as the waist." Yet in the lines about the "battery of Venus" he weaves a fancy cloak of circumlocutions. He probably did not consciously make a connection between a penis and a "penetrating eye," but his language is certainly suggestive. The word "battery" suggests both an assault and an artillery placement, yet the threat of attack evidently comes from the other direction, not from Venus but from the probing, insistent peering of the "amorite" or amorist. On both sides there is an implied drive of love—Venus and Amor—and also a need for defenses from invasive violence. Finally, there is the hard question of what and how Lewis sees—being himself an observer whose every page bespeaks an exceptionally "inquisitive and penetrating eye."

This whole passage should also be considered in relation to an earlier page (for January 6, 1806), where Lewis found much to admire in the local women. There his thoughts touched their minds as well as their bodies:

> The Clatsops, Chinnooks, Killamucks &c. are very loquacious and inquisitive. . . . with us their conversation generally turns upon the subjects of trade, smoking, eating or their women; about the latter they speak without reserve in their presents, of their every part, and of the most formiliar connection. they do not hold the virtue of their women in high estimation, and will even prostitute their wives and daughters for a fishinghook or a stran of beads. in common with other savage nations they make their women perform every species of domestic drudgery. but in almost every species of this drudgery the men also participate. their women are also compelled to geather roots, and assist them in taking fish, which articles form much the greatest part of their subsistance; notwith-standing the survile manner in which they treat their women they pay much more rispect to their judgment and oppinions in many rispects than most indian nations; their women are permitted to speak freely before them, and sometimes appear to command with a tone of authority; they generally consult them in their traffic and act in conformity to their opinions. (Moulton 6:168)

This passage opens and closes with touches of admiration, especially for women who rightly command men's respect. But these lines frame the darker side of women's lives as drudges and servile prostitutes. Of course, many white observers saw native women as mere drudges, just as they saw adequately nourished native people as starving wretches. As Vibert puts it, "The 'squaw drudge' is one of the most prominent and persistent images in travellers' commentaries on Native women throughout North America" (127). Lewis inherited this prejudiced attitude, and the women he saw at the Pacific coast seem to have stuck in his mind and troubled him deeply.

It is tempting to think that he was maddeningly baffled by Indians who eluded his competence. They seemed too coarse, dirty, and oddly shaped to seem fully human, yet too wily, ingenious, and subtly aggressive to be underestimated as adversaries. Their secrets remained beyond his knowing; they might well have given better terms to other white traders; they fascinated yet repelled his eye. He wanted to possess them in his language, but they went on being "very loquatious and inquisitive" in their own. Did Lewis perhaps translate these enigmas into frankly sexual terms—through mental associations with the coarseness of the men's talk, the women's flimsy clothing, and the rapid success many young women had in luring his men and getting trinkets in return? On the first days at the site of Fort Clatsop, the men had to be restrained from giving away too much; many of the young women then seemed "handsom," but some showed evident symptoms of venereal diseases and a few men who sported with them required treatments long afterwards (Moulton 6:73–74; Ronda 208–09).

What is safe to say is that at this point the captains felt pushed to an extreme tension. They did not just see and report but peered, as it were, through drizzle and fog at shapes beyond recognition. Lewis's fears of treacherous traits and his embarrassment over exposed genitals force a reader to share his bewilderment. His journals carry full, cool, temperate accounts of dozens of shocks and dangers. Why not here? When Lewis writes that "the most disgusting sight I have ever beheld is those dirty naked wenches," or when he fidgets with a euphemism like "battery of Venus," his own hand falters and fudges and becomes the most curious object on his page.

Twenty-five years later, John H. Frost came to this same area with his wife and young son, to establish a Methodist outpost.[3] He did not particularly yearn for this site; Jason Lee assigned it soon after the Frosts arrived from the East in 1840, and they did what they were told. They managed to stay for three years before rain, illness, loneliness, and futility drove them back to Boston. Soon after his return, Frost drew on his journal and other notes to add a few chapters to Daniel Lee's longer memoir, published as *Ten Years in Oregon* (1844). Frost traces a plodding narrative line through months and years from arrival to departure, but he develops a few striking events in detail. To readers of Lewis and Clark his pages also brighten at several turns with notes that recall theirs.

The Methodists planned to set up both a mission and a farm on the Clatsop Plains west of Fort Clatsop. Frost and William Kone went there with a settler named Solomon Smith, who had come west with Nathaniel Wyeth's first expedition in 1832. In Oregon Smith had married a Clatsop woman he met at Fort Vancouver. Frost wrote that she "knew something concerning the true God" and could translate for the mission (Lee and Frost 269). In fact, Celiast Smith was the daughter of Coboway, the Clatsop chief to whom Lewis and Clark had given Fort Clatsop when they abandoned it, and her son later recorded her memories of seeing the expedition when she was a child (Wheeler 2:196–97). The Hudson's Bay Company kept a small agency at Fort George, in present-day Astoria, and there was backup support from both Fort Vancouver and the main mission compound on the Willamette. Such were the promising advantages of this new enterprise.

Frost, Kone, and Smith brought tools and supplies up the Skapanowin River by canoe, then carried heavy loads across marshy lands to the site of their first cabins. All in vain. The first heavy rains broke through the roof and drove Kone and his pregnant wife back to Fort Vancouver. The Frosts stayed on at a different log house, which the men put up hastily on the banks of the Columbia. There they endured cold and hunger. Local Indians hunted elk and sometimes feasted on whales that washed ashore, but they proved to be sharp traders, just as they had been with Lewis and Clark. They boasted that they were good at stealing. They came to church services at times, then disappeared.

Learning Chinookan languages such as Clatsop proved difficult or impossible for the missionaries. These languages had special sounds they could not master—just as the Indians could not pronounce some common sounds in English—and there was a much easier alternative. For many decades both Indians and whites managed to communicate through a limited, composite trade language which was not Chinook or Clatsop but the so-called Chinook Jargon. In the nineteenth century it was used widely along the lower Columbia and the adjacent Pacific coast region. It included words derived from English, French, Chinook, Clatsop, and other languages, but it provided a vocabulary of just a few hundred words (including words evidently copied from English and French) and had no complexities of verb conjugation or noun declension. Traders used it. Explorers used it. In the Indian settlements at Fort Vancouver it may well have been the first language many children learned. It was also the language which early ethnographers learned and used—including such pioneer scholars as Paul Kane, Horatio Hale, George Gibbs, and Franz Boas (Brown 91–95, 98). It was simple enough to learn and newcomers picked it up for years before any vocabularies or handbooks were published.[4] Frost and other missionaries were hardly alone in using it and trusting it, and we will see some samples of its use in later chapters. But could it convey the deepest truths about religion? Frost quickly came to have his doubts. "I would speak to them in their own tongue [i.e., Chinook Jargon]," Frost wrote, "which by this time we could speak very well, but we found it altogether insufficient as a medium by which to communicate to their dark minds the meaning of the gospel" (Lee and Frost 298).

The missionaries kept clinging to their sense of purpose, but one after another the Kones and Frosts fell ill. By late 1842, Frost wrote, "my own health had now become so much impaired that I was obliged to desist entirely from labour; the bronchitis, with which I had been afflicted for the past year, became much more severe, and I found my spine and liver to be much affected, so that there was continual pain in my side and back, and my nervous system became entirely deranged" (325). At last the mission doctor came out and "saw proper to operate on my throat by cutting off the palate"; Frost still saw little hope of improvement and sent the doctor back to the Willamette with a letter asking to be discharged (328–29).

This short history points up the severe hardships of early settlement at the mouth of the Columbia. To make matters worse, the Frosts had imagined they could not only survive there but settle in with refined

comforts. Sarah Frost stressed that point to the Northwest historian
Edmond Meany many decades later, in 1907.

Meany happened to meet her by an odd coincidence at a Sioux
reservation in South Dakota, when she was over 90 years old, twice
widowed, and living with a nephew who had long been a reservation
doctor. She was blind and nearly deaf, but she still spoke the Chinook
Jargon and recalled many details from her years in Oregon. She told
Meany that she had brought a full set of good china intact around Cape
Horn and also packed a barrel full of fine gowns—which grew out of
fashion in that barrel before she finally unpacked it back in Boston. "I
had a bureau, too, and a fine bonnet. Now I did not need that bonnet
in Oregon, so I put it in the bureau and left it there. When I got ready
to leave Oregon I took my bonnet from the bureau and found that a
skunk had gnawed a hole in the top and made a nest. . . . I was a good
milliner. . . . So I just put a fine bow of ribbon over that hole made by
the skunk and had a good bonnet again" (Meany 12–15).

To maintain their way of living, John Frost exhausted himself
carrying 100–pound bags of flour, double window sashes, kegs of nails,
and heavy stove parts—not to mention that bureau—over marshy trails
to their log house. Later, he and Solomon Smith made a two-week trek
down the coast and then inland to reach the Willamette mission. Indian
guides helped them find an overland route for their one pack horse.
They then followed that trail back, driving a herd of horses and dairy
cattle along beaches and over steep headlands—a round trip of 320
miles by Frost's reckoning. He explained that going by water (up the
Columbia and then up the Willamette) was much more expensive and
dangerous, and that living without such livestock was not an option:

> Bread stuffs, and sauce &c., cannot be grown without a team.
> Milk, butter, beef and pork can not be made without cattle. And
> cattle and horses could not be brought to this place without driv-
> ing them over land, except by paying more than the worth of
> them to get them here by water, besides loosing nearly the same
> length of time in accomplishing the same object. And no one
> would move in this matter unless Br. Smith and myself would

undertake. Therefore, believing it to be necessary for the existence and prosperity of this missionary station through the blessing of God, we did undertake, and we accomplished what we did. (Frost 355)

As it happened, the Frosts settled on the Columbia just a few months before Lieutenant Charles Wilkes crossed the Pacific and led a naval squadron into Puget Sound and the Columbia River. This was the United States Exploring Expedition of 1838–1842, a large-scale project for the benefit of American empire. In this region it was an elaborate naval version of Lewis and Clark, for it came with the same objectives of mapping and reinforcing claims to the Columbia and adjacent territories. Wilkes came out to Point Adams on May 24, 1841, and spent much of the day with the Frosts and the local Hudson's Bay agent, James Birnie. He scanned the horizon, hoping to catch sight of one of his principal ships, the sloop-of-war *Peacock*, which was long overdue from Hawaii. Then he turned stern eyes on the prospects and pretensions of his hosts.

"Mr. Frost was a shoemaker," this well-born officer wrote in his diary, "& his wife is what his class in life require an active smart body but I find there is little desire in either to bring about the conversion of the natives." He ate at their table and disparaged it, too: "We returned to dinner at Mrs. Frost which she had prepared herself, there was an attempt at showing off that made all her endeavors failures and only proved how she had been brought up which she was desirous of proving had been that of a lady but with ill success" (Wilkes 16:213). Perhaps Sarah unpacked her china—platters, ladles, and all— for this occasion and it looked very odd in a rough log house, under the nose of a punctilious self-styled commodore. Wilkes had been much better entertained at Fort Vancouver, where Hudson's Bay officers had ampler means for formal occasions with lofty visitors.[5]

The *Peacock* finally reached the Columbia River in mid-July, but it ran aground and broke up on the treacherous bar. The ship's crew, instruments, and records all made it safely to shore, where they set up a survival camp with timely aid from the missionaries. Kone, Frost, and Birnie rushed to bring them tents and other supplies. Frost wrote that they merely did what they could to relieve their countrymen, "but it was but very little" (Frost 167). Kone later claimed much more credit for making rescue attempts with Indians and canoes, then cooking all night for the survivors and running supply trips to Baker's Bay (Kone 12–13).

At the mouth of the Columbia, in any case, these successors of Lewis and Clark—military and civilian, naval and agricultural—faced very different hardships. They also happened to face each other, over the best provisions the missionaries could afford.

By working so hard to bring cattle and horses and window sashes to the Clatsop Plains, Frost and Smith also laid the foundations of an enduring settlement. Long after the mission had faded away, the Smiths were still prospering on the land. In fact their descendents can still be found in Clatsop County. Solomon and Celiast were one of the first couples married in Oregon by the missionaries, and they remained together long after other mission couples divorced and laws came into force against intermarriage; they are now buried together in the pioneer cemetery south of Warrenton. One of their children, Silas Smith, went east to be trained as a lawyer, married in New Hampshire, and returned to practice in Oregon. In his later years he was active in the Oregon Historical Society and wrote about early Indian beliefs and practices, preserving stories he had heard from his mother and other family members.

The Smiths do not appear much in Frost's records for two good reasons. They lived a full six miles away from where Frost finally settled, and he did not stay long enough to see how their marriage developed over time. Modern writers, however, have traced the lives of both partners and discussed their intermarriage in detail (Eugene Smith; Peterson del Mar). They brought separate strengths to their joint venture. Celiast returned to the Clatsop region as the daughter of a famous chief, and she retained many old ways; she even kept slaves. Solomon introduced farming with animals and prospered with other enterprises, too; later he was active in Oregon politics. Together they blended two very distinct cultures that went on living uneasily near each other on a small peninsula.

They thus remain a sharp contrast to the famous expedition couple,

Sacagawea and Toussaint Charbonneau. Each of the Smiths was a strong local figure, whereas Sacagawea, despite many legends about her, was a very subordinate figure in the Corps of Discovery and one of many women Charbonneau claimed to possess. The Smiths' long and apparently stable marriage also gives the lie to Captain Lewis's implied judgment that Clatsop women could only be repugnant to any sensible white man.

Frost, however, seems to have looked past the Smiths and what their marriage implied. In the end, he came to see local Indians just as darkly as Lewis had. He also reflected on his experience to make a sharp critique of the mission effort, in a compact statement of themes that others would repeat. To his mind, the Indians of the region moved in a spiritual, moral darkness that the missions were ill-prepared to combat. If Lewis saw Indians as physically ugly, Frost saw them as almost hopelessly depraved.

Frost knew in advance that he had a hard task ahead of him. Before moving down to the Astoria area, he went there with Daniel Lee and met with some of the Indians. He explained his plan, using Lee as an interpreter, and found that they were disappointed that he had not come to trade for beaver or salmon. He believed that he readily understood their habits of mind.

> For it should not be forgotten that they never act from any higher motives, in their transactions with the whites, than the prospect of temporal gain; and it is perfectly reasonable that they should not, since they possess no correct knowledge of the relation they sustain to God, as rational and accountable beings, nor of the future state as a place of retribution. It is true, they have some strange and indistinct notions of the continued existence of friends departed but, as nearly as we could ascertain, the employments of that state were considered to be similar to those of the present; consequently the oldest woman among the Chenooks, a descendant of Comcomly [another chief who met with Lewis and Clark], when she buried a daughter, a number of years ago, it is reported that she caused two slaves to be killed and deposited

in the same canoe with the dead body of the deceased, for the purpose of attending her in the future state. And in addition to the above, we ask, does any man, while in an unconverted state, of any nation or climate, act from any higher motive in anything that he may do than from a principle of supreme selfishness? (Lee and Frost 233)

Depravity and ignorance were not a surprising problem: they were the common conditions of the fallen world. Frost rather complains that the missions were misled and ill prepared. Native people were not eager to be taught, as the mission organizers had claimed, and as a result there was a great waste of funds and energies in Oregon, "for the purpose of effecting that which, in all sober reason, ought never to have been expected" (Lee and Frost 234). From his own experience, Frost also doubted that teaching could have proceeded long and effectively. Language was an insuperable barrier, and so were the very different life patterns open even to native children.

It is acknowledged on all hands that the present prospects in respect to civilizing and Christianizing these natives are exceedingly gloomy. They are by a great majority fewer in number than they were supposed to be; and as each clan has a peculiar dialect or tongue, those who profess to be the best judges believe their language to be not worth reducing with the design of printing the same, and of making it the medium of communication. I am inclined to favour this view of the subject. And the prospect of teaching them the English language is no more promising. In respect to the adults, it would be the nearest thing to an impossibility. Their habits are formed, and they consider everything that has the appearance of work, that does not yield an immediate visible profit, as slavery; hence it is disgraceful, in their estimation, to labour. And as their organs of speech are formed, they cannot make our English sounds; for instance, I never met with an Indian in the country that could speak my name (Frost) properly: some would have it Mr. Plost, and others Floost, and the like; it seemed to be impossible for them to sound *fr*. And then, if they are taken when young, the prospect is but little better; for after they are cleansed from the filth and vermin, and clothed, and fed, and taught for a few years those of them that do not elope, preferring the liberty of the plains and mountains to the confinement, restraint, and labour of a school, suddenly drop into the grave in consequence of the most deadly and loathsome diseases which they inherit from their fathers and mothers. So that at the time the writer left the country, there were more Indian children in the mission grave-yard at the Walamet, of such as had been taken by the missionaries and treated as above mentioned, than there were of such as were alive and in the manual labour school. (Lee and Frost 311)

In the sober reasoning of Frost and several others, the situation in Oregon led step by step into despair. Without willing students, there were no prospects of surmounting the language barriers. Without clear communications, there was no hope of explaining ideas such as law. And without a sense of law, the depraved would remain forever beyond hope of salvation. "Their language is so defective that thereby it is impossible to acquaint them with the true nature of *law*; and until they feel they are condemned in consequence of having transgressed the law of God, how can they be made to feel the need of Christ?" (Lee and Frost 313). This question had practical implications, too. If Indians could not be improved by the ministers, their evil still had to be controlled. Like many others, Frost was shocked by the operations of de facto law as the Hudson's Bay Company enforced it. Early in his stay, he stood by at the hanging of an Indian. "This was the first execution of the kind I ever witnessed," he wrote in his journal, "and I hope it may be the last" (Frost 61). Nonetheless he felt it was "necessary for the safety of the community" that Indians should be conspicuously punished, a notion that echoes in the writings of many others (Frost 58; cf. Hines 392–93).

How then could a clear-eyed man like Frost stay on day after day, and give up only after seeing his own health collapse, along with that of his wife? He offered the lame explanation that by staying he prevented worse offenses. "It may be asked, What good has been effected by [our] toil and sufferings . . . in Oregon? . . . I answer, *Much*. Much crime has been prevented among the natives" (Lee and Frost 331).[6] But a deeper reason was his continuing belief that he was serving God, no matter how futile his work might seem. His own salvation depended on trying to convert others before the Last Judgment, at whatever cost to himself in this world.

This conviction appears even in the imagery he uses to describe the Oregon landscape—in terms of stark contrasts between darkness and light. One night, he saw God's handiwork as "silver rays" upon "virgin waters" and felt reassured that the world could appear that way to a Christian. He had just visited an island where Indian shamans were performing healing ceremonies; when he left, he took comfort in the surrounding moonlight:

> It was now night, but the pale moon had taken up the tale of creating goodness, and was pouring her silver rays upon the expansive bosom of the virgin water, while the owl upon the opposite mountain, more rational than his unfledged neighbours of the island, was pouring forth the praises of his creator God in solemn notes. A few moments' calm reflection upon the exalted privileges of the Christian, who has abundant proof of an all-surrounding Deity in the works of his hand, in connection with the assurance that all things shall work together for good to them that love him, had a tendency to dispel the excitement created by the inhuman and most ludicrous scene which we had just witnessed; and now wrapping myself in my blanket, I stretched out in the bottom of the canoe, and fell asleep. (238)

Weeks later, when Frost and Smith first set up their tents on the Clatsop Plains, he again had to compose himself to sleep, after the scare of meeting a bear. Frost faced it—and overcame it—as an emblem of primordial evil.

> We took courage, and as we approached, the bear withdrew, and retired into the thicket, so that we took possession of the place in peace, struck a fire, pitched our tent, and soon sat down to a hearty supper. . . . We now united in prayer to Almighty God,

imploring his direction and aid, that we might become instrumental in rearing the gospel standard in that wild place, where the enemy of all righteousness had from the beginning held unrivalled dominion. We now laid ourselves down and slept in peace and quietness until morning. (282–83)

Do these final lines mean what they seem to say—that the devil ruled Oregon and Indians were under his sway, even agents of his will? Frost used precisely those blunt terms elsewhere. "What wretchedness have we seen since we have sojourned in his wilderness!" he wrote in his diary. "Is not the day hastening when the peaceful reign of the Messiah shall be established here, where our fellow men are universally led captive by the Devil at his will?" (Frost 160).

Frost was not alone in writing this way. The missionaries' resolute hope was that they might be instruments of light, moving in tiny ways to unfold God's greater strength. "All is dark. The wretchedness of the heathen is untold. The gospel only can ameliorate their condition. And O! how difficult to communicate one truth to their dark understandings. Yet we will continue to try. We will use the means within our reach, and leave the event with God, in whose hand are the hearts of all men!" (Lee and Frost 305–6). These were the cosmic stakes in this moral contest. In his years in Oregon, Frost saw Indians not as deformed bodies (he says very little about their physical appearance) but as wretched, deformed, lost souls.

At the Gorge: Curses and Revelations

Over the centuries, Indians developed a great trading center where the Columbia River breaks through the Cascade Mountains. Here the river fell through narrows, over massive basalt stones—until huge dams deepened the river in the mid-twentieth century. French-speaking trappers and traders used the word *dalle* (flagstone) to name a particular stretch Les Dalles or The Dalles. A major fishery was long established along this part of the Columbia, where many tribes came and caught salmon leaping in their seasonal runs.

As Lewis and Clark came downstream in 1805, Clark made many quick decisions and observations here. He guided the party through dangerous waters—what he called the Short Narrows and Long Narrows—in about seven days. "In those narrows," he wrote, "the water was agitated in a most Shocking manner boils Swell & whorl pools, we passed with great risque It being impossible to make a portage of the canoes" (Moulton 5:328–29). Many times he oversaw the portaging of heavy goods, then ran canoes through the rapids: "however we passed Safe to the astonishment of all the Inds: of the last lodges who viewed us from the top of the rock" (333).

The captains noted that through this portal they were entering another world. For the first time since they left Illinois, houses were made of wood. Salmon seemed to be the principal source of food and wealth, as buffalo had been on the Plains. Some Indians had European clothes and metal goods—sure signs of contact with ships at the coast. At this season the great salmon runs were over, but it was clear that such runs were large and that they supported important exchanges. The fish were dried here, packed in huge bundles, and traded for other goods from far inland and up and down the Pacific coast. Clark later called one of these villages "the great mart of trade" (Jackson, *Letters* 2:527).

The Indians here were also challenging. They were the trading lords of the region and expected compensation for passing through their territory. They might take items as a hint, if gifts were not offered. This was a situation the captains never quite comprehended (Ronda 172). At this point, too, the explorers' two Nez Perce guides pled that they had now done all they could, for they could no longer interpret the local language; they were at the boundary between speakers of Sahaptian and Chinookan languages. In fact, these guides knew they had crossed into hostile territory. They quickly bought horses and fled back to the Clearwater. Even without interpreters, the captains soon understood that the villagers at hand were sharp traders. They had heavy stacks of fine, dried, packed fish, but they held out for high prices: "the natives not being fond of Selling their good fish, compells us to make use of Dog meat for food" (Moulton 5:327–28).

1. George Catlin (1796–1872), *General William Clark*, 1832. Oil on canvas,
28 1/2 x 23 1/2 in. Catlin painted this portrait around the time of Clark's
meeting with the four Indians from the far West. (National Portrait Gallery,
Smithsonian Institution, NPG.71.36)

2. *(above left)* George Catlin (1796–1872), *Hee-oh'ks-te-kin, Rabbit's Skin Leggings.* One of the Nez Perce visitors, as he was painted on his return trip to the West in 1832. (Smithsonian Institution, American Art Museum, Gift of Mrs. Joseph Harrison, Jr., 1985.66.145)

3. *(below left)* Retouched photograph portrait of Solomon and Celiast Smith, taken some time after the early mission period. Solomon Smith was one of the first American farmers to settle and prosper in Oregon; his wife was a Clatsop who had seen Lewis and Clark as a child; they were among the first couples married by the missionaries, and their descendants still live in Clatsop County. (Oregon Historical Society, #CN 014130)

4. *(below)* The small hand printing press used by missionaries at Lapwai to print the first books published in this region. These early books were attempts to translate English texts (including Bible passages and an Indian agent's laws) into Sahaptian languages using a Roman alphabet. (Oregon Historical Society, #OrHi 26237)

5. Barry Faulkner, detail of a mural panel, *The First White Women to Cross the Continent Welcomed by Dr. McLoughlin at Fort Vancouver, 1836*, state capitol rotunda, Salem, Oregon, 1938. Marcus and Narcissa Whitman and Henry and Eliza Spalding are shown facing officials of the Hudson's Bay Company. Along with Jason Lee and his followers, these missionary couples made the first enduring American settlements in the Northwest and helped open the way for other immigrants over the Oregon Trail. (Legislative Administration, Oregon State Legislature)

6. Henry Spalding in later years, posed with two symbols reflecting his abiding beliefs—a Bible and a hoe. Both items brought revolutionary changes to Northwest Indians. (Pacific University Archives)

7. *(left)* The earliest known Catholic ladder, drawn by Father F. N. Blanchet, includes annotations in his handwriting. The ladder represents all of human history, from the Creation to 1840; horizontal lines stand for centuries, dots for single years. (Oregon Historical Society, #OrHi 88606)

8. *(below)* Detail of the Blanchet ladder of 1840, showing (in ascending order) the twelve apostles, the Crucifixion, the development of the Catholic Church and the New Testament, and (in the 16th century) the branching away of Protestants led by Luther and Calvin. (Oregon Historical Society, #OrHi 90423)

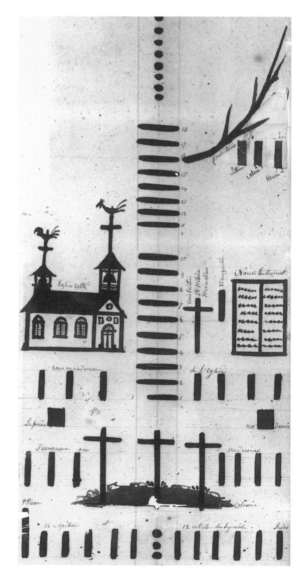

9. Henry and Eliza Spalding's hand-colored Protestant ladder, designed to show the errors of Catholicism and their consequences. In the original, flames and other details are a bright red. (Oregon Historical Society, #OrHi 87849)

10. Paul Kane (1810–1871), *Interior of a Ceremonial Lodge, Columbia River*, 1846. Oil on paper, 9 1/2 x 11 1/2 in. Note the central fire pit and the carvings. It was in a lodge such as this that Henry Brewer witnessed a Winter ceremony, which he described as a "dance" or "performance." (Stark Museum of Art, Orange, Texas, 31.78/210, WOP 13)

The next spring, after the dreary winter and tense feelings about Indians at the coast, Lewis and Clark came back through the Gorge and faced worse insults. One of the natives pelted them with rocks as they struggled in the falls and rapids. John Shields was assaulted. Someone made off with Lewis's Newfoundland dog. Earlier some Indians had tried to help by bringing up a small canoe that broke loose, and now a local chief apologized for the bad behavior of a few. But Lewis's anger reached a flash point. "We ordered the centinel to keep them out of camp," he wrote, "and informed them by signs that if they made any further attempts to steal our property or insulted our men we shold put them to instant death" (Moulton 7:105). He sensed that only their numbers protected the party: "Our men seem well disposed to kill a few of them. we keep ourselves perefectly on our guard" (7:106).

The expedition was eager to move on, but with canoes it was impossibly hard work and Clark had no success in bargaining for good horses. At The Dalles, Lewis wrote out his frustration, calling the natives "poor, dirty, proud, haughty, inhospitable, parsimonious and faithless in every rispect" (Moulton 7:146). In a study of every encounter between Lewis and Clark and native peoples, James Ronda states that the last two days at The Dalles "held more unpleasantness than any comparable time in the history of the expedition" (Ronda 219). In the end, the party had to march onward with just a few pack horses. Lewis ordered cast-off gear to be burnt rather than fall into Indian hands, and proclaimed that he had it in his power to "kill them all and set fire to their houses" if their pilfering continued (Moulton 7:152).

This part of the Columbia proved much more accommodating to the early Methodists. Henry Perkins and Daniel Lee set up the Wascopam mission here in 1838, on the south bank of the river in what is now the city of The Dalles. They, too, had their abrasive moments, but Perkins remained until 1844. Both men became deeply involved with the local people, and they made such extensive records that the anthropologist Robert Boyd has used them to develop a very full historical ethnography: *People of the Dalles* (1996; cited hereafter as *People*).

The Indians here had become less threatening to whites after waves of smallpox, malaria, and other diseases swept inland from the coast.

Thousands had died, and the survivors were terrified by the power of white traders' pestilences. The region was also dominated by the Hudson's Bay Company in the 1830s, and the Methodists and other missionaries soon developed their own support networks, with frequent communications between outposts. These settlements did not depend on trade with Indians; they were set up to be self-sufficient with their own farms and annual shiploads of supplies. The Indians still pestered and pilfered—Daniel Lee's account is peppered with remarks about these annoyances—but both he and Perkins felt secure enough to marry, bring their wives to Wascopam, and stay on with young children. They also interfered boldly against gambling, slavery, and other practices they abhorred.

For the Methodists, the Wascopam mission was the outstanding success story. Here they achieved their one large-scale conversion of Indians, when hundreds accepted Christianity in 1839–40. The young ministers worked long hours studying the local languages and traveling to visit scattered villages, to preach and to teach. Some of the same circumstances that had exasperated the explorers also worked to the missionaries' advantage. Large numbers of Indians gathered here from both sides of the Cascades. They came to fish, trade, and renew social and political ties built up through intermarriage. Both Sahaptian- and Chinookan-speaking tribes came to winter villages in the area and to fishing sites that had been passed down through their families.

When these gatherings brought Indians near, the Methodists evangelized at camp meetings. One historian has suggested that the Wascopam site was chosen with an eye to this particular Methodist practice. More likely the site looked promising for the farms the mission planted: it was an open, level space set back from the river, near a spring. Still, "there were more revivals and camp meetings at The Dalles in three years than there were in the rest of Oregon in ten" (Loewenberg, "Missionary Idea" 161).

Perhaps unwittingly, Perkins and Lee also took advantage of local customs and rituals. Boyd provides full details about these belief patterns and summarizes their convergence:

The mode of experiencing religion at Indian winter ceremonies and Methodist camp meetings was very similar. Although the Indian form emphasized song and dance and public perform-ances, and the Methodist emphasized sermonizing, exhortation, and song, both were communal in nature, characterized by several meaning-laden activities, and compacted into a restricted, marathon period of time that produced heightened emotional states. And each promoted individual religious experiences. In the Indians' case, the heightened emotional atmosphere encouraged each participant to enter a state in which he was in communion with his personal guardian spirit and could act out his spirit songs and dances or, in extreme cases, perform unusual ceremonial acts. The Methodist camp meeting encouraged its participants to release their pent-up feelings, confess their sins, and in general give themselves up to the charged atmosphere of their surroundings, in which they might feel a surge of emotion, which was inter-preted as a spiritual rebirth. Of all the missionary denominations of the Northwest of the late 1830s and 1840s—Catholic, Presby-terian, Congregational, Methodist—only the Methodists shared with their charges such an emphasis on the communal and individual religious experience. . . . [These] conversions mix[ed] the liminal states of a funeral, spirit acquisition, and Methodist conversion indistinguishably into one experience. (*People* 211–12)

Henry Perkins, of course, saw mass conversions as an outpouring of God's spirit. He stressed the wonder of these events when he wrote them up for the Mission Society. His report became a famous article in the *Christian Advocate* (October 14, 1840), and was later reprinted as a tract titled *The Wonderful Work of God among the Indians of Oregon Territory*. (Boyd prints a text edited from two sources in *People* 243–70.)

As this report makes clear, Perkins also understood this event as a very personal story. The revival began and grew from the intimate spiritual reawakening of just two men, Perkins himself and a lapsed Methodist circuit rider who just happened to show up at the mission.

This side of Perkins's report is worth tracing at some length, to bring out the particular wonder of evangelism as he experienced it.

In September 1839, three adventurers came across the Rocky Mountains and appeared at the mission just when Perkins needed help in putting up a new building. (He and his wife were the only white adults there at the time.) Their leader, Benjamin Wright, was an experienced carpenter, and he stayed on for weeks of hard labor. As the men worked together it came out that Wright had once been a Methodist circuit-riding preacher, and he was still deeply troubled by his loss of vocation. He also challenged Perkins one day with a sharp remark: "It was while Mr. Wright and I were on the roof of the house topping the chimney, that he remarked to me 'You are nothing but Congregationalists,' meaning, as I understood him, that we missionaries were a set of formalists. . . . [We] had the form, but not the power of godliness. These remarks went home to my heart as true—as far as I was concerned, and led to a course of earnest thought" (*People* 244–45).

The two men resolved to preach to each other, and they soon caught the attention of several Indians:

> We concluded, for the improvement of our minds and our advancement in the spiritual life, to deliver a sermon before each other every evening before our fireside, my wife being the only one besides who could understand English, and accordingly commenced with all the formality due to an audience. These exercises were greatly blessed to us and as we unfolded to each other the Gospel duties and privileges, we were led to seek more and more an entire conformity to Christ. Seeing us so earnestly engaged from day to day in the services of religion, the attention of some of the natives was arrested, and they began to attend with us, although as mere spectators, for they understood none of these things. At length their curiosity arose to such a pitch that a few of them begged of me to explain to them in their own language what we discoursed to each other.

We had constantly preached to them from the commencement of our mission among them, but without effect, they being entirely indifferent to Gospel truth. I now commenced explaining to them, at the close of every sermon the leading truths which we had discussed, and we now saw, for the first time, that these truths produced a seriousness among them and their interest seemed to increase every evening. (246)

Soon "an old Indian doctor" named Tumsowit joined them in prayer. "Brother W. and I often took him with us in private to pray; and feeling that God alone could teach him effectually, we often plead before the Lord for his conversion. As he was the only one for some time who showed a deep feeling, we took in him a peculiar interest" (*People* 250). Tumsowit experienced a conversion, "and immediately his soul went out in strong desires for the salvation of others. The next day he began to exhort individually those with whom he met to break off their sins" (251).

Other wonders followed. Numbers of Indians began to attend early morning prayer meetings. Yacooetar—a chief of the nearby village, who shared a house with Tumsowit and had been his bitter adversary— became a convert. As these native leaders began to exhort others, the numbers increased to scores of people, then hundreds. In April 1840 the ministers set up an eight-day camp meeting. Daniel Lee wrote that twelve hundred natives attended, and on the final Sabbath "communion was distributed to several hundreds" (Lee and Frost 191–92). These are huge numbers, if the entire native population of this district was indeed about 1,600 at this time (*People* 204–05). Meanwhile, Tumsowit became an active preacher at villages from the mission site down to Fort Vancouver, and Benjamin Wright moved on, preaching to both Indians and white settlers at Fort Vancouver and the Willamette mission (*People* 343, 327).

A year later the outcome of this fiery season was hard to assess. Indian congregations still met and prayed, but many of the converted had fallen back into their old ways. Some also fell under the influence of newly arrived Catholic priests. Many more had dispersed and moved off out of sight. Perkins looked back ruefully and wondered how many Indians "were sincere in taking upon them a profession of piety, or how far grace had operated on their hearts. . . . In too many instances, . . .

their goodness has proved to be like the morning cloud and early dew, and they have 'endured but for a time'" (*People* 267).

Despite these subsequent setbacks, both Perkins and Lee had felt themselves astonished and exhilarated by an inexplicable surge of Indian attention and transformation. To a modern reader it may seem that they were buoyed up by their own misunderstanding. Indians like Tumsowit were not seeking and finding God's grace, but taking on the trappings of white men's power. Boyd neatly describes this double pursuit:

> Prayers must have been seen by Tumsowit as the missionaries' power songs; if he learned them by rote, he would acquire the powers that they gave the missionaries. Tumsowit's time "alone among the rocks and hills on his knees" was the missionaries' equivalent of Christ's forty days and nights in the wilderness, which preceded revelation; to the old shaman and his Indian observers it was a standard power quest. Isolation from family, marathon "searching" to the point of exhaustion—both were perfectly understandable to the Indians. Although the final "salvation" (read vision experience) was not remarkable from either Christian or Indian perspective, the "change was immediately observable," and Tumsowit was accepted as a "new man" (that is, Christian, or more powerful shaman), apparently in both cultures. . . .
>
> Tumsowit's behavior after his conversion follows a pattern that would be understandable to Max Weber; simultaneously, as he began to exhort and spread the word, he was filling the roles of [both Christian] apostle and Indian prophet. (*People* 343)

What this analysis leaves out of account, however, is a further dimension of the missionaries' drive. They, too, were pursuing deep spiritual quests—quests that meant isolation from family, marathon searching, exhausting labor, and grief of soul. This is precisely what the long trip west amounted to for Perkins, the Lees, and the likes of Benjamin Wright. They left everything behind and immersed themselves in life among Indians—squalid, wretched, benighted, disease-ridden, thieving, lying, fornicating, sinful Indians, as they repeatedly described them. Their frank aims and hopes were that they could thereby attain eternal salvation, not only for others but for themselves. They would know their own salvation, too, in immediate experiences of personal revelation.

This pattern is as plain for Perkins as it is for Tumsowit. The most blissful moment of his life, he wrote, was his conversion experience as a young man at a camp meeting in Maine in 1836. "It gave me such happiness that the impression of it never left me; and in all my back-slidings since, I have ever looked back to those few weeks when I enjoyed the fullness of love as the happiest portion of my life—it was heaven below" (*People* 247). But that joy did not last. Perkins fell from that height of feeling and wrestled for years with his own emptiness and unworthiness as a sinner, let alone a minister. He was powerless alone, and books could not help, especially the books he found at hand, "such as served to darken counsel by words without knowledge" (247). As Perkins tells his story, it was in this state of anguish that he had a vision. A tutelary figure appeared out of nowhere, just as vivid and powerful as any bear spirit, coyote spirit, or eagle spirit appearing to an Indian spirit quester. This was Benjamin Wright—whose very name and work have a numinous ring: Mr. Maker or creator, Mr. Right, and as later months proved, Mr. Write. In any case, Wright emerged before Perkins as an older alter ego, just as despairing as Perkins himself, but experienced through years of his own revival preaching. He now exposed his own reconversion quest through the hard questions and exhortations he aimed at Perkins across the hearth. Within a few weeks—on "Monday, the 28th of October, . . . my day of salvation"—Perkins struggled alone and came to a crisis. He emerged from it feeling "that I had now received the Lord's anointing," even that Christ his savior had spoken directly to him a second time, saying, "Be clean" (248).

Just as immediately as had Tumsowit, Perkins then threw himself into new activity, exhorting and spreading the word. His work was just as complex as Tumsowit's, too—another double line of commitment. Among the Indians at hand he began teaching and preparing for his great revival meetings. But he also yearned to exhort his own people. A year later he could hardly be dissuaded from returning to the East to rouse his countrymen. He wrote long letters to the *Christian Advocate*, expressing this yearning. He felt called by God to proclaim the whole truth to people he had known, "and so entirely did these things possess my mind, that my interest in the work of this country [Oregon] was very much diminished, or rather swallowed up, in the interest I felt for friends in my own. For several months I felt no rest in my mind, and suffered severely in my health on account of the constant pressure of this subject; . . . I have not found much rest yet" (*People* 268).

At the high point of his time in Oregon, then, Henry Perkins was lifted and driven onward by an experience of irresistible revelation. It gave him new power. Not far from his mission station, Meriwether Lewis had been driven to an extreme of murderous exasperation by the natives. Perkins reached an extreme of fulfillment among them, crowned by the sense that he was imparting that same fulfillment outward, even to their oldest and wisest.

I called at one house where was an aged doctor, who had seen nearly a hundred years. He remembered the visit of Clarke and Lewis, and described their dress, and the general sensation produced on them by their unexpected appearance, and the trinkets they brought with them. His appearance and conversation interested me much. He seemed a relic of former days—a voice from the past. A whole century he had stood and seen his people rise and fall around him, and many a time he shed the bitter tear for his comrades, while he had seen the oblivious wave of death close over them, and not one ray of light cast athwart the gloom, and no voice to direct him, or them, to a glorious immortality, where friends may meet again. My heart rose in silent praise to Him who had spared his life to hear, like Simeon, of Jesus, and what was more interesting still to me, was, that I could give him the Gospel now through one of his own countrymen. "Tell him," said I to Yacooetar [the interpreter], "of Jesus." Yacooetar commenced—gave an account of his birth—his life—his conversations with his disciples—his instructions . . . of his sufferings and death; . . . of his resurrection[;] . . . of the scenes of a future judgment, and the final destiny of the righteous and wicked after death. When he had finished (and they were both by this time very much excited,) "Ah!" exclaimed the old man, with a loud voice, "this is the talk I want to hear;" and then turning to me, he tried to express his thankfulness that I had come to tell him of these things, and then taking a poker and pulling the coals from the fire, "There!" he exclaimed, "you have come just so, to pull me out of the fire." The old man then joined us in prayer, and has since that time been like a true seeker of the pearl of great price. (*People* 259–60)

Along the Walla Walla: Powerful Medicines

When they left the Columbia Gorge on the return trip, the Lewis and Clark party struggled along with just a few horses, as we have seen. But they soon came upon friendlier Indians with better animals and found means to make satisfying trades. On April 25 Lewis wrote that the party had enough "to transport with ease all our baggage and the packs of the men"; that day they also obtained two riding horses for the captains (Moulton 7:166). That was enough, they felt, to get them to Nez Perce country, where they expected to pick up horses they had left through the winter.

Near the mouth of the Walla Walla River two days later, they met once more with a chief who had welcomed them the previous October. "He appeared much gratified at seeing us return, invited us to remain at his village three or four days and assured us that we should be furnished with a plenty of such food as they had themselves; and some horses to assist us on our journey." At his village he called out for firewood and provisions "and set the example himself by bringing us an armfull of wood and a platter of 3 roasted mullets." Early the next morning he "brought a very eligant white horse to our camp" for Captain Clark. He expressed a wish for a kettle, but when it was made plain that none were to be had, he merely asked for whatever Clark felt was right, and "appeared perfectly satisfied" with a gift of a sword and one hundred balls and powder (Moulton 7:173, 174, 179).

These quoted details are important because they set the stage for what became a three-day meeting between the explorers and this tribe. The captains wrote this chief's name as Yellepit or Yellept, which could mean "friend, blood brother" in Nez Perce or "trading partner" in Sahaptian, according to the expert sources Moulton cites (177n). But what the captains took as a name could also have been a self-description. As soon as he met the party, their busy host began exercising the "yah-lipt" trading practices of this region. They have been described as follows by a native informant of the early twentieth century:

> I come to see you. I bring blankets, furs, beads, clothing and many things with me. These I give to you. I do not say anything. I leave them without words, You are glad to see me. You take me in and feed me. We are Yah-lipt. I am your Yah-lipt; and you are my Yah-lipt. Maybe I have come from another tribe, come with pack horses loaded for my Yah-lipt. I stay several days. Then I say: "Now I go back home." You say "All right!" Then you order your boys, the young Indians to round up your horses. You select maybe ten, maybe twenty of best horses and give them to me. We have had a good time, and I go home feeling fine.
>
> Yah-lipt is not loaning things, is not the way the white people do business. White man goes to another white friend says: "How long? When you pay back?" The white man says "Thirty days, sixty days, I pay you back." That is not Yah-lipt. Indian never says any thing about paying back. Let it alone. Never speaks that he wants paid back. That is good, the Indian way. The Old Indian way of friends! (Lucullus McWhorter manuscript, reprinted in *People* 65)

The old Indian way may have been violated in this case when Yellipt stipulated that he wanted a kettle in return for the fine horse he brought Clark; or the captains might have pressed him to be specific, and he might have responded quickly, not knowing how long he could hold them there. As things worked out, he managed to detain them for a good while and led them to make several exchanges in a relaxed and friendly atmosphere. He seems to have done all he could to make everyone comfortable with food, shelter, entertainment, and more.

Yellipt pointed out a better land route back to Nez Perce country. He called in about a hundred Yakima Indians for an evening of dancing. He delayed till the next day before furnishing canoes to get the party across the river—and then tried to persuade them to stay another night. A captured Shoshone woman could translate his language to Sacagawea, and so for the first time in months the captains were able to converse extensively with Indians: "We conversed with them for several hours and fully satisfyed all their enquiries with rispect to ourselves and the objects of our pursuit" (Moulton 7:178).[7] The exploring party evidently unwound, for they danced for an hour before the Indians danced, and some later joined in with the Indians. When they parted, they had obtained six good horses and provisions for the next stage of their journey. "Accordingly we took leave of these friendly honest people" (7:187).

Ronda states that Yellipt had a clear sense of purpose in these dealings. By entertaining his visitors so well, he was building prestige among his neighbors and angling for long-term trade advantages as a broker of white men's goods (Ronda 221, 167). Another kind of exchange, however, also emerged in this visit. The previous fall Lewis and Clark had come this way and been hailed as supernatural beings, or at least so they thought (Moulton 5:305). Now their hosts offered them a glimpse of Indian spiritual life in their dances: "Some of the men who were esteemed most brave entered the Space around which the main body were formed in Solid Column and danced in a Circular manner Side wise. . . . one of their party who made himself the most Conspicuous Charecter in the dance and Songs we were told was a Medesene man & could foretell things. that he had told of our Comeing into their Country and was now about to Consult his God the moon if what we Said was the truth &c. &c." (Moulton 7:180–81).

Unwittingly, the party may have provoked a contest of medicine songs and more. John Ordway's journal puts it this way:

the head chief told our officers that they Should be lonesome when we left them and they wished to hear once of our meddicine Songs and try to learn it and wished us to learn one of theirs and it would make them glad. So our men Sang 2 Songs which appeared to take great affect on them. they tryed to learn Singing with us with a low voice. the head chief then made a Speech & it was repeated by a warrier that all might hear. then all the Savages men women and children of any Size danced forming a circle round a fire & jumping up nearly as other Indians, & keep time verry well they wished our men to dance with them So we danced among them and they were much pleased, and Said that they would dance day and night untill we return. (Moulton 9:299)[8]

A local medicine man stood out in that hour, but William Clark had stood out earlier that day as a potent healer. Ailing people were brought to him and he provided various treatments, from splints for a broken wrist to eyewash for a common malady.[9] Patients kept coming the next day, and one brought him a good horse as a gift (Moulton 7:186). According to Ordway, "Our officers dressd. their wounds, washed their eyes & gave them meddicine and told them how to apply it &C. the chief called all his people and told them of the meddicine &C. which was a great wonder among them & they were much pleased" (9:299).

"It was great wonder among them." "They would dance day and night untill our return." These could be echoes of Indian rhetoric, which the skeptical captains disdained to record. Clark's medicine was certainly no great wonder to him. None of his remedies was very complicated, in his view, and he seems to have left some behind free of charge. A few days later, he dispensed remedies to several dozen ailing Nez Perces and wrote apologetically about his practice. "In our present Situation I think it pardonable to continue this deception for they will not give us any provisions without Compensation in merchendize, and our Stock is now reduced to a mear handfull. we take Care to give them no article which can possibly injure them. and in maney Cases can administer & give Such Medecine & Sergical aid as will effectually restore in Simple Cases" (Moulton 7:212).

Who can know how deeply Clark's skills and chemicals impressed the people he touched? Decades later he was warmly remembered among the Walla Wallas and Nez Perces. When missionaries came, the powerful Walla Walla chief at that time immediately sent his son to live with them to get a literate education. This son of Peopeomoxmox was renamed Elijah Hedding, after the Methodist bishop who had appointed Jason Lee. He studied with Marcus Whitman, spent years at the mission school at the Willamette, and became a principal intermediary between Plateau Indians and white settlers in the 1840s.

Clark's powerful healing looks particularly fortunate if it is set alongside the tragic career of Dr. Marcus Whitman, the medical missionary who came to this area thirty years later. Whitman set up the Waiilatpu mission near the Walla Walla River in 1836. He was an exceptionally well-trained physician by the standards of that time, but he worked—as Clark obviously did not—under the constant threat of death if he lost a patient. That threat was finally fulfilled in 1847, when a band of Cayuses killed him and twelve others, in retaliation for a plague of measles.

Not much had changed in medical practices in the intervening years. Army officers such as Clark carried an apothecary's outfit of emetics and cathartics and a few surgical instruments; Whitman's equipment was much the same. Meriwether Lewis's training was, however, rather a crash course. He spent a few weeks in Philadelphia learning from Jefferson's friends, including the outstanding physician, Benjamin Rush. But even in his own time Rush was notorious for advocating copious bloodletting, and to readers of the explorers' journals, he remains almost as frightful for Rush's "thunderbolts"—purgative pills he concocted of calomel and jalap (Chuinard 155–56).

Whitman had much more training than did Lewis or Clark. To become a licensed physician usually required two years of apprenticeship with an older practitioner followed by a semester at a medical college. Whitman was exceptional in going back for another term of lectures and so qualifying for a proper M.D. degree from a leading New York school (Drury 1:81). Of course, he did little or no laboratory work, and advanced chemistry, anesthesia, and antibiotics were yet to be imagined; the stethoscope was a recent invention, and the hypodermic syringe was still unknown. In practice, most physicians learned centuries-old means of dealing with illness, childbirth, chronic ailments, broken bones, wounds, and other injuries. They made up their own prescriptions from a small range of ingredients, pulled teeth, did minor surgery, and watched closely as their patients either died or recovered. Presbyterians and Congregationalists required much more formal education for the ministry. Whitman chose medicine as a career because he and his family could not afford seven long years of college and theology school.[10]

It may seem that even short formal training gave doctors an advantage, especially in treating people with no training at all. So it seemed to Clark among the Walla Wallas and Nez Perces. But it would be wrong to think that Indians lacked medical skills. They had many long-tested traditions and remedies of their own. In fact, Clark achieved one of his most astonishing healings by using Indian-style sweat baths as a last resort in treating a severe case of paralysis (Moulton 7:283, 297, 299).

Northwest Indians called in shamans to treat severe illnesses. Often these healers operated by locating and driving out foreign bodies and evil influences. The risk was that shamans had the power to kill as well as cure. They were sometimes called in specifically to kill a weak or unwanted child. If a patient died under treatment, therefore, his survivors might suspect foul play and try to kill his physician. Lewis and Clark did not witness this doctor-killing but many missionaries saw it first hand.

Because of white contact, waves of new diseases swept across the region in the early nineteenth century. To make matters worse, some traders boasted of their powers and threatened to release such evils if they did not get friendly trade and cooperation. Washington Irving retold a notorious incident. The head agent at Fort Astoria in 1812 assembled the Chinooks and Clatsops and gave them a warning after a trading ship had been blown up in waters farther north. " 'See here,' continued he, drawing forth a small bottle and holding it before their eyes; '—in this bottle I hold the small pox safely corked up; I have but to draw the cork and let loose the pestilence, to sweep man, woman and child from the face of the earth' " (Irving 80; ch. 12). Later versions of this "disease in a bottle" story were acted out by captains of trading vessels (Boyd, *The Coming of the Spirit of Pestilence* 112–15). The result of course was widespread fear of white people's powers and medicines.

Doctor-killing resulted not only from revenge but also from distresses brought on by sudden disasters or sweeping changes in a society (*People* 79–82). It became frequent when white people entered the scene—establishing missions and spreading new diseases. The missions brought medical doctors to the West, but at the same time they introduced devastations beyond anyone's healing powers. The idea of "disease in a bottle," meanwhile, reinforced Indian beliefs in sorcery and in white faces as threats of disaster.

Whitman increased his risks by practicing alone in a remote place. His most thorough biographer can find little record of the doctor's medical work, apart from his wife's occasional remarks in a few of her letters, but those letters reveal anxieties about doctor-killing even during the first winter at the mission. A Cayuse chief brought his wife for treatment but became alarmed when she had a relapse. Narcissa wrote that as a result "Umtippe got in a rage about his wife and told my husband, while she was under his care, that if his wife died that night he should kill him. The contest has been sharp between him and the Indians, and husband was nearly sick with the excitement and care of them." The tension eased when this patient was taken to a "te-wat" or shaman and apparently recovered, but soon afterwards another chief died under a shaman's care. "He was a Cayuse and a relative of Umtippe," Narcissa explained; "was sick but six days; employed the same Walla Walla te-wat Umtippe sent for, but he died in his hands. The same day . . . a younger brother of Umtippe went to Walla Walla; arrived about twilight, and shot the te-wat dead" (letter of May 2, 1837, in Drury 1:251).

Such scares went on for a decade, until the doctor, his wife, and eleven others were brutally killed at the mission. The provocation was a result of many tensions that had built up over time. There were rumors that the doctor poisoned Indians by setting out arsenic for wolves, and that he once "cast a spell" on an Indian, who died that very night by choking on a piece of meat (Drury 2:210–13). There were also large-scale disruptions. Hundreds of immigrants were coming over the Oregon Trail and being supported by the Whitmans. In the 1840s Catholic missionaries appeared in the region and began to sow doubts about Protestants. Then one of the region's best-educated Indian leaders, Elijah Hedding, was shot and killed by white men in California in 1844. No one was brought to justice for his death, and Whitman learned that he was a likely object of revenge as an equivalent "educated . . . leader in religious worship and learning" (Whitman letter of May 20, 1845, quoted in Drury 2:135).

Finally, measles suddenly appeared in the Northwest. A severe epidemic came into the Columbia region from California in the summer of 1847, bringing down many white people as well as Indians. At Waiilatpu the mission school was closed and one white child died. But dozens of Cayuses were dying, in a population already reduced to a few hundred. Some of them took Whitman's prescriptions but also practiced traditional treatments—sweating followed by plunges in cold water—that proved disastrous for their high fevers. According to one witness, many of the dying believed Whitman had poisoned them (Drury 2:208–9). A small group of Cayuses plotted against the doctor and, on November 29, they came calling for more medicine, then brandished their guns and tomahawks.

Clark, it thus appears, was remarkably lucky to have practiced among Indians when he did, and with an unbroken series of successful healings. He worked under the aegis of friendly chiefs, treated no one who was in grave danger, and quickly moved on with horses he received from grateful patients. Doctors who came west later soon faced harsher terms. If they practiced more than a few weeks, their work would mean life or death—and death called for retribution.

Marcus Whitman seems to have been particularly resolute, fearless, and decisive. His Methodist colleague Henry Perkins thought so, after working near him for years and supporting Narcissa at the Wascopam mission during the doctor's long absence in the East. Two years after the Whitman murders he wrote a remarkable letter to Narcissa's sister, in which he blamed the event in large part on the doctor's unyielding character. (The letter is reprinted in full in Drury 2:390–94.) According to Perkins, Whitman was everything that Indians were not—independent, brusque, superior, and always busy. "He & an Indian would never agree. How could they? What could such a man have in common with an Indian?" Most acutely, Perkins asked: "How could they symbolize with each other?" This letter survives only in a hard-to-read transcription, and this sentence may be miscopied. Perhaps Perkins's crucial word here was not *symbolize* but *sympathize*, for the next sentences discuss how much better Narcissa was at sympathizing with Indians. The question is a good one, however, with either term. It points back to the wonder that Clark did so well—being another resolute, unyielding, fearless, and sometimes brusque white man in authority, yet managing here to both symbolize and sympathize very effectively.

Along the Clearwater: Power and Law

The Nez Perce treated the explorers very generously, on both their westward march and their return. They fed them when they were starving, supplied them with guides and good advice, looked after their horses while they were away, and supported them during weeks of frustration in 1806, when heavy snows blocked their way home. Good feelings developed on both sides and lasted for decades.

Still, Lewis and Clark dealt with all the native peoples of the West with a firm sense of their own elevation. They were federal officers of the United States, specifically directed by the president to survey and exert their influence in newly acquired territory. Even after they crossed the Rockies and hence moved beyond the borders of Louisiana, they continued to regard Indians as people subordinate to their authority. They called for formal councils, decided who were the most important chiefs, presented them with official medals, exhorted them to make peace with their neighbors, and tried to impress them with the wealth and power of the empire that now embraced them.

In their formal speeches, the captains followed Jefferson's example and referred to the president as the great father or chief and to Indians as his (and the captains') children. Almost every paragraph of their first formal proclamation began with that vocative word. In similar circumstances, Lieutenant Zebulon Pike addressed Indians as "Brothers" at about this time (Pike 1:263–64). Pike, too, was sent west by Jefferson, and he could have been following Jefferson's example. Charles A. Miller notes that Jefferson changed his mode of address to Indians from "Brothers" to "Children" during his first term as president—that is, just as he was sponsoring both Pike's expedition and Lewis's.

> With respect to Indians Jefferson's primary metaphor is the family. . . . As Jefferson uses it, the family consists of a father from the outside—English, French, Spanish or American—and native Americans on the inside. Disregarding facts, as metaphors must, the father, who is white, has either red children or children who are both red and white. The place of the Indians in the family changes over time. As governor of Virginia and early in his presidency, Jefferson considers Indians his brothers, presumably the equal of whites. Eventually, although they remain his brothers, Indians also become his children (while white settlers become children of the states). (Miller 48)

Perhaps Jefferson changed the terms in this metaphor *because* he became president; earlier he might have considered Indians his brothers because like them he was a subordinate "child" of the federal "father." But there is no such subtlety in Lewis's use of the metaphor, unless Lewis considered himself the president's living voice in the field.

Lewis seems to have drafted a long proclamation for his meeting with the Otos in 1804, and then repeated and adapted it for other councils throughout the expedition. He thus addressed Indians as his "children" all along the trail. In two central paragraphs, Lewis summed up the grandeur of these officers and their commands.

> *Children.* Know that the great chief who has thus offered you the hand of unalterable friendship, is the great Chief of the Seventeen great Nations of America, whose cities are as numerous as the stars of the heavens, and whose people like the grass of your plains, cover with their Cultivated fields and wigwams, the wide Extended country, reaching from the western border of the Mississippi, to the great lakes of the East, where the land ends and the Sun rises from the face of the great waters.
>
> *Children.* Know that this great chief, as powerfull as he is just,

and as beneficient as he is wise, always entertaining a sincere and friendly disposition towards the red people of America, has commanded us his war chiefs to undertake this long journey, which we have so far accomplished with great labour & much expense, in order to council with yourselves and his other red-children on the troubled waters, to give you his good advice; to point out to you the road in which you must walk to obtain happiness. He has further commanded us to tell you that when you acccpt his flag and medal, you accept therewith his hand of friendship, which will never be withdrawn from your nation as long as you continue to follow the councils which he may command his chiefs to give you. (Jackson, *Letters* 1:205).

The captains also carried printed forms that could be filled in to certify that a particular recipient was the "friend and ally" of the United States and under its government's protection "so long as he [does] acknowledge the authority of the same" (*Letters* 1:210).

These high-flown phrases and promises, of course, reached Nez Perce ears through a chain of interpreters, including a Shoshone they held as a captive. Nonetheless, Lewis claimed that he and Clark explained "minutely . . . the views of our government with rispect to the inhabitants of this western part of the continent, their intention of establishing trading houses for their releif, their wish to restore peace and harmony among the natives, the strength power and wealth of our nation &c." (Moulton 7:242). These topics took hours. Then the captains made a show of their astonishing technological and scientific equipment. "We amused ourselves with shewing them the power of magnetism, the spye glass, compass, watch, air-gun and sundry other articles equally novel and incomprehensible to them." Clark also continued to treat ailments with the power of his medical kit.

Clark raised their prestige by practicing medicine, but just briefly; both captains held their high councils then mounted fresh horses and safely rode on. They were soon far away from any need to make good on their promises or threats. Decades passed before another American official reached this part of the world. During that time a new generation grew up and a few Indian leaders began learning to read—so that formal documents lost some of their edge of mystery.

The Nez Perces were taught by missionaries of the American Board of Commissioners for Foreign Missions, particularly Henry and Eliza Spalding, the couple who came west with the Whitmans. The Spaldings settled at Lapwai, a few miles up the Clearwater River from its mouth on the Snake. Many months later, Asa Smith and his wife set up a remote mission at Kamiah, sixty miles farther up the Clearwater. Spalding and Smith desired similar ends. Both were strong-willed men, convinced that depravity was the natural condition of human beings, and both were dedicated to saving the benighted. They differed so sharply about means, however, that they had to work miles apart.

Spalding decided that the most effective ministry was to gather Indians near his mission and teach them the arts of husbandry. He set up a school, a model farm, and a mill, and gradually persuaded several Nez Perces to leave off hunting and gathering and cultivate farms of their own. He literally converted some Indians' gun barrels into metal blades for hoes and plows. In this way he aimed to develop a stable, settled congregation, maintain a proper school, preach the gospel, and bring about a complete change in Indians' habits and prospects.

Unfortunately, Spalding was by nature a deeply unhappy man. He blundered and faltered as he began this long-term project, and paid heavily for insisting on doing things his way. Spalding seemed to need a lifetime to get a proper start. Simmering quarrels with Whitman, Smith, and others led to his being dismissed by the mission board in 1842; he was reinstated only after Whitman rode back to Boston to intervene in person to have the order rescinded. After the Whitmans were killed in 1847, all the Plateau missionaries, including Spalding, were pulled from the region. After many years he returned, picked up old threads of his work, baptized hundreds of Nez Perces and Spokanes, and founded Indian churches that endured. In the end, he stayed in the field far longer than any of his colleagues from the 1830s, and he saw wider, deeper changes in Indian life grow out of his work.

Asa Smith came west two years after the Whitmans and Spaldings, inspired by the glowing reports they had published about their reception and early successes. Once on the scene, however, he found much to criticize and even deplore. The idea of teaching Indians to farm looked worse than absurd to him. It was pernicious; it whetted long-ings for worldly success. Smith moved deep into the interior; in order to preach to Indians in their natural condition, he sought a place where good numbers could be found through much of the year. (At Kamiah he was very close to the spot where Lewis and Clark had spent weeks in 1806, waiting for snow to melt on the higher trails.) As a result, he and his wife lived through months of bitter isolation while he studied the Nez Perce language.

Smith was highly educated, especially in languages, and he had a scholar's weaknesses. He scorned Spalding's hardhanded practicality and model farming, but the loss of their milk cow left Smith and his wife despondent. To his credit, Smith compiled a large Nez Perce vocabulary and worked out a complex grammar of the language, a linguistic structure unlike any he had ever seen. Yet he had to admit that while he was learning *about* the language, his colleague Cornelius Rogers was off *learning* the language by buffalo hunting with the Indi-ans and picking up idioms and a more useful colloquial readiness. As he worked at his desk, Smith also wrote long reports about his situa-tion to the secretary of the mission board, and thereby managed to work himself into a state of despair.

Some of the intricacies of these reports are worth unfolding later, but their gist can be stated in few words. Step by step, they led to much the same disillusioned conclusion that John Frost reached on the lower Columbia. Even if he mastered the language, even if he gathered hearers, even if he spoke inspired gospel truths, he could do no good in this place. The Indians around him were not the welcoming eager learners that he had supposed, but depraved, wily, self-righteous hea-thens, beyond hope of deep conversion. "There seems to be no other way in the present state of the church & world," he wrote, "but for these numerous tribes to perish in their ignorance. The idea is indeed appalling, but from the nature of the case, so far as we can see, it must be so" (Spalding and Smith 109).

Other factors contributed to Smith's despair. Smith's wife became chronically ill and depressed. They were isolated. In 1840 some local chiefs came to evict them in "the most insolent manner & absolute terms" (Spalding and Smith 201). They held on through the winter of 1840–41, then returned to New England after three years of further mission work in Hawaii.

Despite their mutual dislike, Smith and Spalding managed to join forces for a time on one common project. They worked to design and print books that would teach Indians in their own language. A small printing press arrived in 1839 as a gift from the Hawaiian missionaries and was set up at Lapwai, Spalding's mission, where Spalding learned to operate it. (The first press to reach the Northwest, it is now in the collections of the Oregon Historical Society.) Soon the missionaries made plans to compose elementary arithmetic and reading books, selected translations from the Old and New Testaments, and a brief hymnal—all in a phonetic alphabet using roman type.

In effect, Smith joined with the others in a plan that Spalding had been nursing for many months. The group decided to abandon the alphabet Spalding had devised, and they corrected mistakes in Spalding's proposed first text. The chief tasks of further composition fell to Smith and Spalding. It was agreed that the missionaries should give up trying to teach English and give their attention "entirely to the Native [languages] as the only safe way of communicating religious truth to the mind" (Ballou 48). Soon Smith was spending hours preparing the second book, a fifty-page elementary reader titled *Nimipuain Shapahit-manash Timash*, which appeared in 1840 (Schoenberg 27–28).

After Smith and Rogers left the region, further imprints came out on an irregular schedule, as hired printers came and went and the remaining ministers found time to prepare copy. In its few years of service, however, this small piece of equipment forced the missionaries to recognize how very complex their relationship was with the Indians around them.

All the ministers—Spalding, Smith, Rogers, Whitman, and Elkanah Walker and Cushing Eells (stationed among the Spokanes)—tried their hands at turning English into phonetic Sahaptian. All were baffled by the difficulty. Whitman begged off early, pleading that he had enough to do as a doctor. Walker and Eells prepared only a sixteen-page primer in the Spokane language, and even at that Walker apologized for the "very imperfect" product which he helped Spalding print. He also wrote in 1841 that reducing the language to writing was a trial, and in the end he deferred to Eells's better education—though "probably there is no point on which we disagree so much as on the language" (Ballou 97). Many ministers labored to translate pages of the Bible, and thus learned just how awkward and inadequate their vocabularies were, and how open to misunderstanding scripture might be, especially given the lack of exactly equivalent words and phrases. Smith was deeply perplexed about how to explain such an essential concept as baptism. Later he complained that Spalding accepted converts without adequate teaching: "No one is able to explain the articles of faith & covenant satisfactorily in the Nez Perce language. Consequently they know not what they are required to believe" (Spalding and Smith 112, 141).

As years passed, these men also learned another hard lesson. Even when provided with books, the Indians did not learn to read as they had hoped. Spalding wrote out the mournful conclusion in 1847.

> It is the opinion of all the members of the mission now present that the Natives do not possess perseverence sufficient to hold them to study a sufficient length of time to enable them to read by the Roman Alphabet. We have come to this conclusion after much labor & experience in teaching in the Roman Alphabet. Consequently we have no encouragement to proceede in our translations. We have no hope that they will be read. (Quoted in Ballou 102)

At about the same time, Spalding was grumbling over what new immigrants were telling the Indians: that they should have been learning to read and write in English, in the first place—"by which language alone people obtain property & which God understands better than any other. But our teaching them in the native is the same as building an impassible wall around them, to prevent them from having intercourse with whites & from getting property" (quoted in Stern 2:70).

Was Smith therefore right after all? Were language and customs insuperable barriers to promulgating the gospel in this part of the world? Smith was long gone by 1847; the others were left to minister by other means than language alone, and to wonder about the power of the scriptures they cherished and had thought they were preaching.

Meanwhile, a different kind of scripture entered Nez Perce lives. In 1842, the first federal Indian agent came to Spalding's mission and promulgated a set of eleven laws, which Spalding promptly set in type in the Nez Perce language and ran through the Lapwai press.

This agent was Elijah White, who had been a mission doctor at Willamette from 1836 to 1840, until he was forced out over various charges of reckless behavior. Before he left, he made threats and tried to raise a violent mob against Jason Lee (Loewenberg, "Elijah White v. Jason Lee" 651, 657). Years later White was also awkwardly involved in an accident that took several lives. He vigorously leapt ashore just before a heavy canoe slipped back into the current and carried an Indian and four white passengers over the Willamette Falls. Many people distrusted him and saw him as heavy-handed; Gray in his later history described him as murderous (270–71).

In any case, White was dismissed by the Methodists but soon came back full of importance. He had gone to New York, then on to Washington where he secured an appointment as an Indian subagent, which made him the first and only federal official residing in Oregon country. This appointment was technically invalid; the law that authorized it failed to pass in Congress after White had left for the West. In the eyes of Hudson's Bay Company officers in Oregon, it also seemed to violate the 1818 treaty; and settlers in the Willamette largely ignored White's authority as they continued to establish their own institutions. Nonetheless, White's arrival caused a stir. He not only carried official papers, but also led a large party of new settlers west over the Oregon Trail, and when he arrived he delivered a letter from the American Board that ordered the closing of the Whitmans' and Spaldings' mission posts. He would continue to assert his official importance until 1845 (Stern 2:130–31).

Soon after White reached Oregon, fresh mission problems gave him the chance to exercise his authority. Narcissa Whitman had been alone at the Waiilatpu mission when she was awakened in the middle of the night by an Indian intruder. She scared him off, fled for safety, and spent the winter of 1842 43 at The Dalles. Then a fire broke out and burned the Whitmans' grist mill. It was already late in the year when White learned of these events, but he led an armed party up the Columbia as fast as he could. To strengthen his authority, he enlisted the support of Dr. McLoughlin's stepson and of Cornelius Rogers, the former missionary who spoke Nez Perce. When he reached Fort Nez Percés he also persuaded the clerk there to join him—despite explicit orders to the contrary from McLoughlin (Stern 2:132). The group rode on to the Whitman mission and then to the Spaldings', and called Indians to a council at Lapwai on December 6. (This is the same meeting mentioned in Chapter One, where White heard Hohots Ilppilp rise and speak, recalling meeting Lewis and Clark and then commending his literate grandson, Ellis.) When the Indians gathered, White read out a newly composed list of eleven laws, other white speakers supported this proposal, and the assembled Indian leaders agreed to observe and enforce them.

White soon reported these actions to the Commissioner of Indian Affairs, and congratulated himself for having established his laws to the cheerful satisfaction of all parties. The Indians, he stated, unanimously agreed to his proposals by selecting a high chief and ratifying the new arrangements. "They desired to hear the laws. I proposed them clause by clause, leaving them as free to reject as to accept. They were greatly pleased with all proposed, but wished a heavier penalty to some, and suggested the dog law, which was annexed" (Allen 186). The laws were as follows:

Art. 1. Whoever wilfully takes life shall be hung.
Art. 2. Whoever burns a dwelling house shall be hung.
Art. 3. Whoever burns an outbuilding shall be imprisoned six months, receive fifty lashes, and pay all damages.
Art. 4. Whoever carelessly burns a house or any property, shall pay damages.

Art. 5. If anyone enter a dwelling, without permission of the occupant, the chiefs shall punish him as they think proper. [Public rooms are excepted.]

Art. 6. If any one steal he shall pay back two fold; and if it be the value of a beaver skin or less, he shall receive twenty-five lashes; and if the value is over a beaver skin he shall pay back two-fold, and receive fifty lashes.

Art. 7. If any one take a horse, and ride it, without permission, or take any article, and use it, without liberty, he shall pay for the use of it, and receive from twenty to fifty lashes, as the chief shall direct.

Art. 8. If any one enter a field, and injure the crops, or throw down the fence, so that cattle or horses go in and do damage, he shall pay all damages, and receive twenty-five lashes for every offence.

Art. 9. Those only may keep dogs who travel or live among the game; if a dog kill a lamb, calf, or any domestic animal, the owner shall pay the damage, and kill the dog.

Art. 10. If an Indian raise a gun or other weapon against a white man, it shall be reported to the chiefs, and they shall punish him. If a white person do the same to an Indian, it shall be reported to Dr. White, and he shall redress it.

Art. 11. If an Indian break these laws, he shall be punished by his chiefs; if a white man break them, he shall be reported to the agent, and be punished at his instance. (Allen 189–90; Gray 228; article 4 is missing from the eleven articles as they are printed in Allen; it is supplied from Gray, along with the bracketed addition to article 5.)

All these laws seem to have grown out of recent local offenses. The punishments also reflect the summary justice enforced by the Hudson's Bay Company for many years and Spalding's own use of the lash on occasion (Stern 2:24–25; Drury 22; Spalding and Smith 172–73). Spalding certainly approved of these laws, for he proceeded to translate and print them himself. He later reported to his mission board: "I have printed the laws & introduced them into the school. They were soon committed to memory by hundreds" (Ballou 98). Unfortunately, no complete copy of this imprint has been found by the modern historians Ballou and Schoenberg, and none are listed in Spalding's inventory of losses for 1847, when he was forced to abandon the Lapwai mission (Spalding and Smith 365). Working alone, he may have printed a very small run and hastily passed them out, to make good on White's promise that the Indians would have their laws in writing.

White's high-handed law-giving had many confusing results. Josephy makes this summary judgment:

> In time, the laws would prove damaging to both the Indians and the white men. On the missionaries' part, they signified the abandonment of any further pretense of divine disapproval of the Indians' bad conduct. The Americans, not God, were now admitted to be the directors of the giving of punishment, and the realization of that fact by the Indians soon stripped the missionaries of what had long been one of their most powerful means of control. On the Indians' part, the laws substituted the hangman's noose, the lash, and cruel imprisonment for the humane, ethical forms of social disapproval under which the Indians, without Christianity or civilization, had long maintained village and family discipline. As the old ways came into question, the ground was inevitably prepared for the dissolution of Indian self-discipline and morale. (Josephy 229–30)

Charles Wilkes had anticipated some of these difficulties when he visited the Willamette Valley in 1841 during the U.S. Exploring Expedition. American settlers there appealed to him to approve their establishing local laws. He objected on several grounds: laws were not yet necessary in their community; the Americans still constituted only a minority of the population and would find it hard to enforce their rules on Catholics, Indians, and members of the Hudson's Bay Company; and the invocation of secular laws would undermine the missionaries' moral code and authority (Wilkes, "Diary" 17:48–49). Marcus Whitman, too, expressed specific doubts about White's laws when he wrote to his

mission board, especially about the separate administration of rules for
Indians and rules for whites. "It is evident that there should be but one
code for both the native and the settler in the country" (letter of 8 April
1844, quoted in Stern 2:154).

Enforcement soon proved awkward. Indians had no leverage to
obtain justice for white men's crimes. And after the murders at the
Whitman mission 1847, White's laws were simply abandoned so that
the accused could be pursued, tried, and punished by the Americans
(Stern 2:190).

In the heat of the moment at Lapwai, however, Spalding gave the
new laws a strong sanction by printing them and urging Indians to learn
them in school. Probably without thinking the matter through, he thus
put them on a par with his other Nez Perce books, and with the schoolwork and religious teachings they represented.

Subsequent events made a cruel turn on the tensions between his
idea of mission and Asa Smith's; the advent of American power and
law would soon demonstrate that both men had been right, and both
had been rehearsing just one string before the arrival of the orchestra.
Smith had held that Indians could not be saved until they learned the
meanings of law, damnation, and atonement. The laws would soon
teach those lessons to Indians with a vengeance, and reveal that rules
given to them would not be enforced against white offenders. Spalding had believed that salvation would come after Indians learned
farming and reading. Within a decade or two, federal laws would force
those lessons, too. Many Nez Perces would be driven off their lands,
onto reservations, onto farms, and into schools. In Spalding's years, the
scattered, understaffed Protestant missions could not begin to prepare
Indian leaders to read and protest effectively. When treaty makers came
in the 1850s, they extorted mere X marks on their papers.

So the line ran, from Lewis and Clark to Spalding and Smith, to
White and later lawgivers. In negotiating with the Nez Perces and even
in offering them years of service, American invaders addressed them
as if from an unattainable height of law or learning. They looked down
from the saddle, as it were, and gave directions, well assured that they

were best fitted to bring Indians the powers and advantages of the written word.

These brief comparative vignettes have followed Lewis and Clark from the mouth of the Columbia upstream to its tributaries at the base of the Rockies, and have isolated and expanded some of the leading themes embedded in their journals: matters of subsistence, conflict, trade, science, and diplomacy. The experiences of the missionaries who came later reveal both how brilliant the explorers could be and how blunderingly lucky they were to scrape through the winter of 1805–6. Those who came after them saw many close companions die or waste away from disease, privation, violence, accidents, isolation, and depression. The explorers came and returned without loss of life or limb, despite dozens of bold risks. The missionaries came to the same settings with their own lofty aspirations, stayed for years, and so faced the unyielding hardship of settling near the Columbia. Even the brightest gleams of success sank to embers in their journals before they were forced to go home or turn their labors a different way.

Yet this contrast also reveals the very limited, brief, even shallow experience of the explorers in this region. They have often been portrayed as a tight yet diverse little society, sustaining each other with various talents and skills: the highly competent captains; the domestic trio of Charbonneau, Sacagawea, and their infant; the trusted black slave York; the plucky soldier-adventurers serving their turns at carpentry, metal work, hunting, fishing, cooking, sewing, and even singing and dancing. A characteristic moment was their joint selection of the winter camp site at Fort Clatsop, a decision in which all the adults were consulted (Moulton 6:83–84). By contrast the missionaries' papers reveal a more complicated diversity in their parties: couples and family groups from New York and New England, native Hawaiian laborers, a black man from California, all intermingling with local Indians in their daily routines and frequently interacting with the British, French-Canadian, Indian, and mixed-blood people of the Hudson's Bay Company.

We usually see the explorers' party in discrete moments of adventure and achievement. Because of the way the journals are composed, they also present Indians in fixed locations as the expedition party moves through their lands and past their lodges. The missionaries appear in denser, overlapping stories, with tangled threads of ongoing tensions pulling tight within their little societies and across adjacent groups. They are Methodists, Presbyterians, Congregationalists, and independents, all uneasy about each others' beliefs and practices. They are men and women; clergy and lay workers; adults and children; scholars and rough laborers. Strung out in little settlements along a dangerous waterway, they depend on each other, but also watch each other with intense vigilance. And none is ever quite set apart, if only because they all rely on the power of the Hudson's Bay Company—even as they struggle against it. Rough adventurers show up, pass through, linger, join their work, and drift away. Catholic priests move in and challenge them with rival teachings. Trains of immigrants arrive, sap their resources, and set up secular establishments that surround them.

And always there are Indians close by but never quite settled and trusted. They are evidently weakened from contact with white invaders and their diseases, but they go on traveling to fish, hunt, and gather berries and roots, and they go on practicing their own rituals. The missionaries—being missionaries—cannot seal their doors against them nor impress them briefly and pass on; but they cannot hold many of them as willing, long-term pupils either.

There is the bitter rub. The captains always knew how to treat Indians warily as their subordinates—as generous trading partners at best, poorly armed adversaries at worst. The mission leaders came out to meet Indian souls. For them, the work of reclaiming the Columbia would mean years of toil among the heathen. They came expecting that—but then learned that the work would prove futile almost from the time they arrived. After a year or two, most of the couples were weakened in body and spirit. Few held fast to the hopes that had brought them west. Many turned, for solace, to hours and hours of writing about the spiritual shortcomings of their neighbors, or about their own fine balance of faith and disillusionment.

3

THE BOOKISH INVADERS

NORTHWEST INDIANS HAD LIVED FOR THOUSANDS OF years along the Columbia before explorers' ships appeared, to interrupt and upset their ways of doing things. They found comforts and fulfillment on their own terms, harvesting food plants, game, and fish; sustaining houses and villages for centuries; developing stories, myths, tools, weapons, and decorative arts suited to this climate and terrain; and connecting with each other across hundreds of miles through intermarriages, trade networks, and festival gatherings (*People*; Ames and Maschner; Rubin).

They lived in small groups—tribes and villages of a few dozen or a few hundred—rather than the cities and empires that emerged elsewhere on the continent. And they passed on their learning through direct contact with their children, in practical training and words not written but spoken or sung aloud and often repeated. Everyone grew up and remained within range of a family or a village and its instructive sounds.

For this reason it is fair and useful to describe their societies as *oral* or connected by voices. That term also has the advantage of being less cumbersome and implicitly judgmental than others. They were not pre-literate or illiterate or even nonliterate, because they lived through gen-erations without any notion of literacy, any need of it, or any remote contact with it.

After the first European and American explorers arrived on the scene, Indians went on for decades without a pressing need to read and write. Indeed, the first companies of whites to reach the Pacific coast were themselves divided between literate commanders and illiterate under-lings. Contact with Indians was mainly face to face and voice to voice, with books far out of sight most of the time, in the officers' quarters or the chief factor's compound. A few crew members, foot soldiers, and fur trappers may have carried books or Bibles, but if they spent much time among Indians the advantage lay in learning Indian ways. As for the commanders, they had what we might call practical or competent literacy. They could keep a log book, write a report, balance an account ledger, or sustain official correspondence, but none were ambitious as writers; nor were they particularly keen to read and reread books, to reflect upon or weigh an author's phrases, unless that author offered some very essential information. Lewis and Clark remain notorious examples; they were brilliant explorers but their awkward spellings and grammar may force an uninitiated reader to wonder why they have ever been admired as writers.

The early missionaries were very different. They brought to this region a new pressure of very intense literacy. Individually and as a group they were daily readers, writers, and reverers of books. Almost every man, woman, and child among them was brought up to under-stand the world in terms derived from printed pages. They brought heavy trunks of books across the continent and around Cape Horn. Many of them felt starved when they were cut off from letters and newspapers for months at a stretch. They looked out at forests that they had just cut and reshaped into houses, ate the simple fare they could grow or trade for, built fires against the damp winters, then turned to authors they cherished or to page after page of their own letters and journals.

Such people were at one extreme of a literate spectrum; the Indians they met were at another. The explicit task of the missions was to reach across this difference and bring Indians into a new understanding of the universe. But to put it not entirely figuratively, the Indians could not hear their literacy any better than they could read the Indians' voices.

This problem baffled the missionaries at first and bitterly perplexed many of them for years. In part, their frustration stemmed from the radical misunderstanding that we have already traced: They had been badly misled by print. What the *Christian Advocate* had reported, the missionaries had read and believed. They crossed the continent or took the long voyage around Cape Horn, expecting that flat-headed Indians, having sent a delegation to St. Louis to plead for the white man's book, were awaiting them and yearning for their teaching. In fact, few Indians along the Columbia were eager for religious conversion, and very few adults could be taught the rudiments of reading.

The missionaries also had little notion of how deeply conditioned they themselves were to life in a literate world. They were plunged into a new setting, where things ran altogether differently. They tacitly expected that people lived much as they did, by the book. That is, they lived in history, reckoning time by clocks and calendars and looking backward to a beginning and forward to an end of time spelled out in the Bible. They lived under laws and regulations worked out by literate legislatures, bureaus, and committees. They made exchanges through money and kept precise accounts of debts and profits. Most important of all, they evaluated human behavior through fixed rules and precepts, and understood depths of character through their experiences as readers.

The Indians they met had long lived without such notions of time, law, money, and individual character. Little wonder if they ignored or resisted new pressures to adopt these notions. In fact, it is hard to conceive how the most willing learner could begin to do so without repeated failure, disorientation, and exasperation—even if one were adopted as a small child and kept in a strict regimen at a school.

At its base, this disparity rested on very different conceptions of what is essential in human life. The missionaries, of course, were intensely concerned about salvation. They viewed Indians as deficient souls at best, in need of instruction, discipline, and providential illumination if they were to escape eternal damnation. Being literate, the missionaries made many records of their encounters with Indians in this region—and those records are saturated with this outlook on human nature.

Indians' conceptions are harder to document and fully describe. A telling clue, however, can be found in Henry Perkins's observations at The Dalles. In explaining how news of the first conversions spread widely and quickly, Perkins wrote:

> An Indian tribe is like a great family, every member connected with another; and as all the members of a family feel a mutual interest, so with all the members of any one tribe.
>
> As soon, therefore, as the love of God was shed abroad in the hearts of a few at this village, these social ties were immediately tested, and they were for going off directly to tell their relatives in the neighboring villages "what a great thing the Lord had done for them." (*People* 253)

Perkins's modern editor has pointed to the first part of this passage as an extremely perceptive remark about kinship ties in this region:

> Those social ties operated in lieu of any developed political institutions; in fact, the networks established by kinship between villages were, in that part of the Northwest, the closest equivalent to a tribal structure in existence. Kin ties were extensive between winter villages, among village clusters, and even beyond the boundaries of ethnolinguistic groups. They formed the warp and woof of native society. As an expression of the role of kinship in Northwest society, Perkins's statement is a gem; a contemporary anthropologist could not say it any better. (*People* 72)

The second part of Perkins's passage, however, is just as striking. It goes on to state that though kinship ties were the vital lines of connection, in the immediate moment they were animated by living voices. Kinsman *ran* to kinsman, "going off directly to *tell* their relatives in the neighboring villages." What emerges from both parts of this passage is that Northwest Indians commonly felt, perceived, and responded to new situations in small, interconnected groups, communicating constantly by voice.

As many observers also noted, it was hard to find formal and effective lines of authority in Indian villages. This was so, even though there were clear lines of hierarchy. Some chiefs were distinguished by wealth, some by prowess, some by advantageous connections to several tribal networks, but only slaves felt obliged to obey their orders. Leaders did not command or decide so much as groups did. In Perkins's words: "every member connected with another . . . and all the members feel a mutual interest."

In such a world, the eternal welfare of an individual soul mattered much less than the immediate well-being of entire households and villages. When the missionaries tried to impart ideas of personal repentance and salvation, they had to pry an individual out of this tightly-linked situation, just to make him individual in the first place, an isolated, reader-like kind of person. They had to slip a razor-sharp paper message between Indians and the living voices among which they lived.

This may be the most crucial, pivotal point about the work of the early missions, at least in secular history. Early explorers, trappers, and traders had given a few Indians medals, coins, and certificates, and sent a few children to distant schools. The missionaries intended to introduce widespread Christianity and literacy at the same time. This work necessarily meant breaking apart the old bonds of voices, customs, and rituals, and introducing authoritative bits of paper to take the place of living speakers, singers, kinsmen, and elders.

As we have seen, the first missions failed to survive long enough to achieve much of this plan, though they reported some moments of success. How did they make any difference at all, especially in convincing Indians to mingle with books? They had one great advantage, which they may not quite have understood themselves: They, too, were an interconnected village society. Their settlments along the Columbia, the Willamette, Puget Sound, the Walla Walla, and the Clearwater had their own bonds of kinship—strongly felt Protestant spiritual kinship—reinforced by frequent visits and correspondence. All these groups were also part of a larger web of East Coast mission societies and their outposts. Altogether there was an overlay of literate villagers atop the kinship-related villages of the natives. It served as a working model of communications by both direct speech and other means. It set bookishness—along with agriculture and connections to global trade—before the Indians through living example.

Just how Indians perceived this example is beyond knowing. But how the missionaries lived by their books and pens—that is the very stuff of their surviving records. Their records reveal dozens of writers communicating with figures at a great distance—far correspondents, sponsoring committees, newspaper and magazine readers. In their private journals missionaries wrote for their own consciences and for God Himself, should He be peering over their shoulders to read their lives. In revealing moments, they sometimes formally addressed each other in writing, especially when they lived too close for comfort.

Their records have often been studied as evidence about the history, politics, economics, and anthropology of early Oregon. They have not been studied as documents about literate habits and strategies. Yet without books and correspondence the missions could not have existed. At every turn, literacy informed the writers' lives. They could not have been Christian without their Bibles, or American without their sense of the Constitution and laws that created the United States. They could not have remained true to their particular denominations without having written doctrines they could cite. Often they related to each other by following lines of instruction that had been written out months earlier in Boston or New York, or by writing back to superiors there. When they argued with others or among themselves, they did so in rounded paragraphs which filled up long documents and even books. Finally, their lives were jolted by Indians who could not comprehend a written page. Faced with this radical barrier to their work, they behaved sometimes ingeniously, sometimes perversely, but always with busy attention to pens, ink, paper, and the idea of a press somewhere that could carry their words to hundreds or thousands of other readers.

Many missionaries would have frowned at the suggestion that they were exceptionally literate or literary. A few had done advanced study in theology or medicine, but most came west with no college education. There was a long-standing notion, especially among the Methodists, that higher learning was a waste of time. They felt, writes a church historian, "that when God called a man to preach, it was sinful for him to waste time getting ready, for God would not have called an unprepared man. The *Discipline* of 1784 advised preachers not to permit study and learning to interfere with soul-saving. 'If you can do but one, let your studies alone. We would throw by all the libraries in the world rather than be guilty of the loss of one soul'" (Sweet 223).

In the 1830s, however, even the Methodists were founding schools, promoting books, circulating a major newspaper, and starting missions that required educated leaders. The Oregon mission is a good case in point. It was inspired by an article in the *Christian Advocate* and promoted by the influence of Wilbur Fisk, who had taught Jason Lee at Wilbraham Academy and then became president of the newly founded Wesleyan University. Many of the early reinforcements sent to the Willamette were graduates of Methodist schools. They included young women who planned to teach Indians, as well as young men who would preach to them.

The *Christian Advocate* was a vital part of these new developments. It had recently grown from a modest four-page weekly religious paper to become the most widely distributed periodical of any kind in America, with a circulation of around thirty thousand. It absorbed competing papers and went on for decades, reaching homes across the country. "It will be conducted on liberal Christian principles," an early issue declared, "and is designed to be an entertaining, instructive, and profitable family visitor." Unlike earlier dull papers of church news, letters, sermons, and personal items, the *Advocate* ran "regular departments on news items, home tips, anecdotal cures for every manner of illness, personal notices (marriages, births, and obituaries), and a miscellaneous section (including departments for ministers, parents, children, ladies, and poetry lovers)" (Krapohl 101–2). When it carried the news of the four Indians visiting Clark in St. Louis, therefore, it went out to a broad American reading public—a public that it was helping to create. Subscribers were not intellectual, perhaps, but they were united in unfolding several pages every week, sharing their contents in conversations with family and neighbors, and knowing that readers across the country were doing the same.

Methodists and other Protestants also pored over their Bibles and books of religious teachings. Protestantism had begun with the Reformation and the rise of printing, and it placed the burden of salvation on the individual and his direct understanding of scripture. New denominations had emerged through centuries of doctrinal disputes, which revealed others' errors and stressed particular core beliefs. A major tension in Oregon, for example, resulted from a sharp difference about the possibility of salvation. Calvinist theology held that Indians, like all other sinners, were doomed to perdition from birth and only a few would be saved, despite the best efforts of the church. Methodists, on the other hand, believed that salvation was possible for all and depended on vigorous evangelizing. Such important distinctions, of course, could be fully explained only through discussion of fine points in printed works. The denominations also had overlapping literatures of sermons, devotional classics, songs and hymns, and stories of saints and heroes.

For many, belief remained a matter of intense experience rather than something learned through study or tradition. It stemmed from a personal, inner illumination that led to moral reform and an abiding hope. But how could one know that the divine experience was authentic, not just a self-delusion? Believers commonly tested themselves against the experiences of others, and the weightiest examples were themselves recorded in books—in fact in books that depended on other books. Methodists looked to the famous writings of John Wesley, especially the moment in 1738 when he felt his heart "strangely warmed" in a religious experience. The warming of a heart might seem to be a moment out of time, a wordless revelation. In fact, Wesley had long prepared for it. He had grown up in a bookish family, attended Oxford and taught Greek there, joined a group of students who met to read devotional classics, served as a strict high-church priest, and sought a more spiritually vital teaching among the Moravians. His religious experiences led him to reject overrefined philosophy and go directly into the fields to preach to the multitudes. But he could never completely move beyond the literary forces that had shaped him. To the end of his life he kept diaries and journals and preached the Bible, and his influence spread abroad through his writings.

All Christians, moreover, turned to the authority of the Bible and thus invoked not only a book but a complex of literary forms and literary interpretations. Its ancient composite text held poetry, history, law, formal letters, and prophecy, and so required many different kinds of literary understanding. Over the centuries it also passed from Hebrew into Greek and then Latin and the modern languages, and so contained layers of cultural associations from many parts of the ancient world and Europe. Reverence for scripture was centuries old in Jesus' time, and it figures in such well-known teachings as his Sermon on the Mount. The most naive and illiterate churchgoers therefore were (and still are) immersed in literary patterns, alerted to fine points of language, and instructed in a long sweep of written history, just by attending regular sermons and hearing frequent repetitions of Bible stories and passages.

Perhaps this pervasive bookishness can be brought out more fully if we consider the striking development of the early Mormon movement in America—at just the time and place that Oregon missions got their start. The Mormon prophet and founder Joseph Smith came from much the same background as Jason and Daniel Lee, the Whitmans, the Spaldings, and many of their early reinforcements; he grew up in an intensely religious family of small farmers, who lived first in New England and later in upper New York state. He had little formal education but was caught up, as his parents were, by the preaching and camp meetings that swept this region. When he was seventeen, in 1823, he was in anguish about which of all the competing lines of evangelism was the true faith, and his torment ended in a personal revelation.

He claimed that an angel led him to a hillside near Manchester, New York, and showed him golden plates engraved with strange characters. Four years later he was directed to take these plates and use special instruments to translate them. After months of concentrated work, he published hundreds of pages of history, prophecy, and poetry, written out in several books and in antiquated language much like the King James version of the Bible.

The Book of Mormon traces the migration of a tribe of Israelites from Jerusalem to the Americas around 600 B.C. and their subsequent divisions, wars, and revelations. Jesus appeared among them after his death and resurrection, but his coming was foretold (and in fact he was worshipped) long before his birth. Other historical passages describe the total annihilation of the light-skinned prophetic tribes many years later, as a dark-skinned, corrupted branch of the original families over-spread the continent. The lone surviving prophet Mormon and his son Moroni, descendants of the former branch, managed to compile and engrave the golden plates. They also summarized the history of another vanished people, who had come to the Americas from the Tower of Babel.

This may sound like loosely improvised fantasies on ancient biblical themes, but the Book of Mormon has held the fascination of many subtle readers and scholars. Was Smith a divinely inspired prophet, unique in America and the modern world, or was he rather an ingenious fanatic, one of many in his time who claimed special revelations and succeeded in leading large sects? The crux for both Mormons and skeptics is how a man like Smith could have produced a book such as this. A careful modern historian insists that the work is much too elaborate to have come from a few months of idle dictation by a youth with no writing experience:

> By any standard the Book of Mormon is a narrative of unusual complexity. Scores of characters like Ether and Moroni, Jared and the brother of Jared, move through the story. The pronunciation guide in the current edition lists 284 proper names: Paanchi, Pachus, Pacumeni, Pagag, Pahoran, Pathros, Pekah, Rahab, Ramath, Ramumpton. Intricate and shattering events are compressed into a few sentences. Migration, war, and intrigue alternate with prophecy, sermon, and conversion. Mormon, as warrior, historian, and prophet himself, interwove political and military events with the history of salvation.

Besides the intricacy of plot, the narrative perspective is complicated. The first six books are pure source material, written by the original prophets and untouched by later editors. But then with only a slight introduction, Mormon takes up the story himself. In his narrative, derived from the available source materials, he quotes other prophets and sometimes quotes them quoting still others. Moroni injects a letter from his father, and Nephi inserts lengthy passages from previous scriptures. Mormon moves in and out of the narrative, pointing up a crucial conclusion or addressing readers with a sermon of his own. Almost always two minds are present and sometimes three, all kept account of in the flow of words. (Bushman 119)

Many attempts have been made to explain this complexity. Some have linked Smith to other authors and collaborators, who might have helped him pull off an elaborate fraud. Some have used theories of psychiatric stress and fanatical drive. For millions of Mormons, of course, his book is the outstanding evidence of his divine authority.

For our purposes, the Book of Mormon points up how oddly bookish Protestant fervor had become in the American Northeast in the 1820s and 1830s. To speak to that world, it would seem, Smith's revelation had to take the form of an elaborate and mysterious book. Mormons even relied on this book alone as they tried to make their first converts. They put copies into people's hands and urged them to read it, thus letting it exert its own persuasive power. Yet at the same time they looked elsewhere themselves—to other revelations that came to Smith and his successors—for their chief points of doctrine and organization (Remini 79–85).

Smith himself had a strange relation to the plates that passed into his hands and then returned to the angel. He could not directly *read* the "ancient Egyptian" characters before him but had to rely on seerstones or specially provided crystal spectacles, in order to interpret them. Some of the plates also remained "sealed up" beyond his knowing. In practice, he peered at the interpreting instruments in the darkened hollow of a hat as he dictated to others (Givens 32). Meanwhile he went on earning a meager living by doing farm work and helping others search for hidden treasure. He found no fortunes, performed no other miracles, gained no personal wealth or comfort, could not even escape the bitter loss of a child who died at birth. A large part of his manuscript disappeared when one of his scribes took it and showed it to others— and no revelation would bring it back. The period of his translating looks numinous and shabby by turns, as he seems chosen and inspired in some moments and yet oddly ignorant in others, a mere instrument for getting the contents of golden plates onto sheets of plain paper.

What he produced, however, was something astonishingly Bible-like, as he and his contemporaries understood the Bible: a book to be read and yet also taken on faith; a work of history that was also imparted by figures living outside of time; a text compiled by learned men over a period of centuries, and yet immediately available and compelling to the humblest modern reader. His book sets Mormonism apart from all other religions, for it denies their truth and adequacy; yet it also mirrors a widespread Protestant Christianity in its time, for which a great Book was essential to spiritual life, even if it was largely unread or unreadable.

Oregon missionaries would have scoffed at Smith's scripture and reviled it. But it is fair to say they handled their Bibles with as much intense reverence. As we have seen in previous chapters, they too were prepared to see personal revelations in the present, especially when odd events coincided with well-remembered Bible lines. The Indians who came to St. Louis seemed to be calling with the same voices that Paul had heard in Acts 16: "Come over into Macedon, and help us." As Daniel Lee put it, this idea reached Wilbur Fisk and others "as a divine mandate" (Lee and Frost 111).

Hundreds of other lines from the Bible were on the mission people's tongues and the tips of their pens, as a matter of daily routine. The Bible supplied astonishing new passages from time to time, as the ministers searched and found texts for their sermons, and in private life the Bible could sometimes seem an inspired oracle. If one ran a finger down a randomly opened page, a verse might leap out with God's own apt word of particular comfort or admonition. Apparently Margaret Bailey and her difficult husband shared a belief in this practice, and so quoted scripture to each other:

> What text do you think accidentally met my eye the day you left here? It was this: "And these two kings shall set their heads together to do mischief; and they shall tell lies over one table; *but they shall not prosper.*" By which I then gained an intimation of what you have since done. And this morning when praying most earnestly to God to preserve you and keep you from every evil, I also accidentally met these texts in scripture: "And I will scatter him, and the wealth I have given him, to the four winds; and because he would not have Me to reign over him he shall wander destitute and forlorn, and famine and want shall be his portion." (Bailey 275)[1]

Quite apart from Bibles and devotional books, the missions also gave concentrated attention at times to personal messages and papers. At least three notable crises blew up, in fact, over such secular bits of written matter. These disputes rose to a level of rage about what someone had written and how to reveal, suppress, or heed particular sheets of paper.

The outstanding case was the letter Elijah White carried west from the American Board in 1842 that dismissed Henry Spalding from his post and thereby revealed that his colleagues had been complaining about him behind his back. For months, Asa Smith, William Gray, and Cornelius Rogers had been murmuring and writing to each other about Spalding, and Smith had been sending long letters of criticism back to the Board. But it took months for a letter to reach New York, and more months for a reply or instruction to come west. The Board's action arrived and embarrassed everyone, for it came only after irritations had already subsided among these colleagues (Smith had already moved on to Hawaii). Moreover, the letter made the awkward stipulation that both Gray and Smith should close their missions, too, and return east. In effect, it lay on the table and ordered the missionaries to do the impossible. There was no point in closing down Spalding's well-developed mission, and no provision to help mission families suddenly decamp and cross the continent. Marcus Whitman called his colleagues together and got their unanimous backing to go east himself to get the order rescinded—and so he set off alone, to counter written orders with living arguments (Spalding and Smith 217–19).

Meanwhile, similar episodes erupted among the Methodists at the Willamette mission. They, too, involved elaborate exchanges of letters and turned on painful written judgments about individual characters. The first was told in detail many years later by Margaret Smith (later Margaret Bailey), because it left her with a permanent scar. Her account is fictional but evidently based on letters and journal records she had made at the time, and had at hand as she wrote.

Smith was in her midtwenties when she came to Oregon in 1837. She had left New England on the understanding that she would teach at the mission school, but when she arrived she was assigned to live with Rev. David Leslie and his family, who had sailed out with her and now treated her as their domestic servant. No papers could be found to prove that she had been sent as a teacher, and both Leslie and Jason Lee found it convenient to employ her otherwise. Soon she was resisting pressures to follow the example of other young women in the mission and marry one of the single men; she preferred to remain single and pursue mission work.

After many uncomfortable months, however, she became involved with William H. Willson, the mission carpenter. Willson seems to have been an unsettled character. He had been a ship carpenter and before that a whaler out of New Bedford, and he eventually tried out many trades in Oregon, including preaching, doctoring, and land speculation. As a suitor he also proved unstable. He pursued Miss Smith, but when she rejected him in 1838 he sent a letter overland, proposing to another young woman in Boston. Jason Lee carried this letter as he set out for the East that year, but he was hardly out of sight before Willson changed his mind again and sent a message after him to retrieve the letter.

The letter was not recovered, but Willson and Smith agreed to board together through the winter. At the end of that time Smith still would not consent to marry, and Willson suddenly had pangs of conscience.

He confessed to Leslie that he had been living in sin, and the two men coerced Smith to sign a certificate that she, too, was "guilty of the crime of fornication." Afterwards Leslie assured her that he had burned that paper, but not before revealing to others that she had admitted her wrongdoing. Some time later, Margaret married William J. Bailey, a rough-hewn, alcoholic doctor, who tried in vain to extract a written apology from Willson for causing an "injurious report" to be circulated about his wife (Bailey 90–99, 149–84).

These trials and conflicts obviously turned on letters and certificates. And there was more. From the time she arrived, Smith kept framing careful letters appealing for justice. She wrote to Leslie and to Jason Lee, protesting her ill treatment, and she weighed every turn of phrase as she replied to their replies. Early on, Leslie complained to Lee that this young woman was falsely accusing him of "uttering falsehoods." Then one day Smith happened upon an odd certificate in the desk of the school room:

> To Whom It May Concern.
>
> We the undersigned members of the Oregon mission, in view of the statements and representations made by Ruth Rover [the name Smith/Bailey uses in her fictional memoir], viz: that she believed Mr. Leland [i.e., Leslie] guilty of selfishness and false-hood, do hereby certify that it is our opinion that those and any other statements by her made, tending to injure his character, are groundless. (Bailey 92)

Evidently Leslie had pressed for a secret meeting to get this endorse-ment; it was signed by all five of the ministers then in the mission. (What Smith saw must have been a draft or copy; the signed certificate seems to have been held by Leslie.) Smith immediately wrote to Lee insisting that "the certificate must be withdrawn and my name removed from it; or, if given at all, bearing my name, it must be done in such a manner as not to convey the impression that *I* am guilty of falsehood" (93). Thereafter, she kept careful copies of her letters to him and his replies, including his letter that quoted one of Leslie's letters in full.

The dispute dragged on. Leslie wanted to hold the signed certificate;

Lee wanted the whole matter kept silent; Smith wanted both men to abide by the formal mission rules, as she read them, and show her some proper respect. The impasse finally ended only through promises of more certificates. "After many altercations between us, Mr. [Leslie] said he did not intend to show the writing to any body unless he should learn that I had spoken of this to others, and was willing to promise in writing that he never would show it only [i.e., unless?] for this reason; and Mr. Lee also said that he was willing to give me in writing their conviction that they did not suspect *me* of speaking untruths in this affair" (Bailey 97–98). Both men delayed and in fact no papers ever changed hands; Smith concluded that the two men realized how absurd their promises were and simply desisted from further persecution.[2]

Many months after these events, Jason Lee returned from his trip to the East and found himself entangled with a more brutal letter-writing adversary. This was Elijah White, the mission doctor who afterwards became the first Indian agent in Oregon. White had stirred up complaints and dissentions in the past. He probably had a hand in initiating a petition to Lee in late 1837, urging him to return home for a time, for his own good and that of the mission. (This was another document with a curious life of its own—first adopted by the members of the mission, then retracted, then put into effect by Lee's own decision to go east in 1838.) During Lee's absence, the doctor engaged in irregular projects and shady transactions. When Lee returned, he insisted on auditing the doctor's accounts—and thus began a feud that lasted through two months and fifteen sharply worded letters.

Robert J. Loewenberg's study of these letters explains that White had one main end in view from the beginning—to detach himself from the mission and heap all the blame for that act on Lee's shoulders ("White vs. Lee" 646). Lee, on the other hand, needed to keep the one mission doctor he had or show good cause for parting with him. (Dr. William Bailey, who was to marry Margaret Smith, was not a mission doctor and practiced among other settlers along the Willamette.) At an early stage of the quarrel, White charged that Lee had "virtually dismissed" him from his post, and he threatened to go home and campaign for the appointment of an abler mission superintendent. He

followed up with a series of baffling claims, threats, offers, and innu-
endoes: Lee should resign forthwith; he should also provide White with
a good character reference; he should make peace if he wanted White
to trumpet his good character hereafter. Lee tried to get White to back
down, but he just became more sarcastic and belligerent.

Others in the mission made matters worse by bringing formal
charges, so that White had to undergo a church trial. Lee presided and
a committee of six pronounced White guilty of disobedience to
church orders, dishonesty, and imprudent conduct. In a late attempt
to back out of this situation, White offered to burn his correspondence
with Lee, but when the trial was over he lashed out again. He called a
public outdoor meeting, and when Lee and others showed up he tried
to turn a mob upon them and have Lee carried off on a rail. Lee, of
course, took careful notes of these events and sent a full report back
to his board.

The war of documents continued long after White was expelled from
the mission. He left Oregon, returned to New York, made loud protes-
tations to the Mission Board, and then threatened to begin a campaign
of negative publicity unless he was fully exonerated in the pages of the
Christian Advocate. He also lodged a formal Bill of Objections against
Lee in the New England Conference, where Lee had been ordained; that
move eventually forced Lee to return east again, to defend himself in
person. Account books, letters, formal charges, trial transcripts, and
board minutes—all those inky papers took part in this clash of characters. Everything seemed to turn on public reputations—on how words
were read even by these men's closest neighbors and associates.

As we have seen, White returned to Oregon in 1842 and exercised
his new authority as Indian agent by dictating a code of laws to the Nez
Perces and other Indians. An echo of his own literate demands came
back to face him as a result. He learned that Indians, too, could insist
on certificates of character. A Molalla Indian named Cockstock had
broken several of White's laws before being killed while leading a raid
around Oregon City in 1843. About a year later, a war party came down
from The Dalles to seek reparations for his death. White acted sensibly for once and found a balance between the Indians' sense of justice

and his own. He pointed out that two white men also had been killed in the Cockstock affair, then offered a few simple presents to Cockstock's widow and nothing to the chiefs. "To this proposition," he wrote, "they most cheerfully consented, and . . . left, having asked for and obtained a written certificate, stating that the matter had been amicably settled" (Allen 237).

The missionary William Gray tried to keep a list of all the Americans who came to the Columbia region after 1834. According to his figures, about 136 American settlers were living in Oregon in 1840, before great numbers began to pour in over the Oregon Trail. Nineteen were ministers, three were physicians, thirty-three were white women, and thirty-two were children—a total of eighty-seven who were presumably literate or born into literate households. Another thirteen were lay members of the Protestant missions; another thirty-six were settlers, most of whom could read (Gray 192). The mission communities were thus tight-knit groups, heavily enmeshed in reading.

Many of these newcomers tried to reach across language barriers to teach Christianity. At their best, they invented novel ways of communicating with Indians, or faced their frustrations honestly and reconsidered their own motives and convictions. They also wrote and wrote about the stages of their experience, enabling us to retrace them in detail. Later, after they had left Oregon or mission life, many tried to sort out their achievements and failures by compiling long books from their letters, essays, and personal journals. Their mission work was and remained essentially literate and literary.

Small as it was, this colony of Protestants was threatened and challenged by an even tinier group, the handful of Catholic priests who came to Oregon after 1838. In part, their threat was political and cultural. The first priests came from Canada, were encouraged by the Hudson's Bay Company, and began ministering to both Indians and French-Canadian settlers. They set up missions very close to some Protestant settlements and drew away converts.

During the period of joint occupancy there was always a question of how the white population would balance out with loyalties to

Britain and the United States. To the Americans, the Canadian priests came as interlopers, encroaching on their territory with false doctrine — and maddening success. Theologically they were wrong; politically they were alien; they even spoke another language, but they quickly attained great influence over a very wide area.

The priests had the enviable advantage of traveling widely through-out the year. As unattached celibates, they could devote themselves to mission work without the household responsibilities of the married Protestants. In the first appeal for an Oregon mission, Wilbur Fisk had called for "two suitable men, unencumbered with families, and pos-sessing the spirit of martyrs" to live among the Indians, "learn their language [and] preach Christ to them" (*Christian Advocate*, March 22, 1833). Just a few years later, Fathers François Norbert Blanchet and Modeste Demers were meeting this description almost to the letter, while Jason and Daniel Lee had become distracted by wives, children, farms, financial arrangements, and deep-running quarrels among their associates.

The priests, moreover, presented a challenge to the Protestants in the way they reached out to Indians. Of all the Christian missionaries, they demanded least in the way of formal learning and long-term dis-cipline before they accepted Indians as Christians or likely converts. The Catholic church had accommodated believers for centuries without requiring that they read; priests interpreted the Bible and administered sacraments appropriate for an oral society. And a priest's physical touch at baptism implied a gentle promise on both sides; instruction and confirmation of belief could follow much later. When the four Indians had come to St. Louis in 1831, the priests there immediately saw that they knew how to make the sign of the cross, and baptized them without delay; when two of the visitors died, they were "interred with all the Catholic ceremonies" (Rosati 599; Palladino 11). In the Northwest a few years later, the mission priests quickly trained large Indian congregations to sing, make ritual gestures together, and repeat common prayers and parts of the Mass. Blanchet and Demers each traveled great distances and often baptized scores of native children when they met at large gatherings.

The Protestants set higher demands. In fact, the more highly educated they were, the more stringent their standards. As we have seen, Asa Smith came to the conviction that any Indian conversion was impossible. Isolated in a remote place with a sick wife, he began to hate Henry Spalding and therefore hate and oppose Spalding's policies. He also became frustrated by his own failure to master the Nez Perce language. These factors all darkened his mood. But he began with dark view of human nature anyhow, and his disgruntlement had a strict Calvinist logic. There could be no salvation without a clear understanding of the gospels. The Indians could not attain this understanding, because they had no conceptions of law, penalty, justice, faith, or covenant, and there was no way to explain or impart these ideas to them (Spalding and Smith 139–43). Smith wrote that the Nez Perces were also complacently self-righteous: "They love not the truth when it condemns them" (Spalding and Smith 146). As a practical result of this conviction, he complained bitterly when Spalding admitted just two Indians to church membership.

Other ministers found ways to be more hopeful. Most believed in God's power to surmount language barriers and mysteriously transform individual souls. Some drew close to particular Indians and felt they witnessed their lasting conversions. Some took part in revivals and reported hundreds of converts, some of whom still kept the faith months and years later. Jason Lee made sober plans for the long term. He and his board required a ten-year commitment of applicants for the Oregon missions, understanding that it would require long effort by many hands before Indians would be converted or even taught very much.

But how to make a beginning? All the missionaries had to begin somehow to reach the people near them. The obvious solution was to preach, using native interpreters if any were available. Sometimes that arrangement worked very well. Henry Perkins and others even gained prestige by having intermediary spokesmen, because native chiefs also used subordinates—sometimes called criers or heralds— who repeated what they said in a loud voice, while the headman himself stood apart and refrained from exercising direct exhortation (*People*

89; Hunn 84). Perkins also had the good fortune to make converts—and proselytizers—of two chiefs early in his work.

Despite these inroads, interpreters could create great misunderstandings. A minister could not know how well his own words were being relayed nor how long an intermediary would live by his lessons and convey good example. Besides, even the most sympathetic convert might have problems in expressing unfamiliar ideas. Elijah Hedding, for example, had applied himself at school to learn the English language and become a good Christian, but he could interpret the Bible only haltingly. Here is Margaret Smith's report of him, her "proof of the capacity of these Indians to learn":

> Conversed to-day with a young Indian from Walla Walla, who can speak English tolerably well, having been for some time under the instruction of Dr. Whitman. He has, since his stay among us, manifested a disposition to absent himself from the lodges of his people and spending the time in our houses, seeking instruction in reading, &c. He has been singing me some of the hymns he has learned, and telling me what he knows about the bible. He says that Jesus Christ came here, and wicked men made holes in his hands, and feet, and sides, and he died and was put in the ground—came up again and went to heaven—and that by-and-bye he will come here again, blow a trumpet and all the people will come to him—to the good he will say, "come, come"—but to the bad he will say, "go away." Also, if good people wish to speak to him he will turn his ear and listen, but if bad people speak to him he will stop his ears. Repeating the names of the apostles he said Judas was bad and put something around his neck and he died. He also spoke of the Holy Spirit, and of angels, but I could not comprehend what he wished to convey concerning them. (Bailey 145–46)

A better solution was for a minister to learn the native language and speak it himself. But this approach, too, turned out to hold unforeseen complications. Whitman tried but soon begged off, claiming he had enough in hand with his medical work. Spalding, Smith, and Rogers applied themselves to learning Nez Perce and found that even though they could speak it well enough to hold simple conversations, they were challenged in trying to represent it in alphabetical characters. They also became very critical of each other's attempts at translation.

Like everyone else, Perkins found Chinookan languages too hard to speak and hear because of their alien sounds, but he closely studied Sahaptian words and structures, just as Smith worked to unfold Nez Perce grammatical patterns. As a result of their work, both these men became deeply puzzled about how to convey some essential religious ideas. The Indian languages either had no equivalents or their closest words were firmly embedded in other beliefs and practices. Perkins could not translate the Lord's Prayer because the word for "hallowed" or "sacred" carried ideas of blood sacrifice rituals and prohibitions—much too complicated for his purposes. He could find no precise word for "prophet," either (*People* 274–75). Smith found the structure of Nez Perce too complex for literal translations. "From the very genius of the language, the verb expresses the precise manner of the action, as well as the action itself—all that we would express in our language by a verb, together with an adverb or other adjuncts. Hence we are obliged to say more than we wish to, & more than the bible itself says" (Spalding and Smith 139). He also ran into blank spaces where English terms had no Nez Perce equivalents—no words and no underlying ideas.

Subtler problems caught at Perkins when he tried to translate the gospel of Matthew. First he could find no accurate term for "blessed" when he addressed the Beatitudes. Then he came to Matthew 5:21–22, an ironic crux in which God's punishments for lighter offenses are said to be heavier than for murder. Here he became perplexed not about Sahaptian and English but about the accuracy of the Bible itself: "Indeed I cannot bring myself to believe that our translators have given us a faithful translation of our Lords words" (*People* 300). At another point the Indians' ideas made him pause. Matthew 4:16 reads: "The people which sat in darkness saw great light; and to them which sat in the region and shadow of death light is sprung up." The Indians had their own "shadow of death," he admitted:

The natives say, when their friends die, that a shadow comes over the world—every thing in it to them looks dark, & it is a long time before the sun shines, or the world appears as bright as before. This "skesh" or shadow, they term "The shadow of death." This to my mind is beautiful.

Probably no minister headed west with the thought that his mind would be improved by heathen ideas, but here Perkins confesses that an Indian expression had taught him something worth knowing.

In place of such close study, most ministers made do with a rough vocabulary of a few hundred words and a strong faith that God would help them communicate somehow. On the lower Columbia many used the Chinook Jargon, the pidgin language of French, English, and native words which had long served in the fur trade. Margaret Smith complained that not one of the ministers had learned a native language when she arrived at the Willamette mission in 1837. "Consequently our labors are confined mostly to the children in the mission family, who are learning English. There is, however, a kind of jargon spoken and learned for purposes of trade, which is familiar to several tribes, and easily acquired, by which some knowledge of their lost condition may be communicated to the adults" (Bailey 105–6).

She once copied out her own short sermon in the Jargon:

Mican tum-tum cloosh? (Your heart good?) Mican tum-tum wake cloosh. (Your heart no good.) Alaka mican ma-ma lose. (By-and bye you die.) Mican tum-tum cloosh mican clatamay Sakalatie. (Your heart good you go to God.) Mican tum-tum wake cloosh mican wake clatamay Sakalatie. (Your heart no good you no go to God.) Mican clatalmay sayyah; hiyas wake cloosh Schochen. (Go ye great way off; very bad devil.) Sakalatie mamoke tum-tum cloosh. (God make heart good.) Wah-wah Sakalatie. (Speak to God.) Sakalatie mamoke hiyas cloosh mican tum-tum. (God make very good your heart.) Hiyack wah-wah Sakalatie. (Quick speak to God.) (*Oregonian and Indian's Advocate*, Nov. 1838: 60, quoted in Bailey 318n2.)

If this is a fair sample of what the ministers were doing, their lessons depended on the repetition and variation of a few phrases, to drive home a simple message: Fear God and change your ways. It is hard to imagine how a grown Indian could signal comprehension except through a rudimentary range of gestures in return: learning to recite or sing prayers and hymns, weeping and trembling to give good evidence of fear, and making conspicuous changes of conspicuous objectionable habits or otherwise obeying very explicit commands. All these means left plenty of leeway for shallow, self-serving conversions.

Preaching, in whatever language, was also supported by other means of communication and persuasion. As we saw earlier, the great revivals in the Columbia Gorge derived in part from the merging of Methodist camp-meeting intensity, on the one hand, and seasonal gatherings and rituals of the Indians, on the other (*People* 210). Many missionaries called on other aids to their teaching—such as the books produced at Lapwai. The most ingenious, even spectacular teaching device, however, was the ladder, which both Catholics and some Protestants used to represent the history of the world.

The ladder took several significantly different forms. The best-known were long strips of paper or cloth, representing all of history from the creation of the world, at the bottom, to either the present year or the attainment of heaven, at the top. They seem to have begun in picture teaching of some sort done by Henry and Eliza Spalding, and were followed by carved wooden towers used in Catholic teaching, then painted cloth or paper ladders developed by the priests, and finally a Protestant ladder or ladders designed to rival and deride the Catholic ladders, which also circulated widely in lithographed or printed form. All these forms involved pictorial symbols or illustrations of Bible stories and patterns.

These devices may seem merely pictorial enhancements of various missions' sermons—"visual aids" in the jargon of modern teaching. As they developed, they also came to reflect the bitter rivalry between Protestants and Catholics. Some early Catholic ladders had conspicuous branches leading off to the right, indicating the false path of heretics and the Reformation. The most famous Protestant ladder answered this insult by tracing a different false path. A straight and narrow column from Eden led up past Luther to a cloud filled with angels—but a broad path also diverged to the left, was cluttered with black-robed churchmen and fiery persecutions, led upward, and then ended with a final pope or bishop being toppled downward into the flames of hell.

This spectacular contrast must have been part of the teaching on many occasions, but a more essential idea runs through the ladder devices. In all of them, the picture elements are based on words. The overall designs neatly translate the Bible and salvation history into a compact, unified visual or tactile form. They also reinforce literate habits of counting, measuring time, relating parallel developments, and noticing significant details. The earliest devices may have been broadly pictorial, but the ladders became increasingly literary, containing stylized pictures tightly intertwined with legends and captions. They were not just held up to catch the eye. They were meant to be read, or retraced with the recollections of words and phrases.

Henry Spalding wrote that he used paintings in his preaching as early as 1836:

My manner of preaching is as follows. We have represented in paintings several events recorded in the Scriptures, such as the passage through the Red sea, the crucifixion of Christ, etc. These I explain first to my crier [i.e., interpreter]. I then go over with the subject to the people, the crier correcting my language and carrying out my history. But this only forms a starting point for these inquiring minds. They return to their tents, and sometimes spend the whole night in perfecting what they but poorly understood on the Sabbath. If one is to leave camp for some distant part of the country, my crier and the paintings are sent for, and the whole night spent in going over with the subjects to prepare himself to instruct others. Several are already preaching in different parts of the nation. I am frequently astonished at the correctness and rapidity with which several will go through with many events recorded in the Scriptures. (Letter of February 1837, quoted in *People* 186–87)

Apparently none of these pictures survives, and it is impossible to know if words were printed on them, if more than one event was shown in any picture, or if pictures were presented in some sort of sequence. Drury says that Eliza Spalding drew these pictures and also decorated her house at Lapwai with other paintings, but he provides no further information (Spalding and Smith 170).

Asa Smith provides some sidelights on Spalding's teaching methods, however, because he sharply criticizes the passage just quoted:

> I have never employed this method at all but I have witnessed the influence of it on this people. I consider it extremely dangerous for a missionary, while he understands the native language very imperfectly, to make use of this method. Mr. S. said they "sometimes spend the whole night in perfecting what they but partly understood on the Sabbath." True they did & filled up the picture from their own imaginations & in this way they have acquired a vast amount of error which I find no easy matter to eradicate. Painting may sometimes be of some use in giving instruction, but to put them into the hands of Indians to give instructions to others, I consider to be very dangerous. (Spalding and Smith 127–28)

Smith also attacked Spalding for his narrative embellishments even when he was not using pictures:

> This extended to all his instruction, whether from historical portions of the bible or from parables. For instances in giving the account of creation, the fall of man &c, he would fill it up with fiction something after the manner of Milton in his Paradise Lost, & give them the idea that it was all in the bible.
>
> In giving the story of Abraham offering up Isaac, he would have a long dialogue between Abraham & his son & tell them so says the Book. In giving the parable of the rich man & Lazarus, he would tell them about the rich man's wife, and what they said to each other when they were in hell, what the devil said, &c, & the Indians would suppose the whole was contained in the bible. Such has been the careless manner of his instruction to the people

& as you may well suppose, we find an abundance of error among the people & it is not an easy thing to correct it. (Spalding and Smith 170)

One can only wonder if any words at all appeared on Spalding's pictures, or if the illustrations were perhaps used to *limit* the embellishments that Spalding added orally and outline the main lines of the story which the criers and others were to memorize.

The first ladder design that incorporated a historical dimension seems to have been invented by Father François Blanchet. He may have heard of Spalding's pictures, but he had already served as an Indian missionary in eastern Canada and he claimed that he hit upon the idea by himself. He used notched sticks at first, in trying to teach Cowlitz Indians in 1839.

As soon as they were refreshed the missionary [Blanchet writes in the third person] began to speak to them of God, of the Incarnation and Redemption. But the great difficulty was to give them an idea of religion so plain and simple as to command their attention, and which they could retain in their minds and carry back with them to their tribe. In looking for a plan [I] imagined that by representing on a square stick, the forty centuries before Christ by 40 marks; the thirty-three years of our Lord by 33 points, followed by a cross; and the eighteen centuries and thirty-nine years since, by 18 marks and 39 points, would pretty well answer [my] purpose, in giving [me] a chance to show the beginning of the world, the creation, the fall of angels, of Adam; the promise of a Savior, the time of His birth, and His death upon the cross, as well the mission of the apostles. The plan was a great success. After eight days explanation, the chief and his companions became masters of the subject; and, having learned to make the sign of the cross and to sing one or two hymns in the Chinook jargon, they started for home well satisfied, with a square rule thus marked, which they called *Sahale stick*. (Stick from above.) (Blanchet, *Historical Sketches* 31–32; see also Blanchet, *Key*, 1–2, and Landerholm 43, 61–62)

Blanchet claims that this device was invented to teach ideas such as Incarnation and Redemption, but his description shows a great concern to explain time. In an oral society, there is no reason to measure time in seven-day weeks, count out centuries and millennia, or think of time as having a definite beginning and ending. Blanchet's wooden "rule" or "square stick" made the Christian, literate time-scheme visible and tangible, and in a form that might also seem magical, like the power sticks used in native ceremonies.

A facsimile Sahale Stick was created in 1963 as a presentation piece for the visit of a new Catholic bishop on Vancouver Island. Relying on later paper ladders, two Saanich Indian carvers made a tall, square post (2 inches by 2 inches by 4 feet) then carved heavy lines across one face to mark centuries with a heavier band for each tenth century. Vertical rows of dots or small curves represented single years—the years of Christ's life between his birth and his death, and then some further years before the establishment of the Christian church. These seem to be the essential features of Blanchet's original design—though the modern carvers added embellishments such as other figures along the sides and a thunderbird at the top (Hanley 16, 169).

Blanchet later claimed that he hit upon this design as if by a divine instinct: "divino velut instinctu . . . excogitata fuit" (Hanley 27). In *The Key to the Catholic Ladder* (1859), Blanchet also claimed that the image of a ladder exactly suited the form of revelation Jacob had received in Genesis 28:

It has been called a *ladder*, from the form which it represents in its development, about the centre, as the eye runs along its plane, from the bottom to the top. It is qualified by the word *Catholic*, in order to convey a sense of its origin and of its character. It is besides, the most real image of the mysterious ladder, which the holy patriarch, Jacob, saw in his dream, resting on earth, at one extremity, and on the heavens, at the other, along which the angels ascended and descended, and on the topmost round of which the Lord leaned, addressing his speech to Jacob. (*Key* 1)

These points may be mere afterthoughts, but Phillip Hanley has pointed out a further striking appeal of this invention. Whether consciously or not, Blanchet repeated a very deep and ancient form of theological teaching. The earliest Christian missionaries, too, had addressed their preaching to non-believers. Their first task was not to inculcate or refine points of doctrine, but to impart a simpler message. It was to announce Christ's life, death, and resurrection and the love of God to humankind that appeared through that mystery. St. Augustine had written a treatise on this form of evangelizing entitled *De Catechizandis Rudibus*, which stressed teaching through a simple but extended Christ-centered narrative:

> The narration is complete when the beginner is first instructed from the text: "In the beginning God created heaven and earth" down to the present period of Church history. That does not mean, however, that we ought to repeat verbatim the whole of the Pentateuch, and all the books of Judges and Kingdoms and Esdras, and the entire Gospel and the Acts of the Apostles. . . . But we ought to present all the matter in a general and comprehensive summary, choosing certain of the more remarkable facts that are heard with greater pleasure and constitute the cardinal points in history; these we ought not to present as a parchment rolled up and at once snatch them out of sight, but we ought, by dwelling somewhat upon them, to untie, so to speak, and spread them out to view, and offer them to the minds of our hearers to examine and admire. But the remaining details we should weave into our narrative in a rapid survey. (Quoted in Hanley 139)

All this, and much more, could be found in the Catholic ladders, for they offered a simple design to the eye and yet could also serve as a framework for further instruction through extended preaching (Hanley 124–25).

Catholic ladders in paper and cloth soon supported that further development. In Blanchet's words: "That plan was afterwards changed from a [carved wooden] rule to a large chart containing the great epochs of the world, such as the Deluge, the Tower of Babel, the ten commandments of God, the twelve apostles, the seven sacraments and precepts of the Church; these being very useful to enable the missionary to teach the Indians and whites" (*Historical Sketches*, 32). The priests made these "large charts," so that they could have images to display when they met with dozens or hundreds of people. These ladders were also easily portable, and they took less time to copy for wide distribution than the carved sticks, though the priests still complained that copying ladders took more time than they could afford (Whitehead 100). They did not make elaborate works of art. The earliest known handmade ladder was designed by Father Blanchet in 1840, and it seems to have been copied and reproduced in at least four other designs.[3] All of these ladders have lines and dots as their central image, with here and there an image of a church or an open book. There are no drawings of human figures, just thick vertical lines to represent outstanding characters such as the holy family or the twelve apostles. At the top of these ladders there is no imagery of heaven. Instead, the bars and lines can be used to calculate the date of the ladder itself; the top point of the ladder is the present year. From the bar for the sixteenth century a barren branch leads off to the right, representing the Reformation, but it bends outward and upward, to show the diverging of different sects into modern times.

By 1842 demand had grown so great that Blanchet asked his superiors to have copies printed and sent to him for distribution (Whitehead 100; White and St. Laurent 74). Around this time an illustration of the Catholic Ladder also appeared in Father Pierre Jean De Smet's *New Indian Sketches;* soon it was copied, used, and adapted around the world (St. Hilaire 57). The printed ladders introduced much new art work, including an image of a steadfast soul being crowned in heaven, at the top of the sheet, and finely etched cuts of the Tower of Babel, Noah's Ark, Moses receiving the Ten Commandments, Solomon's Temple, and scenes of Christ's Passion. The printed sheets were also covered with words, so that the central ladder of time became an inconspicuous narrow backbone on the sheet, surrounded by pictures, Bible verses, and lists of patriarchs, prophets, saints, sacraments, heretics, church councils, and foreign missions. In the late 1840s Blanchet ordered a Paris lithograph which contained dozens of illustrations and details. As Hanley remarks, this version "all but lost the simple, comprehensive impact of the earlier Blanchet creations" (64, 71). Evidently designed for many uses, these sheets required a proficient reader to explain all that they held. In the *Key* he published in 1859, Blanchet printed several short essays elaborating the symbols on his ladders and describing the successive epochs of human history in detail.

Records show that more offensive versions of the Catholic ladder must have existed. Marcus Whitman complained about "the picture of a tree hanging in Chief Factor McLoughlin's room at Vancouver which represents all the Protestants as the withered ends of the several branches of Papacy falling off down into infernal society & flames as represented at the bottom." He also claimed that the priests either made and distributed copies of this same image or preached the same idea using their ladders: "This gives a good idea of their manner of instruction to the Indians as drawn out in manuscript & given to them accompanied with oral instruction of a similar character. The possession of one of these manuscripts by an Indian binds him not to hear any more the instruction of Protestants so far as observation goes" (Whitman to the American Board, November 11, 1841, quoted in Pipes 238). Henry Spalding also complained that the priests "had printed (I suppose in the states) a vast No of small charts on which the Road to Heaven is exhibited & from which Luther is represented as branching off on a road that leads to hell. . . . They tell people that Luther laid down his black gown & cross together & went off on the Road to hell after a wife & never returned & that all American preachers i e all Protestants are on the same road to destruction" (Spalding to the American Board, February 12, 1846, quoted in Pipes 238–39).

These passages should be read with caution, for they may not describe actual ladders so much as reports of them and of oral exhortations that sometimes went with them—or perhaps embellished copies of the priests' ladders made by overzealous converts. Other witnesses, however, reported Catholic images in Indian lodges in British Columbia as "pictures purporting to represent the roads to Heaven and to Hell." A Methodist missionary named Thomas Crosby wrote of pictures showing "a beautiful place labelled 'Heaven,' with all the Catholics ascending to it with wings, and in the lower corner the lurid flames of hell-fire, and Crosby and his friends going head-first into it" (Whitehead 101).

Whatever the grounds of provocation, a few Protestants responded in kind. Blanchet complained in 1840 that Daniel Lee "had the effrontery to make a copy of the historic ladder from ours" (quoted in Hanley 91). Alvan Waller also devised a rival ladder of some kind in 1841, which Father Blanchet claimed was patently inferior to his (Landerholm 85). Finally, Henry and Eliza Spalding created the famous Protestant ladder that is now a prized possession of the Oregon Historical Society.[4] On a scroll that measured almost six feet by two, Spalding and his wife created a large, eye-catching, and dramatic teaching device. They put in bright red flames at many levels next to the broad way of "the man of sin." And to counter the false or heretical branch on the Catholic ladder, they showed that Luther was in fact the first to break free of sinful Catholic errors. In a letter of 1846 to his mission board, Spalding explained that this design would counter claims that Catholics had the one true pathway to Heaven:

> I have planed & Mrs. S. has drawn & painted a chart about 6 feet long and 2 wide containing two ways one narrow & one broad. After representing briefly some of the important events of the world before the christian era & the crucifixion of Christ I come to Paul whom I represent as pointing to one who has turned off from the narrow way where he has left his wife & children & with black gown on & a cross in his hand is just entering the Broad Road. A few of Paul's prophecies concerning the man of sin are translated and printed as proceeding from his mouth such as he shall forbid to marry & after he has left his wife & entered the Broad Road he is represented as the Pope with a sword in one hand & torch or fagot in the other, a king kissing one foot & a bishop the other. . . . [Farther up the Broad Road are various scenes of Catholic persecutions, slaughters, and egregious abuses.

Finally,] Luther is represented as leaving the Broad road and returning to the narrow way. The end of the Man of Sin is represented by his falling back into hell at the approach of the Lord Jesus Christ who is coming in the clouds of heaven with his holy angels. (Quoted in Pipes 239)

This famous ladder burns with color, drama, and the gusto of the Spaldings' animosity. But for that reason it now distorts the very literary character of the Catholic Ladders. They were not paintings, aids to oratory, or weapons of controversy so much as one-sheet versions of the Bible and its pattern of literate history. Even Spalding created a page to be read, for he notes that Paul's prophecies "were translated and printed as coming from his mouth"—as in a crude comic strip. Elsewhere on the ladder many lines are written out in English. This prophecy passage is in the Nez Perce language, however, for attentive Indian followers to study word for word.

Displayed at large gatherings and distributed as gifts; used in church services, class lessons, and one-on-one tutoring—in one form or another the ladders must have been seen by thousands of Northwest Indians. But were they effective introductions to the Bible? Did they lead to a widespread, lasting comprehension of history and salvation? The priests made great claims for them, but among the Protestants no ingenious device seemed to work. Teaching literate ideas, let alone the capacity to read and judge for oneself, took enormous effort and left most of the missionaries deeply discouraged. Many therefore turned to pen and ink for consolation. They wrote up long histories of their experience in the West, as if to salvage something worthwhile—as if to make lasting marks on paper if not on Indians' habits and beliefs.

By making this turn to literacy, many of these writers repeated a cultural shift that had occurred about a century earlier in the eastern states. Larzer Ziff has studied this change in *Writing in the New Nation*, where he uses the terms "immanence" and "representation" to describe different kinds of self that emerged as a result. An immanent self was the living presence of the Holy Spirit in the soul of a believer. This presence might leave traces in a person's writings, but as a living and numinous spirit it could hardly be fixed on paper. Ziff develops the example of the famous New England missionary to the Indians, David Brainerd, whose intimate journal was published by Jonathan Edwards in 1749 and was widely read as a devotional classic. Brainerd's pages give off glimmers of a faithful life worthy of a seeker's emulation.

Ziff points out that in the view of men such as Brainerd and Edwards the created world was complete and a human life had meaning only within the scheme of salvation (the same scheme of universal time that was shown on a Catholic ladder). The soul was complete when it united with God's unalterable plan of time and salvation, which was quite different from any unfolding of mere historic developments. All essential historic changes had already occurred or had been fully plotted in the creation of the world, the incarnation of Christ, and the certainty of the coming end of the world. Each immanent self, however, was still vitally involved in the great drama of salvation. God's design "imparted a cosmic consequence to the lives of ordinary people. Their spiritual experiences became events in world history; what happened in a church revival in a remote part of the colonies was a step in the progress of the divine plan for the universe. The common man could see himself as a participant in matters of far greater public consequence than those that were managed by his social betters in the commercial and political centers of the land" (Ziff 13).

A representative self, on the other hand, was the public identity a writer constructed for wide acceptance by readers in a print culture. Through the the course of the eighteenth century, many a writer mastered the art of creating such a self. And in America this talent converged with the movement to assert national independence and individual rights through revolution. Benjamin Franklin is the outstanding example of a representative self in this period, a figure who fascinated both Americans and Europeans through his facility in creating a winning public image through print. Franklin's *Autobiography* later became a handbook for achieving political, eonomic, social, and moral advancement in the modern secular world. Ziff notes that for Franklin and many others, the congenial form was a narrative, a novel or an autobiography, the story of a unique individual self that developed through time. Such selves were fulfilled not by uniting with God but by achieving recognition, reputation, and wide sales among thousands of secular readers.

It may seem odd to state that the Northwest missionaries repeated this shift from immanence to representation a century after Franklin created Poor Richard in Philadelphia. They were practiced secular readers themselves, as we have seen. But their missionary calling had its roots in a reaction against the secular new world of a Franklin or a Jefferson. In Ziff's terms, the religious Great Awakening of the mid-eighteenth century was precisely "the rebellion of an oral culture valuing immanence against a literary culture valuing representation" (15). For many believers that resistance to secular culture would last for decades. The missionaries who came to Oregon sought nothing less than personal salvation, a personal experience of inner grace—in a word, immanence. As we saw earlier, this was the experience of a lifetime for a man such as Henry Perkins. No book could lead him to it, he felt; no mere act of writing could enable it; none could adequately recapture it. Prayer, anguish, hardship, sacrifice, toil for others, the fervor of evangelism—in short, the disciplines of mission work—offered the best hopes of attaining this gift of the soul.

When they began gathering their notes and assembling histories and narratives, therefore, the mission workers tacitly embraced a new worldliness in their writing. In their personal lives they may have gone on yearning for immanence, but as they wrote with an eye to publication they were turning their mission experience in quite a different direction. Probably none of them realized what a radical shift was involved, but their pens skipped and slipped, as it were, from one meaningful universe to another.

This change of focus pushed Indians into the background. When the stakes were cosmic, the salvation of heathens held the promise of personal immanence; to save others could be the means to save oneself. There was also an element of all-or-nothing danger in this drama. Each Indian was a soul to be met by a Christian soul, but until the moment of conversion that alien soul remained an alien adversary, a subject of the devil—and the missionary's own soul hung in the balance. (Ziff dwells on this point in relation to David Brainerd, and we have noted it earlier in John Frost's writings about the Clatsops.) When mission writers wrote out their narratives, however, this great cosmic contrast had to fade so that a different story could appear: the history of the missions, the history and developing outlook of Oregon, or the earthly travails of particular individuals.

In such stories of literate, representative settlers, the oral societies of Indians had a very subordinate place. Ziff describes how others had already begun the process of drawing Indians into written histories, assimilating them into the imperial narrative of American expansion, and so obliterating Indian ways of understanding the world and time. Jefferson's *Notes on the State of Virginia* was a key text in this development, and, a generation later, so was the *History of the Expedition* that Nicholas Biddle compiled and smoothly rewrote from Lewis and Clark's journals (Ziff 150–73).

In the missionaries' publications, however, we can see this narrative urge straining against the contrary pull of conscience and soul. In many lines a writer may rejoice or anguish about touching alien souls; before his page ends, he nevertheless works to present an appealing self and win the attention of like-minded readers.

Of the early missionaries, Asa Smith was perhaps the most prolific diarist and letter writer during his time in the field. "In his lonely isolation of Kamiah," Drury remarks, "the unhappy Smith had plenty of time to brood on his misfortunes and to write letters" (Spalding and Smith 144). He could write a single diary entry of two thousand words, and two of his letters run to over 9500 words each. These writings include long, meditative accounts of Nez Perce language and behavior, and of his colleagues' beliefs and shortcomings. Smith evidently kept his diary to document his misfortunes and complaints, and before long he began to copy it freely, compiling long memorials of self-justification to send back to his mission board. But if he was lonely, as Drury says, he was far from alone. Sooner or later many of his colleagues did much the same, and took the further step of finding a printer. Set side by side, the published books of the Protestant mission workers begin to fill a shelf; add their diaries, letters, formal reports, and occasional articles, and the shelf begins to sag.

Daniel Lee and John H. Frost's *Ten Years in Oregon* (1844) concludes with weary advice to prospective settlers: stay home or settle on the prairies instead! Yet the authors add two further paragraphs, which seem exactly balanced between concerns for the soul and concerns for secular success, between immanence and representation. They plead for the reader's approval, and then for God's.

> And, again, taking all the very embarrassing circumstances into the account, under which the missionaries have been obliged to labour, I ask the church and a candid public, whether as much has not been accomplished toward the evangelization of the inhabitants of that territory, as could reasonably have been expected?
>
> And now in conclusion, we feel that we have done our duty in preparing this work for the perusal of the public, and we hope and pray that it may have its designed effect, and that the blessing of the God of all grace may attend it wherever it may find its way, and that the writers and readers may employ those talents which have been or may hereafter be committed unto them, in such manner, that when the *Master* shall come to reckon with his servants, we may hear it said, with respect to us, "Well done, good and faithful servants; ye have been faithful over a few things, I will make you ruler over many things: *enter into the joy of your Lord.*" (Lee and Frost 336–37)

Similar strains of self-justification resound in later books, including Elijah White's memoir, also titled *Ten Years in Oregon* (1850); Gustavus Hines's long-titled book about Oregon and his world travels, *Oregon: Its History, Condition, and Prospects* (1851); and William Gray's *A History of Oregon, 1792–1849* (1870). These writers, too, claimed to set the record straight, stressed their own misunderstood good deeds, and limned the fatal flaws of others. White says nothing about his own violent nature, of course. Gray could get along with nobody during his mission years; as a historian he remains a notorious grouch.

The sharpest pen of all, however, was wielded by Margaret Jewett

(Smith) Bailey, who had come to Oregon expecting to teach and then found herself battling tenaciously to sustain her character against pressures from David Leslie, William Willson, and Jason Lee. During the mission years she nursed ambitions as a writer, and she soon saw several of her poems and sketches in print. She also kept a detailed diary. Finally, after years of hardship, including a bitter marriage and divorce, she wrote up her life story as a two-volume novel and had it printed in Portland in 1854: *The Grains, or Passages in the Life of Ruth Rover with Occasional Pictures of Oregon, Natural and Moral.* The book received only a few hostile reviews, probably had a small press run, and did not circulate beyond Oregon. Janice Duncan asserts that all but two copies were destroyed by "outraged citizens of the Willamette Valley" (240). Only one or two copies of the first volume can now be found, and very few readers or historians directly knew Bailey's work before it was republished in 1986.

Her modern editors point out that Bailey "was among the first white women settlers, the first person to publish poetry locally, and the first woman to have a newspaper column and to publish a book, leaving a record of what life was like for one woman in the early days of Oregon" (Bailey 18). But such terms box her in as a woman and an anomaly, and overlook the advantages she exercised as a woman and as a constant writer. As the sole unmarried woman in the missions, firm in her resolve to stay single and do proper mission teaching, she had a unique perspective on mission life. She was both insider and outsider. Moreover, she did not flinch at confronting the ministers who tried to pressure her and ignore her complaints. She pestered them, insisted on getting answers, matched them word for word. In this way she came to observe them intimately at moments of great stress on both sides—and to press two tender points, the place of women in the missions and the missions' commitment to reach Indians effectively.

Bailey is a deft and persistent writer, apparently the only one in the missions who tried to write passable verse or fiction about her experiences. This is not to say she is a master of either art. *The Grains* is a loose and rambling work, hardly a novel but rather a narrative made up of verses, letters, diary passages, documents, and dialogues, with many digressions. Nonetheless it contains long patches of acute prose, including considered portraits of Jason Lee, Cyrus Shepard, David Leslie, and others. It unfolds day-by-day developments of sharp (and sharply worded) conflicts, and it makes very critical observations about Indians and how their evident needs went unmet. Duncan asks if the result amounts to vindictive falsehood or historical truth, but those are very restrictive categories for a memoir such as this, a narrative just emerging out of frustrated religious commitment. Bailey's main character is as hard on herself as she is on anyone else, and, by writing with an edge of deep anger, she cuts away easy pieties about mission heroes. She exposes some of the hardships everyone in the mission knew, when they tried fitting words with deeds.

The Grains thus pulls together many strands of mission literacy and loops them in a final knot. Alone among the missionaries, Bailey attained the luxury of being not just literate or even highly articulate but overtly literary—playfully alert to language and keen to earn respect for herself through writing. Hardships and frustration finally enabled her to break free of her youthful hopes of doing good as a missionary. Instead she became voraciously attentive to unhappy tensions of immanent and represented characters all around her in daily life. She watched them, pen in hand.

In looking back on the missionaries and the Indians, it is easy to suppose that one side had all the advantages—that the literate were obviously better organized and more advanced than the oral societies they addressed, and that in the long run it was inevitable that their ways would prevail. Of the waves of Americans who came to the North Pacific coast before 1850—explorers, traders, missionaries, settlers, and lone adventurers—the missionaries stand out as both the most literate group and the one most committed to teaching native people. Moreover, in the complex global scheme of modern life, fluent literacy now seems essential to holding power. It is the underlying skill that parents round the world work to secure in their children's education. It may thus seem obvious that Indians had to become literate to survive and prosper, or even to resist effectively, once they came into contact with empire-building Europeans and Americans. With these thoughts in mind, a reader may feel that the early missionaries could not help but do some good service to Indians. By teaching even rudiments of reading, and enabling even a very few to speak and read English, no matter how confused their motives, they made at least a start in the right direction.

Such a line of thought may be broadly comforting to modern readers, but it distorts the ways missions engaged with Indians and manifestly failed them. First of all, it merely clothes in softer terms the old notion that might makes right. It exonerates the missions from many errors, cruelties, and absurdities, by narrowing their efforts down to teaching that is relevant to the present—and then praising their wavering intentions as if they were firm accomplishments. It also ignores the direct involvement of the missions in promoting white settlements, which soon shoved Indians firmly out of their way. Second, this way of thinking rests on what may be too facile an assumption: that literacy is power, and an essential power. In fact, Northwest Indians lived without it for millennia, and many tribes have worked hard to preserve and cherish oral teachings for another two centuries—and to reject white people's standards of education. Finally, the notion of literacy as essential power oversimplifies the complex foundations of modern life, and even of life in America in the 1830s. These foundations included literacy, but literacy entangled with many other forces for change.

We will turn to some of these matters again in the next chapter, but to round off the present discussion we can concentrate on just that last point. For all their literate preparation, the missionaries were almost powerless themselves in the face of changes that soon engulfed them.

The most obvious change was the arrival of hundreds and then thousands of American settlers in the region. When the missions began and supporters collected funds and promises, many thought they were continuing the great work of their New England ancestors, who had landed in a wilderness centuries earlier, to make it a godly place. In Oregon, however, wilderness soon gave way to the secular bustle of Manifest Destiny. In just a decade, a new wave of settlers followed the missionaries west. Long wagon trains arrived with weary, hungry, demanding immigrants, who immediately called for more support than the mission stations could supply. Elijah White helped lead one early party. Marcus Whitman led another. Jason Lee and others did their best to advertise Oregon as they recruited reinforcements for their own little settlements. But the great numbers that came caught the missions unprepared, sapped their resources, and completely shifted the character of white society in the new Oregon Territory of 1848.

Other changes followed, and carried hints of coming upheavals. The Hudson's Bay Company retreated to a base of operations at Victoria, and the fur trade faded away. Fisheries, gold, and timber caught the imaginations of new adventurers, and the logic of empire stirred a few of them to think on a grand scale. Still, the missionaries and early settlers remained farm and village folk, as they had been before they came west. They built houses and barns, cleared land, ran small mills with water power, engaged in small-scale trade, and supported a few doctors, lawyers, and skilled artisans. In the 1840s communications remained slow. Factories, steam engines, railroads, and telegraph lines were beginning to hum in the eastern states, but who could know that mechanized warfare would tear those states up within twenty years, and that railroads would span the continent before the century's end? When their missions closed, many Methodists stayed on and became circuit riders, ministers traveling on horseback to far-flung clusters of believers—a form of ministry rooted in the eighteenth century.

Meanwhile subtler changes were developing in the work of other readers and writers. While the Lees, Whitmans, and Spaldings were setting out for Oregon, Charles Darwin was voyaging in the South Seas and recording odd specimens of animals and plants. Charles Lyell was defending new ways of understanding geology. David Friedrich Strauss was completing his critical study of Jesus' life. Such men were changing the ways millions would soon know history. It could no longer be out-lined clearly and simply on a Catholic or Protestant ladder. Just a generation earlier, Lewis and Clark headed west after receiving Jefferson's advice to be on the lookout for living mammoths; Jefferson held creationist notions that no new species could emerge in time, and none could become extinct. But the missionaries in Oregon came face to face with modern science when members of the Wilkes expedition passed through their compounds in 1841. Wilkes's scientists collected specimens and mapped islands and mountains across the Pacific, developing very modern accounts of the gradual creation and erosion of volcanoes and the subtle shifts of the earth's surface over extremely long periods of time.

In their ignorance or denial of such new forces, the Oregon missionaries lived in a pocket of time almost as fragile as the Indians'. Of course, they expected an end of time, and soon. When the gospel reached all the far places of the earth, God's ladder might well be finished. They taught that lesson often, and lived in both dread and hope of what it implied. Then the evil would be horribly punished and the good live forever in bliss. But that was not quite how things turned out. They worked to save Indians from eternal damnation, but then died young themselves or lived on in a world that changed strangely from what they had known and anticipated.

Even their literacy was of a particular, passing character and would soon look antique. They wrote everything by hand, and read books that were set by hand and squeezed through hand presses. Their learning was centered on one great book, the Bible, much of which they committed to memory, and which they listened to and felt in their bodies, through the preaching of their ministers and the group rituals of church services and camp meetings. In their world, law, medicine, and many other callings were learned through apprenticeship and lectures of a few months' duration. How could they imagine a coming age that would demand years of intensive study and training, just to master small fields of expertise? Indeed they tried to break open the clan bonds of the Indians to reach the souls of individuals, never imagining that their own social bonds would be broken apart just as forcibly. When bitter disparities emerged between their paper identities and living characters, such discrepancies caught missionaries by surprise, forcing White, and then Whitman, and then Lee to go east again, appear before their boards, and plead long and hard for proper personal recognition.

What is worse, literacy could not help them out of their deepening predicaments. Far from it. In the form of maps, newspaper appeals, and printed assurances, it had brought them to Oregon. In the form of cruel letters it set them against each other. In the form of science it was grinding away at the platform of belief on which they stood. And for many the way forward was through literary maneuvers that left mission work behind: writing memoirs and novels, publishing secular laws, and fostering schools and churches for white settlers and their families.

Nonetheless, the lifeblood of the missions is now hard to distinguish from the black, dried ink on their pages. Their writings do not just reflect or reveal their work; nor are they just what remains from that work. On page after page, the missionaries' acts of composition, revision, and reflection became the steadiest, most essential work they had in hand. Reading and writing were the means by which they managed their invasion of Oregon and through which the most alert minds measured and remeasured their shocks at facing the impossible.

4

DENYING THE SALMON GOD

MISSIONARIES REGARDED INDIANS OF THE LOWER CO-
lumbia as very strange people. They were human beings, of
course, and capable of achieving Christian salvation; otherwise the missions would have made no sense whatever. But they were
also heathens, uncivilized, habituated to odd practices and beliefs. The
first news of them, which set the mission idea ablaze, made a sensational point of their flattened heads. They found broad faces beautiful
and squeezed their infants' skulls between hinged boards. What would
that process do to their intelligence or even their souls? Captain Wyeth
drew good audiences in Boston in 1833 when he brought a flat-headed
Indian boy onto the platform with him and demonstrated that he could
speak and answer questions. Jason Lee followed his example and
brought young William Brooks east with him in 1838. Brooks not only
dressed and behaved like a conventional young Christian but also
answered many questions in English and even displayed a ready wit.
He helped rake in funds for the missions at meetings in city after city,
until he fell ill and died in Philadelphia (Brosnan 35, 110–11, 119–21, 139).

Lee himself was surprised by Brooks's accomplishments. He wrote that Brooks had not known a word of English three years earlier and had not spent much time in school, yet he rose to the occasion wonderfully. "Though I have seen him at table scores of times with ladies and gentlemen, in various parts of the Union, yet I never in a single instance saw him, by accident or through ignorance, do anything that would be considered *outlandish* even by the polite or well-bred" (*Christian Advocate* of October 4, 1839, quoted in Brosnan 111).

Lee thus held his readers between two poles of expectation. Left to themselves, Indians *would* be outlandish; but once exposed to Christianity, they *could* become fully civilized. He and other writers often stressed both extremes. They made glowing progress reports about conversions, medical treatments, schools, and moral reforms. But at the same time they painted very dark scenes of Indian life apart from the missions.

They reported seeing many Indians living in squalor—poorly clothed, dirty, and showing many signs of disease and malnutrition. They lived from season to season on fish, game, roots, and berries. This diet had looked inadequate to Lewis and Clark even when they were hungry themselves. It would go on seeming meager to the missionaries, who were often farm people and prized their dairy cattle. The missionaries also took in many children left at the missions, and noted that the adults around them seemed driven to beg or steal.

Indians seemed pitiable when viewed through such lenses of prejudice. Close at hand, their ways also seemed different and outrageous. Their offenses ranged from the annoying to the intolerable. Some seemed intractable though petty, such as the constant pestering for worldly goods. Others were ingrained and puzzling. How could bigamy be curtailed, for example, without leaving some wives and children destitute? How could revenge killing be abolished, when white people's laws meted out Indian floggings and hangings? Taken altogether, however, Indians' ways seemed tinged with ingrained evil. Reports of various incidents and offenses add up to a long indictment of depravity. Indians lied and stole. They gambled, drank, and became violent. Their shamans worked up frenzied rituals that ended in slashed flesh. Men beat their wives and children. Indians took captives, held them as slaves, and beat, abused, and even killed them, then threw their bodies out as carrion. They practiced abortion and child killing. They sometimes sacrificed slaves and others as part of their funeral rituals, and even buried people alive. No missionary could imagine a coherent explanation for such things, except the rule of Satan over the wilderness.

The mission people's writings show a steady wariness about Indians' supposed wiles and duplicity, and their ingrained propensities to sin and crime. It is hard to find any passage of admiration for native arts, crafts, skills, or virtues. Very few Indians even have personal names, except for good Christian names assigned in a mission school or at baptism. Only a handful are mentioned at any length, the few who were conspicuously useful as translators, intermediary evangelists, or steady laborers.

Asa Smith perhaps came as close as anyone to broad, direct acquaintance and interchange with a particular Indian's mind, for he worked for months to learn the Nez Perce language from the friendly leader who called himself The Lawyer. Then and later The Lawyer proved himself a steady friend to white people. Smith called him "my teacher" and wrote hopefully about him: "He understands more truth than any other individual & it seems to take some effect" (Spalding and Smith 122). Yet Smith could never shake his suspicion that this man could only have ulterior motives. "Sometimes I think he makes these pretenses in order to please me, as he is very submissive to me, for he feels himself some what dependent on me, & wishes to obtain favors from me" (147). Finally there was a moment of testing in 1840. A Catholic priest came into the area, and The Lawyer resisted his attempts "to get the cross on him." He spoke up, defended the Protestant mission work, and even mocked the priest to his interpreter. Still Smith confided his doubts: "So the Lawyer tells his story. . . . But after all he might fall a prey to Catholicism" (193).

Needless to say, the ministers had no admiration for native beliefs and rituals. If they studied them, it was only to confute them or find some clue or concept by which Christian teachings could be introduced to take their place. They would have been aghast to know that a century later American Indians, including many from this time and region, would be viewed as holy people, keepers of autochthonous wisdom, living portals of American revelations.

This modern attitude has roots in ideas of the Noble Savage, which can be traced back many centuries. It has also been amplified by many new forces. One has been the work of many modern Indians and descendents of Indians, to preserve and restore a deep line of continuity with their past. Their efforts have included popular books about native religion (Vine Deloria's *God is Red* is an outstanding example) and the revival of ancient practices and ceremonies, especially after passage of the American Indian Religious Freedom resolution in 1978. Another force has been the work of modern, secular white readers and writers.

To ease the discontents of civilization, many have idealized an earlier, simpler time, and sought out people living closer to nature and divinity. This pursuit runs from the work of George Catlin to the many books (e.g., by Neihardt, DeMallie, and Joseph Brown) on the teachings of Black Elk of the Sioux, to D. H. Lawrence's celebration of Indians in Mexico and the Southwest, to Carl Gustav Jung's claims that his life was completely transformed through a few conversations with a single Taos elder (Segaller and Berger 132–39).

A third force has been the slow accumulation of patient, disciplined observations by anthropologists. Gathering such information is complicated, of course. Oral societies pass on their teachings through direct contact over long periods—through initiations, dances, songs, stories, and rituals that vary with changing conditions. Written records of a few events cannot fully capture that kind of teaching. Worse yet, literate observers threaten to assimilate and thereby destroy the oral world. Indians past and present have been chary of revealing their sacred things to outsiders. Sometimes they have been hostile, sometimes quietly evasive, sometimes misleading to the best-intentioned inquirers. To survive and continue, many groups have chosen to guard their secrets and risk losing them rather than reveal them and have them published.

To complicate matters further, a layer of legend enfolds some modern ideas of Indian religion. Two particular Northwest Indians have

become world-famous symbols, as wise leaders who spoke propheti-
cally against the white invasion of their region. Chief Joseph of the Nez
Perce met with government leaders in Washington, D.C., in 1879. Soon
afterwards a long speech or essay appeared as his work in the *North
American Review*. He seemed to speak truth to the American officials
who had defeated his people and broken their promises, by presenting
an outline of tragic Indian history. His message was simply phrased and
very moving, with appeals to deep values that might embrace all
people. In fact, he or his interpreters seemed to harmonize native spiritual life with the ideals of the Declaration of Independence: "All men
were made by the same Great Spirit Chief. They are all brothers. The
earth is the mother of all people, and all people should have equal rights
upon it" (Joseph, quoted in Josephy 640).

A few years later, another long Indian speech appeared in a Seattle
newspaper. It was part of a column of reminiscences by a local doctor,
who claimed he had heard it delivered by Chief Seattle to the first governor of Washington Territory around 1853. This speech, too, referred
to the religious life of Indians. Seattle said that guardian spirits would
continue to dwell in his region long after his people had vanished.
Decades later, this speech was further translated and reprinted in several different versions, then excerpted and broadcast around the world
as a manifesto of American Indian beliefs and reverence for the earth
(Kaiser *passim*; Furtwangler 19–46).

As a result, there are now films, songs, novels, poems, posters, children's books, and many mass-market anthologies stressing the sacred-
ness of native American ways. Where the early missionaries saw only
benighted darkness, modern readers are often urged to see intense
light—though much of that light has been generated by later writers'
imaginations.

Fortunately, a handful of missionaries wrote out long reports of a
few Indian ceremonies of the 1830s and 1840s. They cannot be taken
at face value—many of them are disparaging of Indian practices—but
they nonetheless remain valuable as documents that check and challenge both old and new prejudices. In fact, they show the writers' own
perplexities about clashing beliefs; they catch them in the act of seeing

native people clinging stubbornly to coherent, compelling beliefs of their own. Despite their deepest convictions about Indian ignorance and evil, these observers found themselves surprised by the spiritual disciplines they witnessed, so surprised and fascinated that they had to write about them at length.

One of the most extensive accounts is also one of the most intransigent about Indians. Henry Brewer and Alvan Waller witnessed a Winter ceremony at The Dalles in 1846, and Brewer made a long report of it in a letter of 1847. Robert Boyd calls this report "by far the most complete account" of a major religious event in this region—an event that had disappeared by the time anthropologists could study it (*People* 129). He quotes the full passage without interruption and goes on to relate its details to analogous reports from other sources. That is, he mines it as if it were field notes made by a careful student.

In its own terms, however, this letter is a prime document of a minister's deep mental resistance. It may not reveal as much about Indians as it does about convictions that they were wrongheaded, and probably worse. Brewer writes of a "scene" or a "dance," a series of "performances" conducted by "actors" on a "stage." He refers once to the surrounding group as a "congregation" but later calls it an "audience" or a "crowd." He calls one of the participants a "juggler," which is the missionaries' disparaging term for shaman. Altogether he regards the whole evening as a show and a sham.

> I have thought I would devote a few lines, giving you some information of the dance I attended last winter. I have known ever since I have been here that in the month of Dec. the Indians have a great dance but I never would consent to go until last Dec. I accompanied Br Waller, taking along with us some of our most friendly Indians. The scene I saw enacted there that night, beggars all description. It is impossible to give you a correct idea. you need to see it to realize it fully—As we entered the house a tall middle-aged indian was on the stage who had nearly passed through his performance & soon after sat down. The house was

crowded to overflowing. The fire of an Indian house is always in the centre & the smoke escapes through an opening in the roof. The stage or place on which the actors performed was back of the fire. It was composed of thin boards raised probably 8 inches from the ground & covered over with an Elk skin. The next actor that came on the stage was a juggler—I believe they are considered the best actors. He commenced with a low singing noise dancing at the same time taking the lead in the different songs nearly all the congregation assisting. On one side of the house on a high stage were two swinging poles one long and the other a short one. The longer one was ordinarily used by keeping time in striking it against the end of the house, during the height of the performance both were used. Every few moments the actor would swing his right arm & stop to recover strength at the same time some few would make a response however he would stop but a moment & continue on with the old tune or a new one, every time he would increase in exertion. At this stage of the performance the sweat ran in streams down his naked body for he had nothing on but a blanket belted around his loins with a pistol at his side. During the height of the performance the audience rose as by magic & commenced beating with their feet. all voices were at the highest pitch & the two poles were beating most furiously. (*People* 129–30)

Brewer clearly expects his reader to share his skepticism. But as he goes on he also raises other expectations. He has an exciting, sensational spectacle to report—"The scene I saw . . . beggars all description"—and he follows through with fire, noise, frenzy, naked bodies, and grotesque actions including acrobatics and a bloody sacrifice.

About this time two young men stepped up upon the stage behind the actor the younger had nothing on but a pr of pants who immediately threw himself with his back upon the back of the actor with his arms over the shoulders of the actor who at the same time caught hold of them. the other young man held his feet up & in this manner he danced some time—this was about the closing up of his performance—One or two others performed without any thing remarkable when we heard a noise above us & then who should make his appearance before us but a man naked or only his shirt held before him with his arms & breast gashed in different places & the blood streaming down. I began to think he came from "Tother world" It seems he came down through the roof before us—He went through his performance nearly like the one I have described only he had quite a bundle of flax & beads & which were distributed to the female singers I had forgotten to mention that during one part of different perform-ances little images were presented before us in a waving manner or a dancing motion & then would be taken in. When this last actor was about through who should come in but a man painted black with a little image in one hand & a stick with large black feathers attached to it in the other hand. He took his station by the fire with a low grumbling singing, swinging motion, appar-ently unconscious of all that was going on around. About this time a small puppy dog was thrown near my feet, when a young man commenced beating the breath out of his body & before he was half dead threw him into the fire & then pulled him out & took a knife & cut him open while the poor little dog was still half alive & then took the warm blood & commenced giving it to this niger dancer who drank three handfuls of it down freely & then he was ready to mount the stage & dance with energy & life. (*People* 130)

Which is stronger in this report, the writer's fascination or his dis-gust? Brewer ends by stressing his revulsion: "By this time I became so disgusted that I wished myself out of that place, but the crowd prevented it. It was all I could do to stay there" (130). But writing weeks later, he goes on and on with this recollection of surface impressions. What is certain is that he does not see through these strange events. He does not give any hint of understanding a significant pattern here, such as a transfer of power from one of the dancers to another. He seems to see nothing except deception, sensationalism, and manipula-tion of the crowd.

Brewer's final lines could be his return to conventional propriety after indulging in sinister excitement, but they also fit with the strong, even daring counter move of his companion. At the end of the evening, he goes on, "Br Waller gave them a talk, warning them of the folly of such a course & enviting them to give it up after which we left for home as it was nearly midnight" (130–31). It must have taken tough self-assurance to begin such a reproach late at night in a tight crowd of highly stimulated singers and dancers, but such was the temper of many ministers. Henry Perkins once broke into a circle of Indian gamblers to scold them and later he confronted slave holders in a dramatic scene (*People* 248–49, 276–77; Loewenberg, "Missionary Idea," 166–67). Henry Spalding, too, stepped into some rough confrontations about gambling (Spalding and Smith 292, 318). Daniel Lee scolded the participants in a shaman's healing ceremony (Lee and Frost 236). Other ministers also spoke out boldly against drinking, slavery, bigamy, and other practices. They could even be stiff-necked over what now seem minor issues. When Rev. Samuel Parker came across the Plains in 1835 he refused to budge when the guides began to move on a Sunday: he would bear proper witness to one of the Ten Commandments, even though his ways riled his fellow travelers (Josephy 130). Henry Perkins echoed his sentiments a few years later. "The proper observance of the holy Sabbath in this country appears to be the hardest of all things to establish," he wrote, and he seemed gratified when one of the local chiefs put a stop to Sunday fishing by having offenders publicly whipped (*People* 272–73).

Brewer's account seems to reflect a common attitude of doubt and even righteous wrath in the face of Indian practices. There were, however, missionaries able to view Indian beliefs in a more sympathetic light.

On August 15, 1843, Henry Perkins mentioned some elements of a First Salmon ceremony in a formal letter he was composing day by day in journal form. As we have seen, Perkins stood out among the ministers of his time because he learned a local language and faced its complexities of meaning. When he tried to translate the Bible, he found that Indian terms and their associated ideas could seem beautiful and even illuminating. Now a similar reflection occurred when he tried to translate the word "hallowed" in Matthew 6:9.

Perkins saw that Indians had their own term meaning *hallowed* or *sacred*, but he was puzzled about it. He could not quite reconcile their associations with ideas proper to Christianity.

> Finished a translation of the Lords prayer—not however to my satisfaction. It is certainly a most difficult piece of composition to put into an Indian language: It is multum in parvo [Latin: much in little, i.e., great ideas in few words]. The ideas expressed in those two petitions—"Thy Kingdom come, thy will be done" etc comprehend matter enough for a sermon. I have been sadly perplexed to know what language to use—And then again "Thy name be hallowed." The natives have but one word for "hallowed" or sacred, & this is applied in such a manner, that I have had doubts about using it in conjunction with the name of our Heavenly Father. (*People* 274)

As he went on to explain, the ideas the Indians held were bound up with their own sacred ceremonies, which he had evidently observed very closely.

> For instance, the "tu-a-ti-ma"—or medicine men—as they are sometimes called by the whites—practice a sort of invocatory ceremony on the first arrival of the salmon in the spring. Before any of the common people are permitted to boil, or even to cut the flesh of the salmon transversly for any purpose, the "tu-a-ti"—medicine man of the village, assembles the people, & after invoking the "Tah" or the particular spirit which presides over the salmon, & who they suppose can make it a prosperous year, or otherwise, takes a fish just caught, & wrings off its head. The blood, which flows from the fish, he catches in a basin, or small dish, & sets it aside. He then cuts the salmon transversly into small pieces, & boils. The way is thus opened for any one else to do the same. Joy & rejoicing circulate through the village, & the people now boil and eat to their hearts content.
>
> But I wish to call your attention to the *blood*. This is considered

to be "aut-ni"—or as we should say sacred, or hallowed, or sanctified—i.e. it is sacredly set apart, & carefully garded for five days, when it is carried out, waved in the direction in which they wish the fish to run, & then carefully poured into the water. This is but one example of the use of the word. The verb shap,a,aut,sha of which autni is the adjective form, is also used for to *prohibit*. Now if I knew the ideal meaning of the original word which we translate hallowed previously to its being used in the sacred writings, I could pass some judgment upon the propriety of using the Indian word under consideration. The idea which any word naturally conveys to their minds, & the associations with which it is connected, I find we cannot be too intimately acquainted with in conveying religious instruction to the natives. I would like much your advice on the subject. (*People* 274–75)

In these terms Perkins questions his own understanding and appeals to a superior authority (his letter was addressed to Charles Pittmann, the corresponding secretary of the Methodist Episcopal Church). It is only incidentally that he describes the First Salmon ceremony—as a way of fully explicating the native idea of the sacred. Like Brewer in the passage about the Winter ceremony, Perkins frames his description with lines about his own larger missionary purposes. He is trying to translate the Bible, and that is part of an effort to teach a proper prayer and reach Indians effectively in words that cannot be misunderstood or misapplied. Nevertheless, we can see him coming much closer than Brewer to glimpsing a point of solid connection between Christian and native beliefs.

Modern anthropologists and linguists have been puzzled by what Perkins says here. Some of his details about the salmon ceremony are reported nowhere else. His tracing of words to their roots is also speculative and hard to elucidate. Boyd reports that even an ethnosemanticist whom he consulted could rely only on "best guesses" in retracing his reasoning (126–28). Perkins, however, was hardly a scholar in the modern sense, and his effort here is to test the words he knows as a reader and writer against the practices he knows from observation and from his own heritage.

What makes this passage rare is his willingness to pause in order to see through or beyond his own categories of learning. Unlike Brewer, he does not immediately assume that the native leader is a charlatan. He refers to him as the "tu-a-ti" and notes that "medicine man" is itself an inadequate translation—"as they are sometimes called by the whites." In these lines Perkins seems to be thinking very evenly in two languages at the same time. As he goes on to explain "aut-ni," Perkins also seems to think evenly in terms of two cultures. His second paragraph in particular seems to search for common ground between the English words "sacred" and "hallowed" and the tu-a-ti practices of catching blood and setting it aside. The collected blood is not necessarily crucial as blood, as a life fluid, even though Perkins underlines the word. As he puts it very exactly: the blood "is considered to be 'aut ni'—or as we should say, sacred or hallowed or sanctified" because of what the tu-a-ti does with it. "I.e., it is sacredly set apart, & carefully garded." The sacred has to do with an act of setting something apart, guarding it, and creating prohibitions around it.

It is risky to speculate about what Christian or scriptural associations Perkins had in mind here, but a few suggestions may be in order. Anyone familiar with the Bible might recall the prohibited space around the burning bush and the voice that warned Moses: "Draw not nigh hither: put off thy shoes from off thy feet, for the place whereon thou standest is holy ground" (Exodus 3:5, KJV). There is also a dangerous space around the Ark of the Covenant, which went into battle with the Israelites and brought suffering and death to those who came near its prohibited presence (1 Samuel 5:1–6:19, 2 Samuel 6:6–7). Perkins certainly would have remembered the prohibitions in the Ten Commandments, particularly the commandment to keep sacred the name of God (Exodus 20:7). The Lord's Prayer repeats that idea in "Thy name be hallowed," the line Perkins was working to translate properly.

If such associations are at the margins of his thinking here, then Perkins is not just trying to find a proper Sahaptian word for an English word, or shrewdly anticipating native distortions of his attempt at translation. For a moment he is hesitating and weighing an ancient New World religious practice against similarly ancient religious practices and feelings in the Old World. A few days later such problems led him to write out a long passage, confessing again that he was at a stand in balancing Indian arguments and biblical texts (*People* 282–86; cf. Loewenberg, "Missionary Idea" 174–75). "The opinions of the Greeks, Romans, & Jews with regard to evil spirits, or demons, formerly, appear to have been almost precisely what the opinions of these Indians are now," he wrote. "I know not how to account for it" (*People* 282).

His struggle with the idea of the sacred was not merely momentary; it touched a nerve in his work. "Now if I knew the ideal meaning of the original word which we translate hallowed previously to its being used in the sacred writings, I could pass some judgement upon the propriety of using the English word under consideration." That is one jewel of a sentence. It bespeaks a deep curiosity, a willingness to reserve judgment, and perhaps something more. Did Perkins have a glimmer of recognition that embedded within his own language and beliefs there might be practices so closely similar to Indian rituals that an equivalence could be confirmed? Whatever his thoughts, he pauses here in a fascinating literary way. He comes to his questions precisely because he is a very conscientious reader, looking hard at two cultures by comparing the implications of their words. He holds himself to a pursuit of literary exactness and so opens his mind to a broader understanding.

This one sentence, however, ends by returning to the notion of "using" the Indian word in his own translation, displacing Indian practices with Christian ideas, and "conveying religious instruction." One can almost sense Perkins's eyes dilating to catch a little more light but then closing down again to get on with his report.

Just as unfortunately, this passage is brief, ambiguous, obscure, and singular. It may well be as close as any early missionary came to treating native spiritual life with sympathetic understanding, yet we are left wondering how sympathetic it is, in the end. Brewer went into the sacred space of the Winter Ceremony, but only reluctantly, and he came out feeling confirmed in his disgust. Waller stood up and protested.

Perkins enters the deeper space of shared language and fuller attention to a tu-a-ti's procedures, but he too draws back after catching just a hint of the genuine in what he describes.

A third report also describes a First Salmon ceremony and the prohibitions it entailed, but it puts them in a very sinister light. John H. Frost, the Methodist missionary at the mouth of the Columbia, learned of a rough and sudden murder when he first came to his post in 1840, and later heard this ceremony used as an excuse for it.

Frost did not witness the murder directly. He heard about it from Solomon Smith, whose Clatsop wife saw only part of the incident and heard reports of how it ended. Later—and through translation—he picked up a native story that explained it. His accounts are also tainted by the way he presents them. He has one version in his journal, another, somewhat different, in the book he wrote with Daniel Lee. (Frost probably kept short memoranda, as well, for his journal contains long passages that were evidently written up in detail long after the events they describe.) In the version he published, he tells the story as a digression, "for the purpose of relating one of [the] barbarous acts" of the people who surrounded him. This deed introduces them as "ignorant, superstitious, and barbarous" people in general (Lee and Frost 283). He also regarded them as improvident and dull of mind, as his story will show.

These layers of hearsay and judgment make Frost's reports almost worthless as evidence of the event itself. But they remain valuable (if troubling) as evidence of the way a missionary understood natives and their values. Frost's reports create an absolute contrast: what to him was radical evil was part of the natives' essential good. A man was buried alive because otherwise the gods would not bring a good salmon run, and many would starve. In Frost's view, this evil was too deep to be dealt with by persuasion; there could be no grounds of common understanding between his civilization and their callous murdering. He came to advocate suppressing native practices and native gods, for overwhelming and eradicating them with well-enforced American laws and institutions.

As we have seen, Solomon Smith was a Methodist layman who came west with Nathaniel Wyeth in 1834 and later married a Clatsop woman. She "knew something concerning the true God," according to Frost, and she was sometimes his interpreter and informant (Lee and Frost 269). Smith had been away for a time in 1840, and his wife told him the fresh news of the murder when he returned to their settlement.

There had been a feast of elk at a headman's lodge during a hungry season before the fall salmon run. One of the guests was a sick man, who ate well but then left early. Back at his own lodge he roasted more meat for himself, then fell into a deep sleep "so that his sister . . . and the other inmates of the lodge . . . found him in this posture, breathing hard, and sometimes groaning, caused, no doubt by having crammed his empty stomach with such a quantity of heavy food." When it was impossible to rouse him, "they all as one struck up the death-wail" and one of them ran to Mrs. Smith to get a shovel for his burial. Frost recounts the story as he heard it:

> Mrs. Smith followed this messenger to the lodge, where she found the customary preparation for the interment of the dead going forward with haste; but as she found the man, to all appearance, not very near his natural end, she proposed to put off the funeral until the following morning, when, if the man was actually dead, they would bury him decently. This counsel was rejected with much spirit, they declaring that he was *"nowitka mamaluse,"* that is, certainly dead, and without further ado he was rolled up in his blanket and mat, tied with a rope, and slung upon the back of a relative, and away they marched toward the place of burial, rending the air with their wailings. They arrived at the spot, lay down the living corpse, which uttered a pitiful groan; this was to them another conclusive evidence that it was high time he should be buried. Mrs. Smith expostulated. But they upbraided her with being regardless of their welfare; seeing that the salmon, which had just made their appearance, would all leave the river at once, if a dead body should be found above ground! The hole was hastily dug, and finding that she could not prevail, Mrs. S. returned to her house; but was told, by one that did remain, that after the

body was put therein and some dirt thrown upon it, one of the men descended to tramp it down, which caused the poor half-buried man to groan aloud; but they persevered until his groaning ceased, and the "last sad offices" were completed. They now returned to the lodge, distributed the knife and such other articles left by the departed, among the present bereaved relations; and committed his elk meat, which was scarcely cooked before his burial and consequent death, to the flames, as it was against their conscience to eat anything which had been prepared by the dead. And as they had a great abundance of salmon that season, they were no doubt satisfied that they had performed a good work. (Lee and Frost 283–85)

Before it reached Frost this story had at least three or four narrators. No doubt it was embellished with dramatic groans and other pathetic details to make it more vivid in the telling. Even if Mrs. Smith can be wholly trusted, it could be that a dead but still warm body was hurried into its grave despite some loud protests of the next of kin. In Frost's journal version of this incident, however, the facts seem to be otherwise; even a *dying* man had to be buried immediately: "The man was dying, and even if he should lay dead above ground they would get no salmon. Buried he must be" (Frost 72).

There were other live burials which the missionaries knew about firsthand. Frost had heard of slave burials in the past (Lee and Frost 233) and he reported another example of the practice a few months after this event. He said he spoke directly to the men who did it. "They acknowledged the fact, but said that he was 'cultus mischemus,' that is, nothing but a slave" (Lee and Frost 321). The most notorious case was the live burial of a child slave in 1844. He was bound and laid atop older corpses along with the body of a chief's son and spent the night struggling to escape before Henry Perkins could arrange to retrieve and ransom him (*People* 111–12).

In Frost's report about the adult who ate too much, the victim was not sacrificed but buried in haste because of a religious scruple. "The salmon, which had just made their appearance, would all leave the river at once, if a dead body should be found above ground." This point was explained to Frost the next spring when the salmon run began again and he was invited to a nearby lodge. The men told them a Coyote story (a "little wolf" story, about an "imaginary deity," as Frost puts it), about the creation of salmon and their proper treatment.

While the salmon were roasting, the men related one of their traditions, which was of the following import: "A long time ago Talapus," that is, one of their imaginary deities, "came this way from the south, in the form of the little wolf, and made all this land from Cape Lookout to Young's Bay; and finding the people very poor, and having nothing to eat but elk, and bear, and deer, and wild fowl, he made the salmon; and when they commenced to run up the river, he made a seine, and placing the snake on the shore to hold the land line, he went out in the canoe and threw the net. Then coming on shore, he and the snake drew the net to land, which contained a great draught of salmon. He now ordered them to be taken to the lodge and laid with their heads to the west until toward night, when the fire was prepared as above described [i.e., in a procedure Frost mentioned earlier]: and Talapus learned their fathers how to cut the fish and roast them, and told them that for some time they must not eat only in the afternoon of each day, and that if any of them should touch a dead body, or eat vermin, until the strawberries began to ripen, the salmon would all leave the river, unless those who had thus defiled themselves should be prohibited from touching a salmon for a specified numbers of days; and that the same results would follow if their women, under certain circumstances, (who were also prohibited from enjoying the privileges of their houses, as it is their universal custom on such occasions,) should look upon a salmon net; and that until that time arrived when the berries began to ripen, which is about the first of June, they must cook the salmon in precisely the same way, and none of it must be taken out of the lodge in which it was cooked. But as soon as the specified time arrived, they were at liberty to cook the salmon as they might see proper, and sell them to whom they pleased. (Lee and Frost 300–301)

First Salmon ceremonies elsewhere in the Northwest often included rigid protocols, but none seems as detailed as these. This story mentions rules for carrying the salmon, cutting it, cooking it, eating it, and storing it. It also prohibits three kinds of pollution: handling of the dead, eating of vermin, and menstruation. Erna Gunther's surveys of the anthropological records mention some of these points, but none deals directly with eating vermin or handling the dead. The closest analogies seem to be pollution resulting from the eating of meat and eating by the recently bereaved (Gunther, "A Further Analysis," 152–5).[1]

Oddly, Frost took careful note of all these rules and noted their force, yet he went on believing that these Indians' minds were vague, cloudy, or blank about myth and laws. He seems to have recorded and copied out this full story for a simple purpose—to clinch his point about barbarism.

> The fact that they fully believe that this is a law imposed upon them by their deity, and that such distressing results would follow, namely, the removal of all the salmon, if this law should be transgressed, accounts for the most barbarous practice among them—of burying their people alive at the commencement of the salmon season, an instance of which has been already related. (Lee and Frost 301)

On the one hand, he insists here that they obey "this law" scrupulously and bury people as a result. On the other hand, he complains that they cannot be evangelized because the idea of law is beyond their comprehension. "Their language is so defective, that thereby it is impossible to acquaint them with the true nature of law, and until they are brought to feel that they are condemned in consequence of having transgressed the law of God, how can they be made to feel the need of Christ?" (313). Apparently, his mind held just two notions of law: the teachings of the Bible, and the kind of justice he saw enforced when white men hanged Indians for murder (274). Indians had neither notion, as he saw it, and so he despaired of them: "the Christian church will never prosper among a people who are in a state of perfect anarchy" (319).

His thinking was compartmental in other ways, too. He may have regarded his neighbors as dull-minded at best and murderers at worst, but that did not prevent him from dining with them when invited. He took careful note of how they (and their slaves) prepared four good-sized salmon for roasting, keeping the heads to the west and minding other scruples about their preparation, then sat down to a good meal, apparently with no qualms. "The salmon was now pronounced well done, and it was taken down and placed in a shallow trough made of cedar, and our plates were filled with the choice pieces, and placed before us. We now divided our loaf of bread among the company, and all hands commenced feasting, except the man who prepared the fish for roasting, for Talapus had prohibited him from tasting a morsel for certain number of days" (Lee and Frost 301).

Taken together, these records show Frost, Perkins, and Brewer approaching and entering Indian ceremonies and rituals but viewing them, as it were, through a shield of denial. They sought clues and sometimes full accounts of Indian beliefs but refused or blocked out any notion that they could hold beauty or admirable meaning. That was not quite conceivable among the "barbarous" or "savage" people they had come to save. Yet these records reflect more than narrow intolerance. They point to abiding tensions between assimilation and resistance, in their time and our own.

It is only through these and a few other passages, after all, that we can now catch glimpses of some pre-contact Indian ceremonies and beliefs. The missionaries opened a possibility for which the early explorers and traders had little time: regarding Indians as people with spiritual lives worth reaching. They reached out to them with naive hopes, to be sure, and a firm commitment to change their ways. But in the 1830s and early 1840s no one else paid much attention to their souls or their learning or spent time writing up their longer stories and practices. Horatio Hale published *Ethnography and Philology* in 1846, as part of the multivolume report of the United States Exploring Expedition led by Lieutenant

Wilkes. This volume included a pioneering study of Chinook Jargon, but Hale's account of Northwest Indians was very sketchy. George Gibbs made the first extensive survey of Northwest native beliefs in the 1850s, and by that time much had changed under the pressure of white contact. By introducing Christianity, even haltingly, the missions had also altered the ways Indians thought about their own myths. As Gibbs put it: "Not merely have their teachers, where they have had intercourse with priests of any denomination, desired to extirpate the recollection of their former superstitions, but the Indians themselves are prone to mix up a little biblical knowledge with their own legends, thus rendering it . . . difficult to distinguish between the original fabric and the subsequent additions" (Clark 295).

Indians, that is, began to think of their own stories in terms of the Bible. Indeed, with contact they were also forced into thinking about *religion*, which itself may be a literate category for experience. Certainly they were asked to make choices among religions, a perplexing situation for people who had long lived by common myths and practices.

The anthropologist Jack Goody has explained this distinction clearly in terms of Asante society in Africa, and his general point applies here as well. Tribal villages have practices and beliefs, or what can be called a "way." Religions, or distinct practices limited to one group or one part of life, are introduced later; they do not exist except where there are literate observers.

> [There are] aspects of practice and belief in all societies that centre around notions of life and death, of the other world, of spiritual beings and of divination, propitiation and sequences of rites. But in African languages I find no equivalent for the western word "religion" (or indeed "ritual"), and more importantly the actors do not appear to look upon religious beliefs and practices in the same way that we, whether Muslim, Jew, Hindu, Buddhist, Christian or atheist, do—that is, as a distinct set. This difference is suggested in the way we define an African religion, not only by its characteristics as a sect or church . . . but as Kikuyu religion or Asante religion. In other words we define a religion in terms

of the practices and beliefs of a particular group of territorially bounded individuals—a tribe or a kingdom. Indeed one can argue that it was not until the competition from Islam or Christianity that the idea of an Asante religion, as distinct from the more inclusive concept of an Asante way of life, began to take shape, first in the mind of the observer and then in that of the actor. This suggestion is given some support by the fact that when an attempt was made to define such religious systems in a comprehensive way, leaving on one side the "ethnic" designations, European scholars then turned to label such as paganism, animism, heathenism, that describe religions in terms of an opposition to the hegemonic written forms. (Goody 4)

In the Northwest these "hegemonic written forms" were confusing because of conflicts between rival forms of Christianity. Methodists, Presbyterians, and Congregationalists did not quite respect each others' doctrines, and Protestants and Catholics were deeply opposed to each other. Nonetheless, the more fundamental difference was between Indians, living in their "way," and literate Christians, who pressed to "convert" them into practicing set-apart religions and rituals. Goody stresses the relationship of religion to literate thinking.

You cannot practice Asante religion unless you are an Asante; and what is Asante religion now may be very different from Asante religion one hundred years ago. Literate religions on the other hand, at least alphabetically literate ones, are generally religions of conversion, not simply religions of birth. You can spread them, like jam. And you can persuade or force people to give up one set of beliefs and practices and take up another set, which is called by the name of a particular sect or church. In fact the written word, the use of a new method of communication, may itself sometimes provide its own incentive for conversion, irrespective of the specific content of the Book; for those religions are not only seen as "higher" because their priests are literate and can read as well as hear God's word, but they may provide their congregation with the possibility of becoming literate themselves. What

I am claiming here, in effect, is that only literate religions can be
religions of conversion in the strict sense. (Goody 5)

Furthermore, it seems to follow that whether the converts become
literate or not, the first conversions start a radical upheaval in oral societies. A one-way movement has to begin once a literate evangelist
manages to attract even one or two adherents. Once those first conversions take place, the society is evidently divided and it is impossible to
hold to a universal way any longer. Adhering to the old ways becomes
a matter of choice, too.[2] Practices once understood as the unquestioned
way, the commonplace, the expected behavior, have to be considered
and justified against the new alternatives. If the "way" becomes stubbornly or actively resistant, it thereby becomes a sort of opposition
"religion." Even to think in such terms, of course, is to step across a
threshold and into the shadow of literate assimilation.

Thereafter, particular practices also require defense and justification.
And such persuasion requires a reservoir of cultural energy, which may
well be depleted after contact with new diseases, new technologies, new
medicines, new forms of wealth, and other new encroachments.

The missionaries taught lines of the Bible, songs, and forms of regular prayer and practice. They exhorted new practices and vigorously
opposed such sins and abuses as gambling, drinking, slave holding, and
shamanism. They taught new skills, such as farming and carpentry
with modern tools. They set an example by living monogamously, in
separate households, with such things as butter and soap, sheets and
brocade. But it also seems arguable that they began a long and irreversible process of conversion just through the underlying fact that
they were emphatically different—just by their coming west, settling
in, sticking doggedly to their commitments, and conspicuously preaching and demonstrating different values and practices, no matter what
the particular practices might have been. Earlier invaders, the explorers
and fur traders, were less intrusive, for they either needed the goods
and services Indians could provide, or they counted on leaving Indians
in place as a deterrent to invasion by any competitors. The missionaries,
by contrast, made great efforts to effect even tiny changes in the native

people, and by that means alone they began to unravel the former webs of tribal life.

That is, even if the missions achieved very few enduring religious conversions and taught very few Indians to read well or stick to farming or manual trades, they began an irreversible shift in perception about laws and ethics and education. Head flattening, child murder, and hurried burials to appease the salmon—all had to be questioned by native people themselves once white ministers intruded on the scene and found one way and another to insist loudly and persistently to them that these ways were inhuman. This is not to deny that white settlers also used force and violence to suppress native practices, and that Indians found ways to resist for a century and more. It is rather to stress that Indians had minds of their own, were affected by persuasion, and began to realign their lives in the face of hard new questions. Some powerful disruption and reorientation of this sort seems to have occurred when the first students returned from the Red River school in the early 1830s, and their learning provoked other Indians to inquire about white men's ways. The questions became even harder to evade when white people came west to preach, managed to form a chain of settlements in Oregon country, then grew in numbers by hundreds and by thousands. The old "way" could not survive intact, and every practice and belief that was part of it had to be weighed and changed or compromised.

Such enormous changes have swept over this region since the 1830s that the teaching by the invaders now seems a matter for regret. We may rightly read passages from the mission records and wish they had been different. Had these newcomers been more inquisitive, generous, and tolerant, their writings might have unfolded pages and pages of stories, lore, ceremonies, beliefs, history, and poetry, in rich detail. For such riches exist, or once did, as later scholars have shown.

For more than a century, patient anthropologists have combed this region and continued the pioneering work of George Gibbs and Franz Boas to collect and transcribe local stories. Many have learned Indian languages and found talented storytellers who could repeat and explain this material. The texts thus recorded have been studied and restudied. Dozens have been collected from dusty archives and freshly presented in anthologies such as Ella Clark's *Indian Legends of the Pacific Northwest* and Jarold Ramsey's *Coyote Was Going There: Indian Literature of the Oregon Country*. Some, especially from the Columbia River region, have been closely examined for their literary qualities. As a result, modern readers can now find samples of Chinook, Clatsop, Tillamook, Kalapuya, Wasco, Wishram, Cayuse, and Nez Perce legends as close as their public libraries. With a little diligent application, modern readers can also find engaging essays about the subtle artistry these works represent. There can be no doubt that the oral culture of the Columbia region was once rich with traditional materials, which passed from generation to generation through the voices of skilled performers.

This is the music that the missionaries never heard or refused to countenance. Yet their firm denial of this oral heritage, or counter-pressure against it, also has its value. This point takes some explaining because it runs against our own comfortable prejudices as readers, so let me state it again: the mission experience may be most valuable to us just because of these failures of understanding. Such failures serve as an exemplary check on the notion that literacy and better scholarship can take in what the original peoples of the Northwest heard and repeated in their own languages.

No matter how brilliant modern studies of these oral records may be, they rest on the shaky scaffolding of a sequence of transmissions. Modern anthropologists did not reach the Pacific coast until many of the conditions that had supported the old ceremonies and lore were gone. In many tribes, diseases and dislocations had reduced the num-bers of active storytellers to a very few. Dell Hymes remarks, "Native Americans themselves, by and large, had no precedent for maintaining verbal tradition other than through oral learning by successive generations. Conquest, disruption, conversion, schooling, decimation eliminated most such learning." It was only through the work of Boas and his students in the early twentieth century that most of what we have of Oregon languages has been recorded. "We must count ourselves lucky to have records of the verbal arts of even a dozen gifted narrators, a dozen from among the hundreds who must have died unrecorded and are now unremembered" (Hymes 6).

Hymes began his intensive work in Chinookan languages on the basis of information that was barely rescued from oblivion long before his time.

> Charles Cultee, the last fluent speaker of Lower Chinook whom Boas could find when he sought for such in 1890, was also the last fluent speaker to be found of Kathlamet. He had Kathlamet ancestry on his mother's side and had acquired the language while living with her kin on the Oregon side of the river. Cultee spoke several languages—Lower Chinook, Kathlamet, Chehalis (Salish), and Chinook Jargon. Boas shared with him only the trade language, Chinook Jargon, and it was through that medium (and Cultee's remarkable intelligence, as Boas stressed) that a fine set of Kathlamet texts was recorded. Apart from some vocabulary recorded later by the Edward Curtis expedition (perhaps from Cultee, perhaps from a neighbor . . .), Cultee's texts and supplementary explanations are all that survive of the language. My own systematic work with Chinookan began with a grammar and dictionary drawn from the Cultee texts. (Hymes 16–17)

Melville Jacobs too had to depend on a single informant for stories in Clackamas Chinook; his wife Elizabeth recorded Tillamook stories told by another single storyteller. And by the 1930s much more of the supporting culture had fallen away. "The materials which [Victoria Howard] offered," Melville Jacobs admits, "together with fragments of supporting information obtained from other modern Chinooks and from Indians of adjacent groups . . . allow only partial depiction of the social system, cultural heritage, and psychological characteristics of the Clackamas people" (Jacobs vii).

Paper records, of course, could never fully capture the oral performance settings, or compensate for their absence. Elizabeth Jacobs notes that stories were told and retold at particular seasons, and listeners were conditioned to pay close attention and sometimes to take part in the event.

> Tillamooks told myths only in midwinter, approximately during the months of December and January. If stories were told at any

other time, it was believed that rain or even more disagreeable consequences would follow. Myths were not dramatized at the winter dances but were told around the firesides in the homes. Spirit-power songs were chanted or sung as they occurred in the body of a story. Only old people were privileged to recount myths. Children and younger persons reclined on mats as they listened. Children were cautioned not to sit when listening lest they grow hunchbacked. The auditors did not repeat the words, unlike some other Indian groups in the northwestern United States. (Jacobs, ed. vii)

Hymes similarly notes that paying attention was enforced. Wasco children who fell asleep were forced to go cut holes through the ice and take a dip in the river (Hymes 21).

As the old supports fell away, informants began to adapt to what their new questioners expected. Clara Pearson recited Tillamook tales in 1934 as Elizabeth Jacobs transcribed them. Before long Jacobs noted that Pearson was reciting only in English yet she seemed to be translating line after line as she spoke (Jacobs, ed. viii). Pearson was a practiced storyteller in both languages and she knew full well that her stories were being transcribed for readers. Ramsey has discerned a number of subtle touches in the resulting text. "Overall, without doubting all their essential authenticity relative to Tillamook tradition, I find in Pearson's narratives extensive accommodation to an Anglo audience or, to be more precise, to an Anglo *readership*" ("Introduction" to Jacobs, ed. xviii).

In another extraordinary case, the researcher was deeply attuned to both his scholarly audience and his native informant. Archie Phinney was a Nez Perce who did his graduate work with Franz Boas at Columbia University then returned to Lapwai in the 1920s, where he recorded tales told by his own mother. In his words, her repertory was extremely valuable because it extended back "beyond the time when the influences of new intertribal contacts and of wholesale myth-trading at nonreservation Indian schools became apparent in Nez Perce mythology" (quoted in Ramsey, *Reading* 69–70). Yet as he worked with this material he sometimes lost heart, for he could not capture its elusive tones. In

1929 he wrote to Boas: "A sad thing in recording these animal stories is the loss of spirit—the fascination furnished by the peculiar Indian vocal tradition for humor. Indians are better story-tellers than whites. When I read my story mechanically I find only the cold corpse" (letter quoted in Ramsey, ed. xxv).

As Phinney's complaint makes clear, recording scholars always had split loyalties. No matter how sympathetic or even intimate with Indians they might be, they still came to the task at hand with an alien commitment. They were to bring Indian ways into a book, transcribe them as fully and accurately as possible, but transcribe them nevertheless— take them out of the living voices of a rural or village space and preserve them for readers in a library, most likely an academic library. In this process, the written work was bound to involve new echoes and dimensions that derived from the researcher's wider reading. It became a different kind of performance, and had to be fitted into categories of literate experience as the writer developed a thesis or linked up new sequences of documents.

In some respects this process has proved wonderfully enhancing and expansive, as scholars have highlighted resemblances between these records and other literatures. Hymes has unfolded poetry where earlier students found only field data. Out of his training as a Shakespeare scholar, Ramsey has found intriguing turns of poetry, drama, narrative, and characterization. In addition, these readings have highlighted the living talents of the Indians who have gone on with traditional story-telling. Ramsey, for example, has traced several ways Bible stories have been retold and recombined, even in impromptu performances. He also examines a Tower of Babel story that raises doubts about getting to heaven by any kind of ladder (*Reading* 208–21).[3]

But the other side of expert literacy is that it reduces this material by interleaving it with scholarly paraphernalia. Nowadays expert literate attention has become burdened with overrefined professional categories. Scholars are on their mettle to state theoretical justifications for every text they examine, and it takes a daring soul to venture into literature, anthropology, philology, and history all in one plunge. "There is linguistics in this book," Hymes begins his introduction, "and that will put some people off":

> "Too technical," they will say. Perhaps such people would be amused to know that many linguists will not regard the work as linguistics. "Not theoretical," they will say, meaning not part of a certain school of grammar. And many folklorists and anthropologists are likely to say, "too linguistic" and "too literary" both, whereas professors of literature are likely to say, "anthropological" or "folklore," not "literature" at all. (Hymes 5)

The title of Hymes's book is *"In Vain I Tried to Tell You"*—a line from an Indian tale, which fits the obscurity of tales left ignored in academic archives. But this line could also serves as a *cri de coeur* for all forgotten tellers, including Hymes himself. Such is the outcome of specialized literacies and the competing categories and subcategories of modern academic learning.

So far, the lines of transmission are complicated enough: from the lore of a village or tribe to the talents (and idiosyncracies) of an individual tale-teller; from that teller to a sympathetic but disciplined academic listener; from one language to another, largely through the adaptations of informants to the demands of English-speaking researchers; from oral performance to print; and from a transcriber in the field to some editor or compiler or commentator at a desk, who must labor to make these records appealing to more readers than just a few rival experts. But the problems do not end here. A further performance also has to take place in the immediate present, by the reader who picks up the resulting printed pages. And it begins with that choice.

In the modern cacophony of advertisements, news bulletins, serial dramas, songs, stories, concerts, internet messages, annual reports, revised regulations, and voter pamphlets, a reader has to make time and space for steady silent hours with a book. Why choose a particular monograph on oral tales? Why expend the energy that is required to enter Northwest Indian culture—especially when African cultures, Middle Eastern cultures, Hispanic cultures, and others exert rival claims, and the volumes of Chekhov, Shakespeare, George Eliot, and Plato always deserve a close rereading?

For reasons we have just surveyed, Northwest oral literature demands a special taste and a special effort of historical imagination, too. It calls for a sense of vanished languages and vanished settings, and an informed reader may rightly squirm in the chair with the thought that each page has been translated and embellished beyond recognition. To their credit, Hymes, Ramsey, and other editors and commentators squarely admit these problems and work nonetheless to reassure common readers of the material's authenticity, even as they invite readers to share what they have found and admired in this material.

Still, there is something to be learned from the attitude of the missionaries. Perhaps better said, there is something to be acknowledged about the stubborn missionary attitude, because it still whispers in every reader's ear. As we have seen, the missionaries strongly and assuredly resisted Indians' legends and ceremonies. They felt they knew better, and frankly pushed back with stern energy to teach their own stories. They were poor scholars and poor anthropologists, in light of what we know now. Their example admonishes us, however, if we look at it honestly.

They were readers, sure of their values; and so are we. They valued literacy above oral culture; so do we, whenever we sequester ourselves with a book. They came to harvest the souls of Indians, just as ruthlessly or zealously as the Hudson's Bay Company came to harvest beaver pelts. In attempting to absorb what we take to be original Indian culture, do we not mean to harvest something just as selfishly or smugly—though with nothing like the risk of life and health the missionaries took?

We can see that the mission workers were earnest and naive. Only in rare glimpses did they sense their own ignorance and wonder if the people whom they came to convert had their own myths, arts, and talents worth knowing. At best, they caught only fleeting glimpses of such riches. If we press the comparison with ourselves, it could be a scourge for the vain assurance that higher education is essentially a reader's domain.

Ramsey offers a very appealing reason for studying the early oral tales. People who now live in the Northwest, he writes, can see the land anew and dwell there more fully.

> For anyone who cares about the mountains, lakes, rivers, forests, deserts, seashores, weathers, and climates of the Oregon country, these stories will strike a deep chord, filled as they are with a vivid sense of place. As a settled region Oregon is still too new for white men's legends to have taken deep root—no sooner does a promising story get told about Dirty Pat McGinty's escapades on the Upper MacKenzie, than someone denies it all on historical grounds—"Naw, it wasn't that way at all!" One remembers Robert Frost's description of the American land "vaguely realizing westward, / But still unstoried, artless, unenhanced . . ." But in these stories from the Coos, the Wascos, the Paiutes, the very terrain they lived on is storied and enhanced, is lifted imaginatively into indisputable myth; the natural features that still delight and haunt us are given supernatural dimensions they otherwise lack, are given a truly native "local habitation and a name." (*Coyote* xix–xx)

The beginning assumption here may well be true, that people whose families have lived only a few decades in the Northwest feel a cultural embarrassment, a lack of inner depth to match the outer grandeur of the mountains, ocean, plateaus, and mighty rivers that surround them. Perhaps, as Ramsey states, they need a literature to ease or deepen the sense of belonging to this terrain.[4] But Ramsey's further point is questionable. Can Indian tales in translation serve that end, and provide an "indisputable myth," a solid and "truly native" foundation to this region, and even "supernatural dimensions" to the "natural features"?

This notion comes dangerously close to identifying Indians with the land and romanticizing both, as well as blurring the distinctions Ramsey carefully spells out elsewhere between tales read on a page and tales told in a ceremonial gathering. Furthermore, as this paragraph unfolds, Ramsey appeals to four or five overlapping literatures as he tries to turn readers toward the deepest, most authentic voices of the landscape. As well as Indian tales he refers to white folk tales, and to the historical records—another form of print literature—that undermine them. He then states that "one remembers" lines written by a famous poet of New England.[5] If Indian tales seem deeper and truer than white tales, they are nonetheless offset by remembered white voices. The terms for what Indian stories do—make the terrain "storied" and "enhanced"—come from the voice of Robert Frost. Or, taken another way, they fulfill lines by Shakespeare about giving airy nothing "a local habitation and a name."

Of course, the main point of this passage is that Frost is wrong: the West did not lack stories and meaning before white people invaded it. We need to learn Indian tales to realize how well inhabited this land has been for centuries. But the embarrassment persists. No one can read them in English—not even Ramsey—without reading them with memories and cross references from other reading in English.

"It is no exaggeration," Ramsey goes on, "to claim that you can't really 'possess' the countries of the Columbia and the Klamath until you have experienced a sense of those places evoked in the Indian stories set in them" (*Coyote* xx). It would be comforting to endorse that point firmly, except that the word "possess" stands out so awkwardly. Why is it set off in quotation marks? Ramsey could be implying that what is at issue is mental possession rather than legal ownership of plots of ground. No doubt he is also recalling the rest of Frost's poem; it opens, "The land was ours before we were the land's," and goes on to develop the idea of possessing and being possessed. But that word still sticks out sorely, because literal possession and dispossession cannot be washed out of it. White Americans have dispossessed Indians of their lands across this region. White readers have also dispossessed Indians of their dominion here by overwhelming their vital oral culture. If we take Indian stories as the necessary mediation between invasion and full possession, we are caught in the act of appropriation, too. We, too, follow the Oregon Trail, retrace the footsteps of the missionaries, and accept these translations as our birthright, our means of keeping Indians in their subordinate place—as facilitators of our possession.

The mental clash of the missionaries and Indians, however, points to a way out of such arrogance, not by offering relief from it, but by reminding us of a different embarrassment—namely, that we can never take possession of this storied land. There are sharp limits in our capacities for understanding, just because we are readers. Indian ways of knowing are not our ways of knowing. We are doomed to be deaf to them, and implicated in denying them. At the same time, our minds are inadequate to hold this region without them. Until we learn the land as intimately as they have learned it, and until we adapt our own beliefs and ceremonies to its unforgiving climate and contours, our possessing will remain largely an illusion.

Currently, Indian children in western Oregon are learning an early language, but their situation illustrates how hard it is to get back to origins, even with the best will in the world. The Confederated Tribes of Grande Ronde are supporting a preschool program with income from gambling—a sin from one point of view, an ancient Indian custom from another, and (in casinos with card games and machines) a Euro-American business enterprise from yet another. Some of the children's ancestors were taught at the Methodist missions, long ago; now the Confederated Tribes are investing in another kind of teaching. At best this language training enables the children to communicate on small matters in a kind of in-group code and to preserve uniquely Indian vocal sounds and patterns from the past. Its proponents are also using it as a lever for self-determination in the present. A recent Oregon legislature passed a bill enabling tribal elders to teach endangered languages in the public schools, and there are pressures to make such language training qualify for second-language credit.

The language being taught, however, is not a precontact Indian language but Chinuk Wawa—the Chinook Jargon of the early trade period—and it is taught through a strict immersion program, five hours a day, five days a week. According to a recent newspaper feature story, only a handful of elders now living can use this language fluently. One of the teachers is not an American Indian but a highly trained linguist. The youngsters learn orally, but words are also spelled out phonetically in a modified Roman alphabet. "The door, the clock and other items are labeled in Chinuk. Popular children's books, with characters such as Olivia the pig, are translated in Chinuk" (Lynn 4). The strain between oral and literate cultures goes on, with popular bookishness now called in to preserve remaining whispers from the past.

This is a good image on which to close: family elders teaching the young, and mediating between nationally famous books and culturally specific ways of talking, ways they had to learn from their own parents and elders. There is no doubt that books lie at the heart of modern, global interconnectedness. Almost everywhere in America our food, clothing, and energy now come to us through complicated transactions involving long-distance transportation and communications. We have to rely on advanced literacy to meet our basic needs, and parents around the world rightly push their children to read, and make sacrifices to get for them the benefits of literate skills. But bookish learning also excludes and suppresses another kind of knowing, the interdependence of families and villages, who live within constant direct hearing of each other's voices and in constant touch with each other's lives.

Old records such as the missionaries' bring us back to the edge of that form of human life. But to cross beyond that edge we have to stop reading and return to listening, and modern bookish adults have few ancestral voices to turn to. Our ears grow untuned for hearing them as our critical eyesight sharpens.

The mission writers now tantalize us with what they have recorded of those voices, even sketchily. Through their pages it is possible to catch glimpses of a world along the Columbia that was very different not two centuries ago, when the river grew silver with salmon every year. Still, we are forced to see through the eyes of the missionaries, and at best we recognize that our way of understanding, like theirs, keeps the oral world forever at a distance. That world speaks to us in languages now obliterated, which we can never comprehend, try as we will. And thereby it preaches to us that our ways, our religions, our notions of civilization are not as all-embracing and complete as we may suppose.

APPENDIX

THE DISOSWAY AND WALKER LETTERS

THE FOLLOWING LETTERS BY GABRIEL DISOSWAY AND William Walker were published on the front page of *The Christian Advocate and Journal* for Friday, March 1, 1833, and were the immediate cause of a movement to raise funds to send missionaries to the Columbia River region. They are reprinted here from that source. Disosway's letter consists of two parts, which introduce and then comment on Walker's letter. Much confusion has resulted from the fact that Disosway's references to "November last" and Walker's implied reference to recent events were both out of date at the time of publication in the *Christian Advocate;* Walker had visited St. Louis on his way to look at lands in western Missouri, in the fall of 1831. Perhaps Disosway miscopied the date of Walker's letter as 1833 instead of 1832; he could also have changed it after delaying publication in order to gather more information. The sharp split between his opening passages (on the Wyandots) and his closing call to action (on the Flatheads) could also indicate that he reconsidered the importance of Walker's letter once he received it. That is, he might have originally designed his letter to the press as a report on the Wyandots, in anticipation of receiving Walker's report on their lands. If he received or reviewed Walker's letter at a much later date, he might then have added the exhortations concerning missions farther west and so sent this somewhat disjointed, three-part article to press.

THE FLATHEAD INDIANS

The plans to civilize the savage tribes of our country are among the most remarkable signs of the times. To meliorate the condition of the Indians, and to preserve them from gradual decline and extinction, the government of the U. States have proposed and already commenced removing them to the region westward of the Mississippi.—Here it is intended to establish them in a permanent residence. Some powerful nations of these aborigines, having accepted the proposal, have already emigrated to their new lands, and others are now preparing to follow them. Among those who still remain are the Wyandots, a tribe long distinguished as standing at the head of the great Indian family.

The earliest travellers in Canada first discovered this tribe while ascending the St. Lawrence, at Montreal. They were subsequently driven by the Iroquois, in one of those fierce internal wars that characterize the Indians of North America, to the northern shores of lake Huron. From this resting place also their relentless enemy literally hunted them until the remnant of this once powerful and proud tribe found a safe abode among the Sioux, who resided west of lake Superior. When the power of the Iroquois was weakened by the French the Wyandots returned from the Sioux country, and settled near Michilimackinac. They finally took up their abode on the plains of Sandusky, in Ohio, where they continue to this day.

The Wyandots, amounting to *five hundred*, are the only Indians in Ohio who have determined to remain upon their lands. The Senecas, Shawnees, and Ottawas have all sold their Ohio possessions, and have either removed, or are on their way to the west of the Mississippi. A small band of about seventy Wyandots from the Big Spring have disposed of their reservation of 16,000 acres, but have not accepted the offered lands of the government in exchange. They will retire into Michigan, or Canada, after leaving some of their number at the main reservation of Upper Sandusky.

The wonderful effects of the Gospel among the Wyandots are well known. Providence has blessed in a most remarkable manner the labors of our missionaries for their conversion. Knowledge, civilization, and social comforts have followed the introduction of Christianity into their regions. To all of the Indians residing within the jurisdiction of the states or territories the United States propose to purchase their present possessions and improvements, and in return to pay them acre for acre with lands west of the Mississippi river. Among the inducements to make this exchange are the following: perpetuity in their new abodes, as the faith of the government is pledged never to sanction another removal; the organization of a territorial government for their use like those in Florida, Arkansas, and Michigan, and the privilege to send delegates to congress, as is now enjoyed by the other territories. Could the remaining tribes of the original possessors of this country place implicit reliance upon these assurances and prospects, this scheme to meliorate their condition, and to bring them within the pale of civilized life, might safely be pronounced great, humane, and rational.

The Wyandots, after urgent and often repeated solicitations of the government for their removal, wisely resolved to send agents to explore the region offered them in exchange, before they made any decision upon the proposal. In November last the party started on the exploring expedition, and visited their proposed residence. This was a tract of country containing about 200,000 acres, and situated between the western part of Missouri and the Missouri river. The location was found to be one altogether unsuitable to the views, the necessities, and the support of the nation. They consequently declined the exchange.

Since their return, one of the exploring party, Mr. Wm. Walker, an interpreter, and himself a member of the nation, has sent me a communication. As it contains some valuable facts of a region from which we seldom hear, the letter is now offered for publication.

Upper Sandusky, Jan. 19, 1833

Dear Friend:—Your last letter, dated Nov. 12, came duly to hand. The business is answered in another communication which is enclosed.

I deeply regret that I have had no opportunity of answering your very friendly letter in a manner that would be satisfactory to myself; neither can I now, owing to a want of time and a retired place, where I can write undisturbed.

You, no doubt, can fancy me seated in my small dwelling, at the dining table, attempting to write, while my youngest (sweet little urchin!) is pulling my pocket-handkerchief out of my pocket, and Henry Clay, my only son, is teasing me to pronounce a word he has found in his little spelling book. This done, a loud rap is heard at my door, and two or three of my Wyandott friends make their appearance, and are on some business. I drop my pen, dispatch the business, and resume it.

The country we explored is truly a land of savages. It is wild and romantic; it is a champaign, but beautifully undulated country. You can travel in some parts for whole days and not find timber enough to afford a riding swich, especially after you get off the Missouri and her principal tributary streams. The soil is generally a dark loam, but not of a durable kind for agriculture.—As a country for agricultural pursuits, it is far inferior to what it has been represented to be. It is deplorably defective in timber. There are millions of acres on which you cannot procure timber enough to make a chicken coop. Those parts that are timbered are on some of the principal streams emptying into the great Missouri, and are very broken, rough, and cut up with deep ravines; and the timber, what there is of it, is of an inferior quality, generally a small growth of white, black, and bur oaks; hickory, ash, buck-eye, mulberry, linwood, coffee bean, a low scrubby kind of birch, red and slippy elm, and a few scattering walnut trees. It is remarkable, in all our travels west of the Mississippi River, we never found even one solitary poplar, beech, pine, or sassafras tree, though we were informed that higher up the Missouri River, above Council Bluffs, pine trees abound to a great extent, especially the nearer you approach the Rocky Mountains. The immense country embraced between the western line of the state of Missouri, and the territory of Arkansas, and the western base of the Rocky Mountains on the west, and Texas and Santafee on the south is inhabitated by the Osage, Sioux, (pronounced Sooz), Pawnees, Comanches, Pancahs, Arrapohoes, Assinaboins, Riccarees, Yanktons, Omahaws, Black-feet, Ottoes, Crow Indians, Sacs, Foxes, and Iowas; all a wild, fierce, and war-like people. West of the mountains reside the Flat-Heads, and many other tribes, whose names I do not now recollect.

I will here relate an anecdote, if I may so call it. Immediately after we landed in St. Louis, on our way to the west, I proceeded to Gen. Clarke's, superintendent of Indian affairs, to present our letters of introduction from the secretary of war, and to receive the same from him to the different Indian agents in the upper country. While in his office and transacting business with him, he informed me that three chiefs from the Flat-Head nation were in his house, and were quite sick, and that one (the fourth) had died a few days ago. They were from the west of the Rocky Mountains. Curiosity prompted me to step into the adjoining room to see them, having never seen any, but often heard of them. I was struck by their appearance. They differ in appearance from any tribe of Indians I have ever seen: small in size, delicately formed, small limbs, and the most exact symmetry throughout, except the head. I had always supposed from their being called "Flat-Heads," that the head was actually flat on the top; but this is not the case. The head is flattened thus:

From the point of the nose to the apex of the head, there is a perfect straight line, the protuberance of the forehead is flattened or levelled. You may form some idea of the shape of their heads from the rough sketch I have made with the pen, though I confess I have drawn most too long a proboscis for a flat-head. This is produced by a pressure upon the cranium while in infancy. The distance they had travelled on foot was nearly three thousand miles to see Gen. Clarke, their great father, as they called him, he being the first American officer† they ever became acquainted with, and having much confidence in him, they had come to consult him as they said, upon very important matters. Gen. C. related to me the object of their mission, and, my dear friend, it is impossible for me to describe to you my feelings while listening to his narrative. I will here relate it as briefly as I well can. It appeared that some white man had penetrated into their country, and happened to be a spectator at one of their religious ceremonies, which they scrupulously perform at stated periods. He informed them that their mode of worshipping the supreme Being was radically wrong, and instead of being acceptable and pleasing, it was displeasing to him; he also informed them that the white people *away* toward the rising of the sun had been put in possession of the true mode of worshipping the great Spirit. They had a book containing directions how to conduct themselves in order to enjoy his favor and hold converse with him; and with this guide, no one need go astray, but every one that would follow the directions laid down there, could enjoy, in this life, his favor, and after death would be received into the country where the great Spirit resides, and live for ever with him.

Upon receiving this information, they called a national council to take this subject into consideration. Some said, if this be true, it is certainly high time we were put in possession of this mode, and if *our* mode of worshipping be wrong and displeasing to the great Spirit, it is time we had laid it aside, we must know something more about this, it is a matter that cannot be put off, the sooner we know it the better. They accordingly deputed four of their chiefs to proceed to St. Louis to see their great father, Gen. Clarke, to inquire of him, having no doubt but he would tell them the whole truth about it.

They arrived at St. Louis, and presented themselves to Gen. C. The latter was somewhat puzzled being sensible of the respon-

† Gen. Clarke accompanied Lewis in his travels through these regions. [Note in original, probably added by Disosway or the editor of the *Christian Advocate*.]

sibility that rested on him; he however proceeded by informing them that what they had been told by the white man in their own country, was true. Then went into a succinct history of man, from his creation down to the advent of the Saviour; explained to them all the moral precepts contained in the Bible, expounded to them the decalogue. Informed them of the advent of the Saviour, his life, precepts, his death, resurrection, ascension, and the relation he now stands to man as a mediator—that he will judge the world, &c.

Poor fellows, they were not all permitted to return home to their people with the intelligence. Two died in St. Louis, and the remaining two, though somewhat indisposed, set out for their native land. Whether they reached home or not is not known. The change of climate and diet operated very severely upon their health. Their diet when at home is chiefly vegetables and fish.

If they died on their way home, peace be to their manes! They died inquirers after the truth. I was informed that the Flat-Heads, as a nation, have the fewest vices of any tribe of Indians on the continent of America.

I had just concluded I would lay this rough and uncouth scroll aside and revise it before I would send it, but if I lay aside you will never receive it; so I will send it to you just as it is, "with all its imperfections," hoping that you may be able to decipher it. You are at liberty to make what use you please of it.

Yours in haste,

WM. WALKER.

G. P. Disosway, Esq.

The most singular custom of flattening the head prevails among all the Indian nations west of the Rocky Mountains. It is most common along the lower parts of the Columbia river, but diminishes in travelling eastward, until it is to be scarcely seen in the remote tribes near the mountains. Here the folly is confined to a few females only. The practice must have commenced at a very early period, as Columbus noticed it among the first objects that struck his attention. An essential point of beauty with those savage is a *flat head*. Immediately after the birth of a child the mother, anxious to procure the recommendation of a broad forehead for her infant, places it in the compressing machine. This is a cradle formed like a trough, with one end where the head reposes more elevated than the other. A padding is then placed upon the forehead, which presses against the head by cords passing through holes on each side of the cradle. The child is kept in this manner upward of a year, and the operation is so gradual as to be attended with scarcely any pain.—During this period of compression the infant presents a frightful appearance, its little keen black eyes being forced out to an unnatural degree by the pressure of bandages. When released from this process the head is flattened, and seldom exceeds more that one or two inches in thickness. Nature with all its efforts can never afterward restore the proper shape. The heads of grown persons often form a straight line from the nose to the top of the forehead. From the outlines of the face in Mr. Walker's communication I have endeavored to sketch a Flat Head for the purpose of illustrating more clearly this most strange custom. The dotted lines will show the usual rotundity of a human head, and the cut how widely a Flat Head differs from the rest of the great family of man.—So great is this difference as to compel anatomists themselves to confess that an examination of such skulls, and ocular demonstration only, could have convinced them of the possibility of moulding the head into this form. The "human face Divine" is thus sacrificed to fantastic ideas of savage beauty. They allege also, as an apology for this custom, that their slaves have round heads, and that the children of a brave and free race ought not to suffer such a degradation.

This deformity, however, of the Flat-Head Indians is redeemed by other numerous good qualities. Travellers relate that they have fewer vices than any of the tribes in those regions. They are honest, brave, and peaceable. The women become exemplary wives and mothers, and a husband with an unfaithful companion is a circumstance almost unknown among them. They believe in the existence of a good and evil Spirit, with rewards and punishments of a future state. Their religion promises to the virtuous after death a climate where perpetual summer will shine over plains filled with their much loved buffalo, and upon streams abounding with the most delicious fish. Here they will spend their time in hunting and fishing, happy and undisturbed from every enemy; while the bad Indian will be consigned to a place of eternal snows, with fires in his sight that he cannot enjoy, and buffalo and deer that cannot be caught to satisfy his hunger.

A curious tradition prevails among them concerning beavers. These animals, so celebrated for their sagacity, they believe are a fallen race of Indians, who have been condemned on account of their wickedness, by the great Spirit, to their present form of the brute creation. At some future period they also declare that these fallen creatures will be restored to their former state.[*]

How deeply affecting is the circumstance of the four natives traveling on foot 3,000 miles through thick forests and extensive prairies, sincere searchers after truth! The story has scarcely a parallel in history. What a touching theme does it form for the imagination and pen of a Montgomery, a Mrs. Hemans, or our own fair Sigourney! With what intense concern will men of God whose souls are fired with holy zeal for the salvation of their fellow beings, read their history! There are immense plains, mountains, and forests in those regions whence they came, the abodes of numerous savage tribes. But no apostle of Christ has yet had the courage to penetrate into their moral darkness. Adventurous and daring fur traders only have visited these regions, unknown to the rest of the world, except from their own accounts of them. If the Father of spirits, as revealed by Jesus Christ, is not known in these interior wilds of America, they nevertheless often resound the praises of the unknown, invisible great Spirit, as he is denominated by the savages. They are not ignorant of the immortality of their souls, and speak of some future delicious island or country where departed spirits rest. May we not indulge the hope that the day is not far distant when the missionaries will penetrate into these wilds where the Sabbath bell has never yet tolled since the world began? There is not, perhaps, west

* Vide Lewis and Clarke's Travels; Cox's Adventures on the Columbia River; and North American Review. [Disosway's note.]

of the Rocky mountains, any portion of the Indians that presents at this moment a spectacle so full in interest to the contemplative mind as the Flat-Head tribe. Not a thought of converting or civilizing them ever enters the mind of the sordid, demoralized hunters and fur trader. Those simple children of nature even shrink from the loose morality and inhumanities often introduced among them by the white man. Let the Church awake from her slumbers, and go forth in her strength to the salvation of these wandering sons of our native forests. We are citizens of this vast universe, and our life embraces not merely a moment, but eternity itself. Thus exalted, what can be more worthy of our high destination than to befriend our species and those efforts that they are making to release immortal spirits from the chains of error and superstition and to bring them to the knowledge of the true God.

G. P. D.

New-York, Feb. 18, 1833.

NOTES

CHAPTER I

1. The features and power of indigenous religions have been much discussed since Spier's seminal work; important later studies include the writings of Deward Walker, Christopher Miller, and Larry Cebula. Walker argues persuasively that "Euroamerican influence, even though indirect, probably had produced conditions in the Plateau before 1800 sufficient to account for a cult movement of the type hypothesized by Spier" (250). In other words, there could already have been a Christian influence that affected the Indians who created the reported prophecies about white people and their religion. Miller and Cebula do not deal at length with Walker's critique; they seem to persist in believing that wholly indigenous spiritual practices and traditions produced a native religion, including prophecies, that prepared Indians to resist white evangelizing.

2. I have quoted letters, journals, and other similar sources exactly as they are in the original, and have not included editorial interruptions to indicate obvious misspellings and other errors.

3. Krapohl explains in detail how the *Christian Advocate* absorbed other journals in its early years, so that in the spring of 1833 its full title was *Christian Advocate and Journal and Zion's Herald*. Hereafter I cite it by its long-running title, *Christian Advocate*, and refer to the dates of various articles and letters, which can readily be found in its four-page issues. I quote from the microfilm copy in the University of Washington library.

4. Biographical information about Disosway can be found in Hampton; Brosnan 10; and Townsend, Workman, and Eayres 365, but all these sources are disappointingly brief and general.

5. The senior William Walker was married to a half Indian woman who "had

great influence in the nation" according to Finley. "The old gentleman, his wife, and his sons, were all good interpreters, spoke the Indian tongue fluently, and all except old Mr. Walker, became members of the church" (Finley 238). In a preface dated 1827, the publisher of a famous memoir about Stewart acknowledges that its materials "were collected and arranged by William Walker, who resided at the Wyandott Nation at the time of Stewart's first visiting them, and does to the present" (Walker vii). The senior William Walker had died in 1824, however, and his son (1800–74) became a headman of the tribe. This younger Walker was well educated, had been a student at Kenyon College, and served as an interpreter for the governor of Michigan Territory. He later moved west with his people after bargaining for better terms on the sale of their Ohio lands, and served as provisional governor of Nebraska Territory in 1853 (Waldman). Oliphant has reprinted Walker's report on his exploring trip to western Missouri in 1831, along with an enraged critique by the Indian agent who had tried to set up the exchange of lands.

6. Many modern works cite the full text of the Disosway and Walker letters from an appendix in Chittenden (3:912–25), which omits the original footnotes.

7. "In 1839, Gabriel Disoway wrote a brief sketch of the beginning of the Oregon Mission in a large ledger book which Jason Lee brought back to Oregon and in which the official history of the Mission was to have been written. This was never done, but in 1847 the book was used as the official record book of the Oregon-California Mission Conference of the Methodist Church. This book is now in the Northwest collection of Willamette University" (Gatke 21n4). Unfortunately this original document has disappeared. Photocopies of the Disosway essay, however, are now filed at the Willamette University library and also at the United Methodist Archives in Salem. The essay does not add any revealing details about the Walker or Disosway letters in the *Christian Advocate*.

8. Johnson (202–3) briefly mentions a letter in the Bancroft collection at the University of California, which contains reminiscences of "a retired clergyman of the Methodist Episcopal Church" who was ordained in St. Louis around 1831. This letter "refers to the Walker letter as overdrawn and incorrect." It seems odd that Johnson cites such a later reminiscence as an authority, in the course of attacking Henry Spalding's later reminiscences of the same event. I omit discussing both accounts because my concern is contemporary writings that influenced the beginnings of the missions.

9. M'Allister also scoffs at the idea of western hardships, claiming that the West is wonderfully salubrious. "Many of our fellow citizens have gone from this

country so diseased as to render it doubtful they could ever reach the mountains and have returned from thence with constitutions restored, to the astonishment of all that knew them."

10. Sheer curiosity was the apparent motive behind another Nez Perce's travel to St. Louis at about this time. Hahastusti or High Bear made a long sightseeing tour by going to St. Louis in 1835 and then traveling on to Mexico. When he returned, he began to teach and exhort Catholic practices (Stern 2:46–47, quoting Nez Perce sources).

11. Jason Lee and the early Presbyterian missionary Samuel Parker tried to see Clark when each of them passed through St. Louis, but had to deal with other officers and informants during Clark's absences (Hulbert and Hulbert 5: 146, 232, 251).

12. Catlin worked up a famous account of one of them, known as The Light, who was killed by some of his people after flaunting his formal army uniform and claiming mysterious powers. See Catlin 1:56, 67; 2:194–200; for full details see Ewers, "When Washington Saw The Light."

CHAPTER 2

1. Daniel Lee did not marry the young woman mentioned here, but he met and married Maria Ware soon after she sailed to Oregon in 1840. Jason Lee himself was the first to be married in Oregon, to Anna Maria Pittmann. She came to Oregon as a mission teacher in 1837, met Lee on her arrival, and was married to him two months later. He had agreed to preside at the marriage of Cyrus Shepard (who came west with the Lees) and Susan Downing, but he surprised the congregation by leading Miss Pittman forward first, as Daniel Lee rose to officiate (Brosnan 88–90; Allen 75–76).

2. Clark copied the lines about the "battery of Venus" in his entry for November 7, 1805, and placed them in quotation marks. This fact has led Moulton (2:25–27) to follow Dunlay in thinking that Clark's journals at Fort Clatsop must have been copied much later from Lewis's journals, in fact written out at some time after Lewis's full essay dated March 19, 1806. This is not a necessary conclusion. Lewis probably wrote the "battery of Venus" lines and other draft passages from time to time and finally copied them out in complete form at the end of the Fort Clatsop period. Clark thus could have copied this part of Lewis's draft much earlier. This procedure also explains an otherwise puzzling discrepancy in Clark's March 19 copy of the passage about "dirty naked wenches." He

includes words that Lewis omits—which might well happen if both men were copying from an earlier draft or drafts.

3. Frost appears as J. H. Frost on the title page of the book he wrote with Daniel Lee, and experts disagree about his name. Both Meany and Brosnan call him Joseph; both Loewenberg and Pipes call him John; Gatke uses one name in his index, another in his text. I follow Pipes, who edited his diary.

4. One of the earliest handbooks, by the Catholic missionary F. N. Blanchet, is reprinted in facsimile in Vaughan, ed., *Paul Kane*, after p. 54. Thomas lists many other early handbooks and notes the numbers of words they list (167–71). Lillard and Glavin (75–85) show the title pages of later handbooks published in British Columbia, and print a very brief sample lexicon. Samarin provides a trenchant critique of the claim that Chinook Jargon was an indigenous trade language before the arrival of white explorers.

5. Wilkes ate with Methodists in the Willamette Valley on June 8, and again he found fault: "We dined a la Methodist on Salmon, Pork, potted cheese, and strawberries, tea & hot cakes, they were all brothers and sisters some with coats, some without, red flannel shirts, and dirty white arms, higgledy piggledly. I shall not soon forget the narrow cramped up table, more crowded round it than it would hold, with the wooden benches, high backed chairs & low seated ones, perchance all the tall ones seized the high seats and the low in stature were even with the well filled board. The meal was eaten by us all in brotherly love, but hunger assisted me or I never should have been able to swallow mine" (17:50–51).

6. Sarah Frost repeated this rationalization in more absurd terms many years later in a letter: "Mr. Frost told the Indians that they must not kill, or steal, or lie, or commit adultery; they must love God, and love each other. They promised to do as he said, and they literally kept their word as long as we remained among them" (Atwood 91). Apparently she returned home and forgot several murders and other outrages that shocked her in Oregon.

7. How the captains communicated with Indians of the lower Columbia remains a mystery. Their journals report conversations and information they must have received from local informants. But they were without translators after their Nez Perce guides left them in the fall of 1805. Apparently they used sign language and some terms from an early form of the Chinook Jargon, and they claimed that many local Indians understood some English. Their difficulties can be gauged by considering the alternative. When Sacagawea translated, as she did here, she needed a translator from the local language (the captive Shoshone woman); Sacagawea then turned to her husband, Toussaint Charbonneau, and

translated into Hidatsa; Charbonneu translated into French; and a French-speaking soldier translated into English for the captains. Awkward as it was, this chain of translations was evidently a welcome relief from trying to communicate by other means.

8. Joseph Mussulman, a retired professor of music at the University of Montana, has developed a program of songs the Lewis and Clark party might have sung as their "medicine songs" in this exchange, and he has led modern audiences in singing them at many Lewis and Clark gatherings. His research has also been published in *We Proceeded On*, the journal of the Lewis and Clark Trail Heritage Foundation. The popular songs of Jefferson's day included "Yankee Doodle" and hymns such as "Amazing Grace," and a patriotic song beginning, "Ye sons of Columbia," set to the tune of our present national anthem.

9. He reasoned that eye irritations were caused by high winds and blowing sand on this part of the river, a conclusion that Nathaniel Wyeth also drew many years later: "The savages are civil and as much as one in ten has lost an eye as I suppose from the effects of the fine sand being blown about or the violent wind for which this part of the river is noted" (Wyeth 183).

10. Many doctors of the time merely picked up a few skills through very brief apprenticeships and then learned as they practiced. Margaret Jewett Bailey married a doctor who practiced in the Willamette Valley, after she had been involved with another man who set up as a doctor for a time, after such skimpy preparation. She eventually pilloried the latter man in verse:

> He said his prayers and learned the creed,
> And went to sea, and knew to read,
> And whiskers wore, cravat and glove,
> And blew the flute, and talked of love,
> And tailored some, then took to teaching,
> And coopered more, then went to preaching,
> But losing favor as a rector,
> He next resolved to be a doctor,
> And studied "Thomas," "Bell," and "Burns,"
> And "Cooper's Surgery" by turns,
> And made some pills, but still was he
> As feeble minds will always be,
> Puny and poor when all was done,
> Like plant in shade which seeks the sun. (Bailey 155–56)

CHAPTER 3

1. Bailey presents these Bible moments as a commonplace practice which readers would recognize (cf. Bailey 256, 309). This passage appears as a series of brief paragraphs in the text cited.

2. Another war of letters took place at Fort Vancouver in September 1836, over the management of the school there. Dr. John McLoughlin issued orders as Chief Factor, against the written protests of the Anglican chaplain, Herbert Beaver. Both men also appealed in writing to higher authorities in the Hudson's Bay Company. McLoughlin prevailed, but Herbert went home to publicize his complaints in a Church of England magazine (Woolworth 237–46). "It is strange today to think that in a small, contained settlement where Beaver and McLoughlin had only to walk a few minutes to speak with one another that they would adhere to the formalities of written correspondence five times in a single day" (237). But so they did. The immediate upshot was that McLoughlin asked the newly arrived Narcissa Whitman and Eliza Spalding to take over the school— and Beaver wrote them a formal note asking them not to.

3. The Blanchet ladder of 1840 came to the Oregon Historical Society in 1990 and is well illustrated in the White and St. Laurent article of 1996. Four other versions are illustrated in Hanley 36, 46, 50, and 58. Large, fold-out copies can be found in Landerholm and Bagley.

4. This ladder has been reproduced in a large foldout opposite the opening page of Pipes's 1936 article in *Oregon Historical Quarterly*.

CHAPTER 4

1. Silas Smith recorded further details about First Salmon practices among the Clatsops, which he learned from his mother and other contemporaries of Frost. He also describes "Talipas" or Coyote, though he does not relate this particular story (Smith 259).

2. Several patterns of resulting factions have been described and even diagrammed by Berkhofer (125–51).

3. Retelling of this sort continues into the present, of course. Roy I. Wilson identifies himself on a recent book cover as both "a retired United Methodist pastor and the traditional spiritual leader of the Cowlitz Indian Nation." He has designed a beaded stole with the design of the Catholic ladder on one long panel

and corresponding symbols from Indian myths on the other. His brief book traces these parallels in detail.

4. The work of Eugene Hunn points to another possibility. Hunn directly studied the land along the mid-Columbia, under the instruction of an Indian elder and his family, in order to compile a combined ethnographic study and "folk ecology" of the region. "I have spent many days exploring the land that is the focal point of this culture," Hunn wries. "I have come to recognize its plants and animals and their habitats, to know them in their winter, spring, summer, and fall aspects; I have through persistent repetition learned to name these features: in English, in Latin, and in the Indian languages. I have been apprenticed to an Indian man. . . . Through this continuing apprenticeship I have acquired . . . a sense of the mystery of a way of life radically different from my own" (Hunn 7). Few of us can be so fortunate as to spend fifteen years learning Indian languages, stories, and engagement with the land from expert friends; but note that Hunn also learned all the features of the land in English and scientific Latin.

5. The Frost poem quoted here is "The Gift Outright" and it is hard to pin down how it should be remembered. It was originally written in the spring of 1941 but was given another turn when Frost recited it at the inauguration of President John F. Kennedy in 1963. In its first form it was about New England colonists; as a televised inaugural poem it embraced the entire continent and complemented Kennedy's claims to be opening a New Frontier.

WORKS CITED

Allen, A. J. *Ten Years in Oregon: Travels and Adventures of Doctor E. White and Lady, West of the Rocky Mountains.* Ithaca: Andrus, Gaunlett, 1850.

Ames, Kenneth M., and Herbert D. G. Maschner. *Peoples of the Northwest Coast: Their Archaeology and Prehistory.* London: Thames & Hudson, 1999.

Appleman, Daniel E. "James Dwight Dana and Pacific Geology." In *Magnificent Voyagers: The U.S. Exploring Expedition, 1838–1842,* edited by Herman J. Viola and Carolyn Margolis, 88–117. Washington, D.C.: Smithsonian Institution Press, 1985.

Atwood, A[lbert]. *The Conquerors: Historical Sketches of the American Settlement of the Oregon Country.* Cincinnati: Jennings and Graham, 1907.

Bagley, Clarence B. *Early Catholic Missions in Old Oregon.* 2 vols. Seattle: Lowman and Hanford, 1932.

Bailey, Margaret Jewett. *The Grains, or Passages in the Life of Ruth Rover, with Occasional Pictures of Oregon, Natural and Moral.* Edited by Evelyn Leasher and Robert J. Frank. Corvallis: Oregon State University Press, 1986 Original edition, Portland: Carter & Austin, 1854.

Ballou, Howard Malcolm. "The History of the Oregon Mission Press." *Oregon Historical Quarterly* 23 (1922): 41–52, 95–110.

Behrmann, Elmer H. *The Story of the Old Cathedral.* Revised edition. St. Louis: Church of St. Louis IX, King of France, 1984.

Berkhofer, Robert F., Jr. *Salvation and the Savage: An Analysis of Protestant Missions and American Indian Response, 1787–1862.* Lexington: University of Kentucky Press, 1965.

Blanchet, François Norbert. *Historical Sketches of the Catholic Church in Oregon During the Past Forty Years (1838–78).* 2d ed. Portland, 1884.

———. *The Key to the Catholic Ladder.* New York: T. W. Strong, 1859.

Boyd, Robert. *People of The Dalles: The Indians of the Wascopam Mission*. Lincoln: University of Nebraska Press, 1996.

————. *The Coming of the Spirit of Pestilence: Introduced Infectious Diseases and Population Decline among Northwest Coast Indians, 1774–1874*. Seattle: University of Washington Press, 1999.

Brosnan, Cornelius J. *Jason Lee: Prophet of the New Oregon*. New York: Macmillan, 1932.

Brown, Joseph Epes. *The Sacred Pipe: Black Elk's Account of the Seven Rites of the Oglala Sioux*. Norman: University of Oklahoma Press, 1953.

Brown, Richard Maxwell. "Language and Exploration: The Role of the Chinook Jargon." In *Encounters with a Distant Land: Exploration and the Great Northwest*, edited by Carlos A. Schwantes, 86–101. Moscow: University of Idaho Press, 1994.

Bushman, Richard L. *Joseph Smith and the Beginnings of Mormonism*. Urbana: University of Illinois Press, 1984.

Catlin, George. *Letters and Notes on the Manners, Customs, and Conditions of North American Indians*. Reprint. 2 vols. New York: Dover, 1973. Original edition, London, 1844.

Cebula, Larry. *Plateau Indians and the Quest for Spiritual Power, 1700–1850*. Lincoln: University of Nebraska Press, 2003.

Chittenden, Hiram Martin. *The American Fur Trade of the Far West*. 3 vols. New York: Harper, 1902.

Chuinard, Eldon G. *Only One Man Died: The Medical Aspects of the Lewis and Clark Expedition*. Reprint. Fairfield, Washington: Ye Galleon Press, 1989. Original edition, Glendale, California: Arthur H. Clark, 1979.

Clark, Ella E. *Indian Legends of the Pacific Northwest*. Berkeley: University of California Press, 1953.

Coues, Elliott, ed. *History of the Expedition under the Command of Lewis and Clark*. Reprint. 3 vols. New York: Dover, 1965. Original edition, New York: Harper, 1893.

Cox, Ross. *The Columbia River; or, Scenes and Adventures during a Residence of Six Years on the Western Side of the Rocky Mountains*. 3d ed., 2 vols. London: Henry Colburn and Richard Bentley, 1832.

Deloria, Vine, Jr. *God Is Red: A Native View of Religion*. 2d ed. Golden, Colorado: Fulcrum, 1994.

DeMallie, Raymond J., ed. *The Sixth Grandfather: Black Elk's Teachings to John G. Neihardt*. Lincoln: University of Nebraska Press, 1985.

DeVoto, Bernard. *Across the Wide Missouri*. Boston: Houghton Mifflin, 1947.

Drury, Clifford M. *Marcus and Narcissa Whitman and the Opening of Old Oregon*. 2 vols. Glendale, California: Arthur H. Clark, 1973.

Duncan, Janice K. "'Ruth Rover'—Vindictive Falsehood or Historical Truth?" *Journal of the West* 12 (1973): 240–53.

Dunlay, Thomas W. "'Battery of Venus': A Clue to the Journal-keeping of Lewis and Clark." *We Proceeded On* 9, no. 3 (1983): 6–8.

Ewers, John C. "William Clark's Indian Museum in St. Louis, 1816–1838." In *A Cabinet of Curiosities; Five Episodes in the Evolution of American Museums*, by Whitfield J. Bell, Jr., Clifford K. Shipton, et. al., 49–72. Charlottesville: University Press of Virginia, 1967.

———. "When the Light Shone in Washington." In John C. Ewers, *Indian Life on the Upper Missouri*, 75–90. Norman: University of Oklahoma Press, 1968.

Finley, James B. *Life among the Indians*. Cincinnati: Cranston & Curts, 1857.

Foley, William E. *Wilderness Journey: The Life of William Clark*. Columbia: University of Missouri Press, 2004.

Frost, John H. "Journal of John H. Frost, 1840–43." Edited by Nellie B. Pipes. *Oregon Historical Quarterly* 35 (1934): 50–73, 139–67, 235–62, 348–75.

Furtwangler, Albert. *Answering Chief Seattle*. Seattle: University of Washington Press, 1997.

Gatke, Robert Moulton. *Chronicles of Willamette: The Pioneer University of the West*. Portland: Binfords and Mort, 1943.

Gibbs, George. "George Gibbs' Account of Indian Mythology in Oregon and Washington Territories." Edited by Ella E. Clark. *Oregon Historical Quarterly* 56 (1955): 293–325, and 57 (1956): 125–67.

Givens, Terryl L. *By the Hand of Mormon: The American Scripture that Launched a New World Religion*. New York: Oxford University Press, 2002.

Goody, Jack. *The Logic of Writing and the Organization of Society*. Cambridge: Cambridge University Press, 1986.

Gray, William H. *A History of Oregon, 1792–1849*. Portland: Harris & Holman, 1870.

Gunther, Erna. "An Analysis of the First Salmon Ceremony." *American Anthropologist*, n.s., 28 (1926): 605–617.

———. "A Further Analysis of the First Salmon Ceremony." *University of Washington Publications in Anthropology* 2 (1928): 129–73.

Hale, Horatio. *Ethnology and Philology. United States Exploring Expedition* . . .

under the Command of Charles Wilkes, vol 6. 1846. Reprint, Ridgewood, New Jersey: The Gregg Press, 1968.

Hampton, Vernon B. "Disosway, Gabriel Poillon." In *Encyclopedia of World Methodism*, edited by Nolan B. Harmon, vol. 1, pp. 689–90. 2 vols. Nashville: United Methodist Publishing House, 1974.

Hanley, Philip M. *History of the Catholic Ladder*. Edited by Edward J. Krowach. Fairfield, Washington: Ye Galleon Press, 1993.

Hines, Gustavus. *Oregon: Its History, Condition, and Prospects, Containing a Description of the Geography, Climate and Productions with Personal Adventures among the Indians during a Residence of the Author on the Plains Bordering the Pacific while Connected with the Oregon Mission: Embracing Extended Notes of a Voyage Around the World*. Buffalo: Geo. H. Derby, 1851.

Howay, Frederic W., ed. *Voyages of the "Columbia" to the Northwest Coast 1787–1790 and 1790–1793*. Boston: Massachusetts Historical Society, 1941.

Hulbert, Archer Butler, and Dorothey Printup Hulbert, eds. *The Oregon Crusade: Across Land and Sea to Oregon*. Vol. 5 of *Overland to the Pacific*. Denver: Colorado College and Denver Public Library, 1935.

Hunn, Eugene S. *Nch'i-wána, "The Big River": Mid-Columbia Indians and their Land*. Seattle: University of Washington Press, 1990.

Hymes, Dell. *"In Vain I Tried to Tell You": Essays in Native American Ethnopoetics*. Philadelphia: University of Pennsylvania Press, 1981.

Irving, Washington. *Astoria, or, Anecdotes of an Enterprize beyond the Rocky Mountains*. Edited by Richard Dilworth Rust. Reprint, Lincoln: University of Nebraska Press, 1982. Original edition, *The Complete Works of Washington Irving*, vol. 15. New York: Twayne, 1976.

Jackson, Donald. *Voyages of the Steamboat Yellow Stone*. New York: Ticknor and Fields, 1985.

———, ed. *Letters of the Lewis and Clark Expedition with Related Documents 1783–1854*. 2d ed. 2 vols. Urbana: University of Illinois Press, 1978.

Jacobs, Melville. *The People Are Coming Soon: Analyses of Clackamas Chinook Myths and Texts*. Seattle: University of Washington Press, 1960.

———, ed. *Nehalem Tillamook Tales*. Told by Clara Pearson; recorded by Elizabeth Derr Jacobs. Revised ed., with new introduction and notes by Jarold Ramsey and appendix by Dell Hymes. Corvallis: Oregon State University Press, 1990. Original edition, Eugene: University of Oregon Books, 1959.

Johnson, C. T. "The Evolution of a Lament." *Washington Historical Quarterly* 2 (1908): 195–208.

Joseph, Chief. "An Indian's View of Indian Affairs." *North American Review* 128 (1879): 415–33.

Josephy, Alvin M., Jr. *The Nez Perce Indians and the Opening of the West.* Reprint, Boston: Houghton Mifflin, 1997. Original edition, New Haven: Yale University Press, 1965.

Kaiser, Rudolph. "Chief Seattle's Speech(es): American Origins and European Reception." In *Recovering the Word: Essays on Native American Literature,* edited by Brian Swann and Arnold Krupat, 497–536. Berkeley and Los Angeles: University of California Press, 1987.

Kone, William W. "Historic Reminiscences in Clatsop Nearly Fifty Years Ago." *Astoria (Oregon) Weekly Astorian,* 27 April 1889. Reprinted in *Cumtux: Clatsop County Historical Society Quarterly* 14, no. 3 (Summer 1994): 10–14.

Krapohl, Robert H. "*Christian Advocate.*" In *Popular Religious Magazines of the United States,* edited by P. Mark Fackler and Charles H. Lippy. Westport, Connecticut: Greenwood Press, 1995.

Landerholm, Carl, ed. and trans. *Notices and Voyages of the Famed Quebec Mission to the Pacific Northwest.* Portland: Oregon Historical Society, 1956.

Lee, Daniel, and J. H. Frost. *Ten Years in Oregon.* New York: J. Collord, 1844.

Lillard, Charles, and Terry Glavin. *A Voice Great Within Us.* Vancouver, British Columbia: New Star Books, 1998. This publication is also issue number 7 of the serial *Transmontanus.*

Loewenberg, Robert J. "Elijah White vs. Jason Lee: A Tale of Hard Times." *Journal of the West* 11 (1972): 636–62.

———. "The Missionary Idea in Oregon: Illustration from the Life and Times of Methodist Henry Perkins." In *The Western Shore: Oregon Country Essays Honoring the American Revolution,* edited by Thomas Vaughan, 151–80. Portland: Oregon Historical Society, [1975?].

———. *Equality on the Oregon Frontier: Jason Lee and the Methodist Mission 1834–1843.* Seattle: University of Washington Press, 1976.

Lynn, Capi. "Reviving a Native Tongue." *Salem (Oregon) Statesman-Journal,* 2 March 2003, section A.

Mandeville, John [pseud.]. *The Travels of Sir John Mandeville.* Translated by C. W. R. D. Moseley. London: Penguin Books, 1983.

Marshall, William I. *Acquisition of Oregon and the Long Suppressed Evidence about Marcus Whitman.* Seattle: Lowman & Hanford, 1911.

McDermott, John Francis. "William Clark: Pioneer Museum Man." *Journal of the Washington Academy of Sciences* 44 (1954): 370–73.

Meany, Edmond S. "Last Survivor of the Oregon Mission of 1840." *Washing-ton Historical Quarterly* 2 (1907): 12–23.

Miller, Charles A. *Ship of State: The Nautical Metaphors of Thomas Jefferson.* Lanham, Maryland: University Press of America, 2003.

Miller, Christopher D. *Prophetic Worlds: Indians and Whites on the Columbia Plateau.* Reprint, Seattle: University of Washington Press, 2003. Original edition, New Brunswick: Rutgers University Press, 1985.

Minutes of the Board of Managers of the Missionary Society of the Methodist Episcopal Church. New York, April 15, 1819–. Manuscript volumes. General Commission on Archives and History, United Methodist Church, Madison, New Jersey.

Mockford, Stuart B. "Jason Lee's Peoria Speech." *Oregon Historical Quarterly* 59 (1958): 19–26.

Moulton, Gary E., ed. *The Journals of the Lewis and Clark Expedition.* 13 vols. Lincoln: University of Nebraska Press, 1983–2001.

Mowry, William A. *Marcus Whitman and the Early Days of Oregon.* New York: Silver, Burdett, 1901.

Mussulman, Joseph A. " 'The Greatest Harmoney': 'Meddicine Songs' on the Lewis and Clark Trail." *We Proceeded On* 23, no. 4 (1997): 4–10.

Neihardt, John G. *Black Elk Speaks: Being the Life Story of a Holy Man of the Oglala Sioux.* Reprint, with an introduction by Vine Deloria, Jr., Lincoln: University of Nebraska Press, 1988. Original edition, New York: Morrow, 1932.

Oliphant, J. Orin. "The Report of the Wyandot Exploring Delegation, 1831." *Kansas Historical Quarterly* 15 (1947): 248–62.

Palladino, L. B. *Indian and White in the Northwest: A History of Catholicity in Montana, 1831 to 1891.* 2d ed. Lancaster, Pennsylvania: Wickersham, 1922.

Peterson, Jacqueline. *Sacred Encounters: Father De Smet and the Indians of the Rocky Mountains.* Norman: University of Oklahoma Press, 1993.

Peterson Del Mar, David. "Intermarriage and Agency: A Chinookan Case Study." *Ethnohistory* 42 (1995): 1–30.

Pike, Zebulon Montgomery. *The Journals of Zebulon Montgomery Pike, with Letters and Related Documents.* Edited by Donald Jackson. 2 vols. Norman: University of Oklahoma Press, 1966.

Pipes, Nellie B. "The Protestant Ladder." *Oregon Historical Quarterly* 37 (1936): 237–40.

Ramsey, Jarold. *Reading the Fire: The Traditional Indian Literatures of America.* Revised edition. Seattle: University of Washington Press, 1999.

————, ed. *Coyote Was Going There: Indian Literature of the Oregon Country.* Seattle: University of Washington Press, 1977.

Remini, Robert V. *Joseph Smith.* New York: Lipper/Viking, 2002.

Ronda, James P. *Lewis and Clark among the Indians.* Lincoln: University of Nebraska Press, 1984.

Rosati, Joseph. "Letter of Msgr. Rosati, bishop of St. Louis, to the editor of the *Annales*" (31 December 1831). In *Annales de la Propagation de la Foi,* No. 25. 2d ed. Lyon, 1843.

Rubin, Rick. *Naked Against the Rain: The People of the Lower Columbia River 1770–1830.* Portland, Oregon: Far Shore Press, 1999.

Samarin, William J. "Chinook Jargon and Pidgin Historiography." *Canadian Journal of Anthropology* 5 (1986): 23–34.

Schoenberg, Wilfred P. *The Lapwai Mission Press.* Boise: Idaho Center for the Book, 1994.

Scofield, John. *Hail, Columbia!: Robert Gray, John Kendrick, and the Pacific Fur Trade.* Portland: Oregon Historical Society Press, 1992.

Segaller, Stephen, and Merrill Berger. *The Wisdom of the Dream: The World of C. G. Jung.* Boston: Shambhala, 1990.

Smith, Eugene O. "Solomon Smith, Pioneer: Indian-White Relations in Early Oregon." *Journal of the West* 13, no. 2 (April 1974): 44–58.

Smith, Silas B. "Primitive Customs and Religious Beliefs of the Indians of the Pacific Northwest Coast." *Oregon Historical Quarterly* 2 (1901): 255–65.

Spalding, Henry H., and Asa Bowen Smith. *The Diaries and Letters of Henry H. Spalding and Asa Bowen Smith relating to the Nez Pierce Mission 1838–1842.* Edited by Clifford Merrill Drury. Glendale, California: Arthur H. Clark, 1958.

Spier, Leslie. *The Prophet Dance of the Northwest and its Derivatives: The Source of the Ghost Dance.* General Series in Anthropology 1. Menasha, Wisconsin: George Banta, 1933.

St. Hilaire, Theodore J. "Pedagogy in the Wilderness." *Oregon Historical Quarterly* 63 (1962): 55–60.

Stern, Theodore. *Chiefs and Chief Traders: Indian Relations at Fort Nez Percés, 1818–1855, vol. 1.* Corvallis: Oregon State University Press, 1993.

————. *Chiefs and Change in the Oregon Country: Indian Relations at Fort Nez Percés, 1818–1855, vol. 2.* Corvallis: Oregon State University Press, 1996.

Sweet, William Warren. *Methodism in American History.* Nashville: Abingdon, 1953.

Thomas, Edward Harper. *Chinook: A History and Dictionary.* 2d ed. Portland: Binfords and Mort, 1970.

Townsend, W. J., H. B. Workman, and George Eayrs, eds. *A New History of Methodism.* Vol. 2. London: Hodder and Stoughton, 1909.

Vaughan, Thomas, ed. *Paul Kane, The Columbia Wanderer.* Portland: Oregon Historical Society, 1971.

Vibert, Elizabeth. *Traders' Tales: Narratives of Cultural Encounters in the Columbia Plateau, 1807–1846.* Norman: University of Oklahoma Press, 1997.

Waldman, Carl. *Who Was Who in Native American History.* New York: Facts on File, 1990.

Walker, Deward E., Jr. "New Light on the Prophet Dance Controversy." *Ethnohistory* 3 (1969): 245–55.

[Walker, William]. *The Missionary Pioneer, or a Brief Memoir of the Life, Labours, and Death of John Stewart, (Man of Colour) Founder, under God of the Mission among the Wyandotts at Upper Sandusky, Ohio.* Published by Joseph Mitchell. New York: J. C. Totten, 1827.

Wheeler, Olin D. *The Trail of Lewis and Clark 1804–1904.* 2d ed. 2 vols. New York: Putnam, 1926.

White, Kris A., and Janice St. Laurent. "Mysterious Journey: the Catholic Ladder of 1840." *Oregon Historical Quarterly* 97 (1996): 70–87.

Whitehead, Margaret. "Christianity, a Matter of Choice." *Pacific Northwest Quarterly* 72 (1981): 98–105.

Wilkes, Charles. *Narrative of the United States Exploring Expedition During the Years 1838, 1839, 1840, 1841, 1842.* 5 vols. Philadelphia, 1845.

———. "Diary of Wilkes in the Northwest." *Washington Historical Quarterly* 16 (1925): 49–61, 137–45, 206–23, 290–301; 17 (1926): 43–65, 129–44, 223–29.

Wilson, Roy I. *The Catholic Ladder and Native American Legends.* Bremerton, Washington: Roy I. Wilson, 1996.

Woolworth, Stephen. "'The School Is Under My Direction': The Politics of Education at Fort Vancouver, 1836–1838." *Oregon Historical Quarterly* 104 (2003): 228–51.

Wyeth, Nathaniel J. *The Correspondence and Journals of Captain Nathaniel J. Wyeth, 1831–1836.* Edited by F. G. Young. Sources of the History of Oregon, vol. 1, parts 3–6. Eugene: University [of Oregon] Press, 1899.

Ziff, Larzer. *Writing in the New Nation: Prose, Print, and Politics in the Early United States.* New Haven: Yale University Press, 1991.

INDEX